The New Testament Church and Its Ministries

The New Testament Church and Its Ministries

Bill Scheidler

Available from:

BIBLE TEMPLE PUBLISHING
9200 NE FREMONT
PORTLAND, OREGON 97220
(503) 253-9020

ISBN 0-914936-43-3
Printed in U.S.A.

ACKNOWLEDGEMENT

I would especially like to thank my spiritual parents, K. R. Iverson and K. J. Conner for the spiritual impartation that they have had in my life without which this book would have been impossible.

PREFACE

All over the world God's Spirit is moving in the earth today to call out a people for His name. God is preparing the world for the second coming of Jesus Christ. He is ordering world events and watching over His Word with a careful eye. God is at the same time preparing the Bride of Christ for a marriage that is not too far off in the distant future. That Bride is the Church of Jesus Christ. God is moving by His Spirit in these days to get the Church ready for the coming of the Lord. The Bride that Jesus returns for will have to be a prepared bride. The Bride that he returns for is to be a glorious, wrinkle-free bride that reflects the glory and image of her heavenly husband. In these days of preparation, God wants to bring the Church to a place of strength and power in the earth. He wants the Church to actually become all that it was intended to be. He wants to use the Church as a powerful instrument in the earth to extend His Kingdom and purpose. He wants to build a faith in His people that can make all of this possible.

This book is intended to help the Body of Christ better understand God's glorious purpose in the Church and their individual part in that purpose. It is intended to give the people of God a vision from God's perspective rather than man's. It is intended to feed the faith of the family of God so that we might begin to see the Church of Jesus Christ actualize all of the things that God has purposed.

This book is a manual for the serious Bible student. For this reason I would encourage the reader to have his Bible nearby while reading this text, looking up and meditating on all of the passages cited. As you are faithful, God will surely build into you a new love for His Church and a new desire to see it established as a place of refuge in these last days. God bless you as you read!

Bill Scheidler
Author

TABLE OF CONTENTS

Chapter 1
THE CHURCH — THE MYSTERY

There is something very exciting about the word "mystery". The very word challenges the hearer to investigate that he might uncover and know what is the mystery. Man has always had a desire to know and to penetrate beyond the limits of natural knowledge. Thousands of people spend millions of dollars each year in the purchase of "mystery novels". Television and cinema productions having an element of mystery have a tremendous appeal. There is something very challenging and exciting about attempting to unravel anything that has been termed a "mystery".

Mystery writers and producers expend a considerable amount of energy and care to ensure that their mystery production will be all that they claim it will be. They begin by weaving a thread of seemingly unrelated happenings and conclude by bringing all of the pieces together as smoothly as a completed jig-saw puzzle. The best mystery writers are able to drop continual clues throughout the account and yet maintain the suspense and conceal the outcome until the very end. The readers of these novels are continually trying to second guess the author and at times are very distant from the proper conclusions. More often than not the reader is actually surprised by the unexpected outcome of the mystery.

In many respects God is a good mystery writer. He has given His Word to man in which all of His plans and purposes are concealed. God begins by weaving a thread of seemingly unrelated happenings through which he has inserted divine clues. As the drama has unfolded over the centuries of time, many have attempted to understand and sort out the mysteries of the kingdom. Too often man has failed in his understanding because he has attempted to render a verdict before all of the facts were in *(Proverbs 18:13)*.

God has purposely concealed certain things and veiled them in mystery form and yet there is a time for the full unveiling of those purposes. Daniel was told that he was to seal up the words of his prophecy until the time of the end *(Daniel 12:4)*.

There are many things that God has reserved for the time of the end. As we approach the time of the end, we can expect more and more knowledge, understanding and wisdom to come to the people of God. This is one reason why it is so important that we do not rely totally on the biblical interpreters of the past when we approach God's Word. If we take God at His Word there are things that will never be fully or properly understood until the time of the end.

A. A MYSTERY DEFINED.

There are many different present day usages for the term "mystery" but we are more concerned about the New Testament usage of this word. The New Testament usage of this word seems most often to correspond to the religious usage found commonly among the ancient Greeks.[1]

> "Among the ancient Greeks 'the mysteries' were religious rites and ceremonies practised by secret societies into which anyone who desired might be received. Those that were initiated into these 'mysteries' became possessors of certain knowledge, which was not imparted to the uninitiated, and were called 'the perfected'."[2]

Perhaps a more simplified definition of a mystery would be "that which can only be known by the initiated."

We know that there are many things relative to the kingdom of God that the natural man who has not been initiated by the Spirit of God cannot understand *(I Corinthians 2:6-16)*. In fact, without the Holy Spirit there is absolutely no way in which he can know them. Therefore if man is to have any knowledge at all of divine mysteries he is going to have to be initiated by God Himself.

[1]IDB Cap. 3 C.F.D. Moule, pp. 479-481
[2]A.W.F. Vine, Expository Dictionary of New Testament Words.

B. GOD, THE REVEALER OF SECRETS

God has veiled much of what he has given to man in mystery form. And yet we must remember that these things that are a mystery to us are not a mystery to God. On the contrary God is the source of all knowledge and He has a full and perfect understanding of everything *(Colossians 2:3)*. Not only has God known all of His works from the beginning *(Acts 15:18)*, but He is also the one and only One who is able to declare the end from the beginning *(Isaiah 46:9-10)*. If there are certain things that have been concealed from man up to the time of the end, we must remember that none of these things is concealed from God Himself.

Even though God has all of the answers and is the fountain-head of all wisdom and knowledge. He has chosen to conceal His true knowledge and wisdom from three classes of people. God conceals His knowledge and wisdom from (1) the slothful, (2) the foolish, and (3) the unregenerate. If we are lazy in our approach to God we cannot expect to find answers to our questions. It is only as we are diligently pursuing after the Lord with all of our heart that we can expect to find Him as the Revealer of Secrets *(Jeremiah 29:13)*. There is a sense in which God actually hides Himself from the slothful. If we are diligent, however, we have the blessed privilege as kings and priests unto God of searching out all of the treasures and gems of truth that God has so carefully concealed in the field of His Word *(Proverb 25:2)*.

God is also careful about revealing Himself to fools. The biblical definition of a fool is one who is void of true understanding and perspective. A fool is one who is not able to handle truth properly. A fool is one who will use truth for his own selfish gain. A fool is one who will hear the truth and yet that truth never becomes a part of his life. The Pharisees of Jesus' day were much like this. This is why most of what Jesus said to them is veiled in parables. Jesus knew that if they did know the truth they would not respond with their hearts *(Matthew 13:11-17)*. Jesus was not one to cast pearls before swine *(Matthew 7:6)*.

In addition God hides the riches of His glory from the unregenerate who have absolutely no appreciation for the eternal things. The unregenerate man is living in the realm of the tangible, the earthly, the sensual and the temporal. The true riches of God are intangible, heavenly, spiritual and eternal. To the unregenerate all of this is mere nonsense and utter foolishness. Therefore God takes no pleasure in unveiling divine mysteries to the uninitiated *(II Corinthians 4:3)*.

To all of these groups of people the mysteries and secret things of God are hidden, but God does have a desire to let *His people* in on what he plans to do. God desires to reveal the mysteries of His kingdom to all those who have separated themselves unto Him. This willingness of God to share mysteries with His people is indicated by the closeness of God's relationship to His people whom He has referred to as a bride or wife. The marriage relationship is the closest and most sacred of human relationships. An atmosphere of openness is to pervade the marriage relationship. This is no different with God. We are a special people unto Him and as such He does not desire to keep anything from us that He plans to do.

This is clearly seen in God's relationship to Daniel. Daniel had an intimate relationship with His God who *"giveth wisdom to the wise and knowledge to them that know understanding"* *(Daniel 2:21)*. As a result when Nebuchadnezzar needed to know the interpretation of his dream it was not to the wise men, the astrologers, the magicians or the soothsayers that God revealed His mind, but it was to His beloved Daniel *(Daniel 2:27-30)*. God let Daniel in on special secrets because Daniel had a true attitude of humility and he recognized that it was not because of any special merit within himself or any special wisdom that he possessed that God had revealed truth to him. When this incident was all over even the Gentile king Nebuchadnezzar had to admit that our God is a "God of gods, and a Lord of Kings, and a Revealer of Secrets" *(Daniel 2:47)*.

It is a blessed thing to realize that when we fear the Lord *(Psalm 25:14)*, and keep a proper attitude of humility *(Luke 10:21)*, we can expect God to come to us as a revealer of secrets. Even when it comes to some of the weightier matters, God wants to 'tip us off', so to speak, in regard to His plans and purposes. He wants to 'keep us posted' right up to the second coming of Christ *(I Thessalonians 5:4)*.

Part of the ministry of the Holy Spirit as the great initiator is to let God's people in on what He plans to do. He is the one who reveals the deep things of God, the things that God has prepared and the very purposes of God to the spirit of man *(I Corinthians 2:9-11)*. He is the one whose ministry includes showing us the things of the Lord even the things which are to come *(John 16:15-16)*. He is the one who will guide us and lead us into all truth. Even as God by His Spirit revealed His plans and purposes to the faithful Simeon prior to the first coming of the Lord *(Luke 2:26)*, so also we can expect God by His Spirit to give the faithful insight into His plans and purpose in these days prior to the second coming, that we may stand with Simeon in terms of our preparedness to meet the Lord when He comes as the salvation of His people.

It is so important for us to recognize that God wants to have a special relationship to His people. He wants to reveal Himself in a special way. He wants to share Himself with His friends. He wants to entrust us with stewardship over the "mysteries" of God (I Corinthians 4:1).

C. MYSTERIES IN THE BIBLE.

There are many things that are referred to as mysteries in the New Testament. Notice the following list:

The Mystery (-ies) of the Kingdom (Matt. 13:11, Mk. 4:11, Luke 8:10)
The Mystery of Iniquity (II Thess. 2:7)
The Mystery of Godliness (I Tim. 3:15-16)
The Mystery of Faith (I Tim. 3:9)
The Mystery of Translation (I Cor. 15:51)
The Mystery of the Seven Stars (Rev. 1:20)
The Mystery of the Woman-Babylon (Rev. 17:5, 7)
The Mystery of the Marriage of Christ and the Church (Eph. 5:32)
The Mystery of God (Rev. 10:7, Col. 2:2)
The Mystery of Christ (Col. 4:3, 3:4)
The Mystery of the Gospel (Eph. 6:19)
The Mystery of His Will (Eph. 1:9-10)
The Mystery (Eph. 3:3-4, Rom. 16:25, 11:25)

Many of these "mysteries" in the New Testament are vitally related to each other, but the last five on the list are particularly associated. The last book of the Bible announces a time when the mystery of God which had been declared even by the prophets of old should be finished. Here there seems to be a culminating of God's plans. Just what this plan of God involves has itself been the subject of much discussion and yet we have to believe that it is possible for the people of the Lord to have spiritual insight into this great mystery. There are great clues as to the plan in a careful examination of some of the other phrases mentioned. Paul speaks of a "mystery of Christ" for the preaching of which he had been put in bonds (Colossians 4:3). Paul was in bonds because of his revelation of the relationship of the Jew and Gentile. Does that have something to do with the "mystery of Christ" and the ultimate plan of God? Paul in a similar portion refers to the new relationship between the Jew and Gentile as the "mystery of His will" (Eph. 1:9-10). What does the coming together of the Jew and Gentile into one have to do with the ultimate purpose of God? To answer this question we are going to have to open our hearts to the ministry of the Holy Spirit, the great initiator, as He speaks to us through the Word of God.

"For this cause I Paul, the prisoner of Jesus Christ for you Gentiles, If ye have heard of the dispensation of the grace of God which is given me to you-ward: How that by revelation he made known unto me the mystery; (as I wrote afore in few words, Whereby when ye read, ye may understand my knowledge in the mystery of Christ)."

Ephesians 3:1-4

Chapter 2
THE CHURCH — THE ETERNAL PURPOSE

The mystery of God that Paul refers to involves the eternal purpose of God. God gave Paul an understanding in this area that had been hidden in times past. The revelation that Paul received totally transformed his life and ministry. When we come to a revelation of what God for all time has been moving toward, we too, will be changed in our perspective and life motivations, for God has a glorious purpose for His people.

One of the most important things for us to see is that God has but *one* eternal purpose that He is working toward. God is not double-minded, uncertain, or unstable, but He is very methodical, determined, and definite in everything that He does. God is not one to begin several projects and leave them all incomplete, but He has always completed that which He begins.

Since we have one God, it stands to reason that He has but one plan. Because God is one and there is no other God beside Him there can only be but one truth. Because God is one and truth is one and God is unchanging then it stands to reason that God does not change His dealings with man but continually works all things after the counsel of His own will. God is not double-minded. He has but one will, one plan, one law, and one goal *(Malachi 3:6)*. If God were limited by human faculties of reason and sense—perception as we are, He would be more like us in terms of accomplishment. But since God has infinite faculties (i.e., omniscience, omnipotence, omnipresence, immutability, omnisapience) He is able like no one else to declare the end from the beginning and see His plan come to fruition.

Sometimes, it is sad to say, we picture God much like the gods of the Greek pantheon playing a little heavenly chess game with peoples lives, changing His approaches to fit His moods and tampering with lives just for the sport of it. We need to clear our thinking. Our God is not motivated by changing whims, for He has no such thing. He is not motivated by a sense of adventure. God is motivated by a pure heart of love, and that heart of love has devised an eternal plan that will glorify Him for eternity.

One thing that has hindered us from knowing God's eternal purpose is our limited perspective and frame of reference. We tend to look at God's plan in terms of what we have seen happen in our life time rather than what has happened for all time. We tend to look at God's plan by looking at one working of God, rather than looking at the workings of God from the beginning to the end. A good way to visualize the problem is by comparing the total plan of God to a parade. There are many elements that go into a parade but none is complete without the other. If we were observing a parade through a knot-hole in a fence, because of our limited perspective, we might totally misunderstand the nature of a parade. If we looked for one moment and saw a clown we might draw the conclusion that a parade is like a circus. If we looked at another moment in time and saw a horse with a rider we might be tempted to conclude that a parade is like a rodeo. But a parade is not a circus or a rodeo. The only way you will be able to really understand a parade is to gain a better perspective. You will have to get above the fence and see the end from the beginning. In doing so you will see where the clowns fit in, where the horses fit in, and how they all fit together.

Too often when seeking to understand the purposes of God we have looked at God's dealings with the Jew and made that the whole. We have looked at God's dealings with the church and have made that the whole. We have looked at God's desire to destroy the works of darkness and have made that the whole. We have looked at God's desire to make us worshippers and have made that the whole. We have looked at God's desire for good pleasure and we have made that the whole. But the thing God is wanting us to do is to come up and sit with Him in heavenly places where we can get a true perspective of God's eternal purpose. When we do this we will see that all of the aspects or portions of truth have a place and fit beautifully into the whole. There is a place for the Jew; there is a place for the church; there is a place for character development and worship. They are all important. There is no contradiction. They all relate to the whole. Everything God has done has been essential for the ultimate realization of the divine purpose. When we see that one purpose, all of God's dealing with man come into proper perspective, and we begin to see how we as individuals fit into the plan of God that he has had from before the foundation of the world.

IJn.   IN THE BEGINNING WAS THE WORD ...

A. DETERMINED BY GOD

As we look into the eternal purpose of God the first thing that we need to see is that the eternal purpose of God was determined in the council of the Godhead. John tells us that "There are three that bear record in heaven, the Father, the Word, and the Holy Spirit; and these three are one." (I John 5:7). Because of this fact God Himself is able to establish His word and confirm His Word "in the mouth of two or three witnessess" (II Cor. 13:1). This is exactly what God did in eternity past. God established the purpose in Himself according to His good pleasure (Eph. 1:9). He did not consult man or angels because they were all to be a part of that plan.

B. ESTABLISHED BEFORE TIME BEGAN

The eternal purpose of God was settled by God before the foundation of the world (Ephesians 1:4). Our place in that overall scheme was also determined before the world began (II Timothy 1:9, Titus 1:2). God did not haphazardly begin His creative works. Before God did anything He had a plan. He had a blueprint. He had a goal in mind to which all of His creative energy, redemptive energy and sanctifying energy, would move. All of God's actions are calculated carefully. All of God's doings are in perfect harmony. All is related to the one goal, the one purpose for the universe, the earth, the angels and man. All relate to the mystery of His will.

C. HIDDEN IN AGES PAST

Even though God has always had but one purpose in his dealings with man, that purpose was not fully understood by man in the Old Testament age (Ephesians 3:5). In fact, when the prophets prophesied of the things that would come unto us they only wondered; they did not understand (Matthew 13:17). God was reserving the full revelation of this mystery for another time. The only comfort that God gave to the prophets was the consolation of letting them know that what they were saying was for a later time (I Peter 1:10-12). The patriarchs and the prophets were living in days of shadow and form when the revelation of the mystery was kept secret, yet this, too, had its purpose in God which was to culminate in the coming of the Lord Jesus Christ and the sending of the Holy Spirit which would make the realization of the purpose possible. The irony is that it was going to be through the very Scriptures penned by these men in ages past that this mystery was going to be made known (Romans 16:25-26).

D. MADE MANIFEST IN THE PRESENT AGE

Paul, more than anyone else in the New Testament age, seems to be the one to whom God brought this understanding. While others were wrestling over many peripheral areas because of their limited perspective, Paul's eyes seemed to have been opened as to the magnitude of God's plan. He is able to say that God had given him knowledge of the mystery by a special revelation.

> "For this cause I Paul, the prisoner of Jesus Christ for you Gentiles, if ye have heard of the dispensation of the grace of God which is given me to you-ward: How that by revelation (as I wrote afore in few words, whereby, when ye read, ye may understand my knowledge in the mystery of Christ) Which in other ages was not made known unto the sons of men, as it is now revealed unto his holy apostles and prophets by the Spirit."
>
> Ephesians 3:1-5

Continually we are reminded by Paul that this purpose is now made manifest (Romans 16:25-26; Colossians 1:26). There was a change in dispensations in which it suits God's purpose to open our understanding in this area. We are no longer in the age of shadows, we are living in the light of the Holy Spirit who is ready to illuminate our understanding. We are not living in the age of the prophets when they desired to know but could not know. We are living in a day when God has a desire to reveal these things to us

E. UNFOLDED LITTLE BY LITTLE

Because the full understanding of God's purpose was reserved for a certain age, nowhere in the Scripture does God tell us in outline form the beginning from the end. God has given some tremendous, divine clues throughout His Word that when pieced together make up a magnificent whole.[1] In attempting to unravel some of the divine mystery of God's purpose we must of necessity begin with God Himself, because when the purposes of God were established no one was there but God. In the beginning God dwelt alone *(Genesis 1:1)*. Before there ever was an angel, a star, a galaxy or a man, God's purpose was established. God did not do anything without purpose but all His ways were known to Him from the beginning *(Acts 15:18)*. It follows then that if we are going to understand God's purpose we must look for clues in the biblical revelation of the nature of God.

But how can we know the nature of God? Man cannot know God's nature unless God first reveals Himself to man. God's ways are past finding out unless He chooses to reveal them to us. The beautiful thing about our God is that He has chosen not to remain a mystery but He has a desire to make Himself and His nature known to His creation. The Scriptures of the Old and New Testament are a testimony to this desire of God. God has broken into history and moved by His Spirit on the hearts of man to bring to man a Word that is breathed by the very mouth of God. In this Word, God has given man an opportunity to know Him in His nature and purposes. Apart from this Word we can only know God's power and being, but through this Word He has given us a true picture of His nature. What kind of God do we serve? What kind of God rules the universe? What are His character qualities? What is His attitude toward His creatures? What limits has He chosen in which to operate and function? All of these and other questions can only be answered by God Himself. God has given us the answers to these questions but they must be searched out in the Word. God did not give us a "Summa Theologica" on the nature of God. Yet these answers are available to the humble seeker of God's truth. God generally hides Himself from the half-hearted. But if we are diligent, there is no reason why we cannot discover an answer to all of these questions in God's Word.

One of the most important revelations as to the nature of God that is foundational to our study of the plans and purposes of God prior to the foundation of the world is that of the immutability of God. God has told us that he does not change. God will change His mind in relation to judgment on His people when they change their mind, but He never changes in His essential character, His being and His nature *(Malachi 3:6; James 1:17; Hebrews 6:18)*. The implications of this are very important to us because it means that if God is indeed unchanging in His character, nature and being, then He is the same today in those qualities as He was 2000 years ago. It means that He is the same now as He was 2,000,000 years ago. It means that He is the same as He was when in eternity past He was dwelling alone. He is the same today as He was before there ever was an angel, a star, a galaxy or a man. If God is eternal now, He was eternal then *(Psalm 90:2)*. If God is Spirit now, He was Spirit then *(John 4:24)*. If God is light now, He was light then *(I John 1:5)*. If God is omnipotent now, He was omnipotent then *(Revelation 19:6)*. If God is omniscient or all knowing now, He was omniscient then *(Romans 11:33)*. The same is true in regard to God's moral attributes. Even though God's moral attributes require an object on which they may be expressed, yet we still have to believe that they are descriptive of the very heart of God. Therefore, if God is holy now, He was holy then *(Isaiah 6:3)*. If God is just now, he was just then *(Psalm 145:17)*. If God is love now, He was love then *(I John 4:8,16)*.

One of the most foundational and central revelations of the nature of God that Jesus Christ emphasized in His life and ministry was the concept of the fatherhood of God. Of all the tremendous revelations of grace and truth that come by the Son of God, this manifestation of the Father is by far the most significant.[2] In the Gospel of John this is made very clear when John says, *"No one has ever seen God; but God's son, He who is nearest to the Father's heart, has made him known".*[3]

---

[1]Note to reader:
It should be remembered that if we come to a correct understanding of the whole, all the pieces should fit. If at anytime in our interpretation we have to strain or stretch any verses we must challenge our understanding of the whole. It is very important for us to be objective and open in our appraoch to the Scripture. We have to be careful how much we cling to our traditional interpretation when God says Himself that there are certain things that will be sealed or shut up until the time of the end. If that is true then many interpreters who did not live in God's fulness of time or the time of the end cannot be expected to have all of the correct conclusions.

[2]Note: It is interesting that the word "father" is alphabetically the first word in the Hebrew Language.

[3]John 1:18 — New English Bible (See also Matthew 11:27 and Luke 10:22).

8

The important thing for us to see is that if God is a Father now and has the heart of a Father now, He had the heart of a Father from the foundation of the world. In the Old Testament age God was as much a father as in the New Testament age. The truth of it, however, is not explicitly outlined the Old Testament, yet every so often God gave them a clear word that He was a father to this people, (See: *Exodus 4:22-23; Deuteronomy 32:6,11; II Samuel 7:14-15; Psalm 2:7; 68:5; 89:26; 103:13; Proverbs 3:11-12; Isaiah 63:16, 64:7-8; Jeremiah 3:4,19, 31:9; Malachi 1:6; 2:10*).

The coming of Jesus, however, initiates a new age, the age of grace and truth, the age of fulfillment. Into this age comes Jesus with a powerful revelation of God as our Heavenly Father, having the heart and passions of a father. It is in this central revelation of God as a father having the heart of a father that we find a tremendous clue to the establishment of the purpose of God from the foundation of the world.

When God was dwelling alone in eternity past He had the heart of a father. It is only through our fatherhood that we can fully understand some of the feelings that are present in the heart of a father. Our own fatherhood reveals to us some of the things that a father desires more than anything else. God had the heart of a father and, therefore, he also had the desires of a father. He had the desire to reproduce Himself, to have many offspring, to reproduce His ministry in His offspring, to have fellowship and relationship with that offspring and to have a bride for His only begotton son.

1. A DESIRE FOR REPRODUCTION OF SELF

There is a desire in the heart of every father to have offspring that reflect the image of the father or that bear the family resemblance. God, too, is interested in an offspring that would be a true reflection of Him. He is interested in reproducing His character in His creation.

2. A DESIRE FOR MULTIPLICITY OF SEED

One of the greatest promises to the fathers of the Bible is that of multiplicity of seed. Even though children are now, in our day, looked at by many as a curse, they were originally designed to be a great blessing. The great promise that Abraham treasured above all was his fatherhood of many nations. As a father, God shares in this desire. Having only one Son did not fully satisfy the heart of God. God has a desire for many sons.

3. A DESIRE FOR REPRODUCTION OF MINISTRY

In the heart of every father is the desire to develop ministry in his offspring that they might share in the ministry of the father. This desire is reflected in the eastern custom of the training of the children in the vocation of the father. Jesus was trained under the hands of Joseph to follow him in his occupation. The Father also desires to bring His offspring into partnership with Him in His occupation, that of ruling the universe.

4. A DESIRE FOR WORSHIP, PRAISE AND FELLOWSHIP

In the heart of every father is the desire for appreciation to be expressed from his children and for there to be a high level of communication between him and his children. There is a desire for the cultivation of a deep personal relationship. God has this desire in relation to those whom He fathers. This is not to be a relationship based on coercion, but a relationship built on free will. In addition to these main desires there is a secondary desire in the heart of a father.

5. A DESIRE TO PROVIDE A BRIDE FOR HIS SON

In the Old Testament the father had the right to arrange the marriage of his son *(Genesis 24)*. God, too, would arrange a divine marriage for His Son by providing a worthy bride for Him.

When God began His creative work, all of this was in His heart. He began by creating an order of beings that would be servants to His higher order. He began by creating the angelic hosts. After which he created the universe of worlds. These Angelic hosts were to be the ministering spirits of the kingdom of God. They did not satisfy the heart of the Father, but they were to be ministers to those who would. Those created beings had a divine order to them much like a well-organized army. They are even referred to as the heavenly host. The main function of this creation was to worship God and do His bidding. One of the highest beings in this created order was Lucifer, the light bearer. He was entrusted with a spectacular ministry as the covering cherub in relation to the very throne of God. He was a superbly created being who had access to God's very presence. His primary ministry seems to have been in relation to music and worship. Most likely he was the worship leader of the universe whose job it was to direct all of the heavenly worship to God Himself.

How long this continued we do not know, but the day came when Lucifer, who was a channel of worship to God, began to look at himself and to notice what a beautiful creation he really was. As he did, he began to desire some of the worship that rightfully only belonged to God. He desired to be exalted above all the other creatures of God and coveted perhaps even that place which God had prepared for a future creation. He was much like Nimrod who rebelled against the thought of being a servant to another order. Nimrod was from the Canaan line which God had appointed unto service, yet he rebelled and desired rulership and worship for himself.

When this iniquity was found in Lucifer, he led a rebellion in heaven which involved a third part of the angels, and another kingdom was established opposed to the kingdom of God. When Satan fell every angel's loyalty was tested. Most of the angelic host remained loyal to God and are presently fulfilling His intended purpose.

When Satan fell God did not destroy Him, because just as God had used him as a vessel of honor, so He was going to use him as a vessel unto dishonor. He was going to use him in a negative way to help mature the offspring that he would produce. God did, however, remove Satan from his place of ministry in the heavenly hosts. He did prepare a place of final judgment for Satan and his angels, but He reserved his ultimate judgment until a later time when he would no longer be useful to the fulfillment of God's original purpose. In fact, He was going to give the privilege of dealing with Satan to the new creation that he would bring forth. When Satan fell he not only took many angels down with him but he also marred the worlds that God had created. *Genesis 1:2* describes the wasted condition to which a good earth had fallen.

God began the restoration of all that he had made to prepare the earth for the coming of his greatest creation—man. All that God did in Genesis 1 was to prepare for man. Man was going to be the creature who would satisfy the Father's heart. God revealed His heart in Genesis 1-2 when he declared His purpose. Notice how the language of this chapter shows the heart of the father.

a. "Let us make man in our image." This corresponds to the desire for the reproduction of Himself. Man's character is to conform to God's character. He is to be in the likeness of God.

b. "Be fruitful and multiply." This reflects His *desire for multiplicity of seed.* Adam and his wife were to replenish or fill up the earth with an offspring all reflecting the same image and likeness.

c. "Let them have dominion." This dominion over the earth was to be preparatory for dominion over greater things. God had a *desire for man to rule* with him, but he was to prepare him by giving him degrees of responsibility. If we are faithful in small things He will entrust us with greater things.

d. "The voice of the Lord God walking in the cool of the day." This was not a strange occurence on the day of the fall, it was a common occurence for God to fellowship with His creation. The man and woman were created *for His good pleasure.*

e. "It is not good that the man should be alone." It is the normal thing for a man to have a bride. So it is with God's Son. Even as God built a woman for Adam He had *a desire to build a many-membered bride for His Son (Matthew 16:18).*

f. "And subdue it." Man had the responsibility of subduing the earth. The implication here is that he had an enemy to face. There is the implication that some being would come with whom Adam must contend. That being was Satan himself. Yet when God's plan was finished man would have the privilege of subduing even Satan *(Romans 16:20).* When God placed man in the garden it was man's responsibility to subdue the earth. By his faithfulness in tilling and dressing the garden, the whole earth would have become a garden of Eden.

When God created man, Satan viewed it as a threat to him and his ultimate victory. Satan's primary purpose was no longer bringing glory and service to God, but trying to frustrate the purposes of God and win man over to his kingdom. In order for him to frustrate the purpose of God he had to try to corrupt God's creation which was destined to fulfill God's purpose. This is when we find Satan introduced in Genesis 3.

Satan was successful in seducing the man but he was not successful in frustrating God's purpose. While Satan caused man to fall from the image of God, to forfeit the dominion, and to corrupt his way, yet God made a provision for man in the seed of the woman *(Genesis 3:15).* It would be through this seed that the ultimate purpose of God would be realized. *That purpose being to have a many-membered man in the image of God who would qualify for rulership and dominion and for the honor of being eternally linked with the Son as one flesh.*

In one respect the purpose of God would be greater in that He would do the greatest miracle of the ages before the face of Satan who chose to exalt himself. He would take a weak, death-doomed creation and through the humility and sacrifice of His Son, and through their faith and reliance on God, make them into all that God desired from the beginning. He would demonstrate to Satan what true wisdom really is.

We can rightly ask ourselves, did the Fall catch God by surprise? Did he suddenly have to alter His purpose? The obvious answer is in the negative. To even imply that a finite being can frustrate or surprise an infinite being is to thoroughly misunderstand the greatness and the omniscience of our God. As created beings we could never catch God by surprise. God in His omniscience has absolute foreknowledge. When He created Satan He knew he would fall. When He created man He knew he would fall. Why did He go ahead and create it all if He knew what we would do? Because He also knew what He would do in regard to man's fall. He also knew that through the incarnation man could ultimately come to full stature. He was able to look beyond to the finished product that was set before Him and He felt it was worth the price. Jesus had this attitude about the cross. Because of the joy that was set before Him, because of the glory that would follow He endured the cross and despised the shame. God therefore was willing to pay the price, because in His infinite foreknowledge He knew that the final product of the creation-redemption process would satisfy His father's heart.

In *Genesis 3:15* God comes to the man and comforts him in the hope of a redeemer who will make the realization of God's purpose for him possible. Six facts about this salvation of man are upheld by this passage:

1. Salvation is initiated and worked by God. Apart from this man has no hope.
2. God's plan of salvation will destroy Satan, the enemy. His head, the seat of his authority, is to be crushed.
3. God's plan includes all of mankind, all of the offspring of Adam and Eve, not merely one nation or individual.
4. God's plan will be realized through the work of a mediator that is born of a woman.
5. God's plan involves the suffering of the redeemer, his heel is to be bruised.
6. God's salvation will be experienced as a part of history even as the fall is part of history.

All of the pre-incarnation history is seen as an expectant preparation for the coming of the Redeemer. From *Genesis 3:15* on, the primary thrust of the recorded word is the preparation and realization of the seed of the woman who would make it possible for man to be restored to God's intended plan and go on to fulfill His intended purpose. From this point on we can see God's concern over all the aspects of His purpose in preparing a people for his manifold purpose. God's concern is that His people experience all aspects of the birthright and blessing (involving rulership, priesthood, fruitfulness, character, and victory over enemies) which relate to this one central purpose. All of the covenants that God made with man deal with nothing but different aspects of this one purpose. The whole Bible is a revelation of the unfolding drama of this one central purpose of God. The plan is initiated in the first chapters of Genesis and it is achieved in the closing pages of the book of Revelation.

F. WILL NEVER BE FRUSTRATED

Man is fickle and more often than not when he begins something he gets discouraged in the middle and the project ends up in a pile in the corner of the attic or basement. Man is impatient and when he sees that a desired project may take some tedious hours of work he is liable to abandon the project. Man is easily frustrated in his tasks because often times he does not realize the difficulty of a task until he is in the middle of it. When he realizes some of the frustration involved, he is prone to abandon the project and try something else. Man is affected by moods and whims, emotions and changing desires.

God is totally opposite to man in this regard. God, who knows the end from the beginning, takes all things into account before He ever begins anything. He is not like the man building a tower who failed to count the cost at the outset. God knew what the cost would be. He knew that His plan would cost Him the incarnation and the crucifixion and yet He was willing to pay the price. God knew all the things that Satan would do to frustrate His purpose, but He deemed it worthwhile to go ahead. Now that God has begun, He is totally consumed with the realization of His original goal. Being omniscient there was absolutely nothing that He did not foresee and allow for. Being omnipotent there is absolutely nothing that will stand in the way of God's achieving His goal. When God sets a goal or establishes a purpose, the thing is as good as done.

The Scripture is very clear on this point. Notice the confidence that Isaiah expresses in the purposes of God.

> *"The Lord of hosts hath sworn, saying, Surely as I have thought, so shall it come to pass; and as I have purposed, so shall it stand: That I will break the Assyrian in my land, and upon my mountains tread him under foot: then shall his yoke depart from off them, and his burden depart from off their shoulders. This is the purpose that is purposed upon the whole earth; and this is the hand that is stretched out upon all the nations. For the Lord of hosts hath purposed, and who shall disannul it? and his hand is stretched out, and who shall turn it back?"*

Isaiah 14:24-27

The obvious response to these questions is "no-one". Once God has determined or purposed something no-one can disannul it. Once God has begun to work no-one will be able to turn His hand back. No-one!! This includes man, angels and even Satan himself! God will use any tool or vessel necessary to accomplish His goal.

God likens this whole principle in His character and nature to the cycle of the rains. He compares the cycle of the rain and snow to the cycle of His Word. Just as the rain and snow that fall from heavens do not return to heaven until they first accomplish their intended purpose (i.e. watering the ground, producing fruit), so it is with the Word that goes forth from His mouth, it always accomplishes the purpose for which it was sent, it always brings forth the intended fruit of the earth *(James 5:7)* before it returns to Him again.

> *"For my thoughts are not your thoughts, neither are your ways my ways, saith the Lord. For as the heavens are higher than the earth, so are my thoughts than your thoughts. For as the rain cometh down, and the snow from heaven, and returneth not thither, but watereth the earth, and maketh it bring forth and bud, that it may give seed to the sower and bread to the eater. So shall my word be that goeth forth out of my mouth; it shall not return to me void, but it shall accomplish that which I please, and it shall prosper in the thing where to I sent it."*

Isaiah 55:8-11

God's Word has gone out, and just as sure as it has gone forth it will accomplish all that He desires it to accomplish. He will fulfill His purpose.

G. IS BEING ACCOMPLISHED IN THE NEW TESTAMENT CHURCH

While God has been working toward this one central purpose since the beginning of time, it is going to be through the Church that this ultimate purpose is going to be realized.

> *"Unto me, who am less than the least of all saints, is this grace given, that I should preach among the Gentiles the unsearchable riches of Christ; And to make all men see what is the fellowship of the mystery, which from the beginning of the world hath been hid in God, who created all things by Jesus Christ:*

To the intent that now unto the principalities and powers in heavenly places might be known by the church the manifold wisdom of God. According to the eternal purpose which he purposed in Christ Jesus our Lord;"

Ephesians 3:8-11

It is in the Church where all of God's intended purposes will come to realization. The Church is God's final instrument that He is using to bring about everything He intended. He is going to use the Church and His operation through the Church to bring us to completion, maturity, perfection and to the lost image *(Ephesians 4:12-16, Colossians 3:10, Romans 8:28-30)*. He is going to use the Church to meet His desire for a bride for His Son *(II Corinthians 6:14, Ephesians 5:32)*. He is going to use the Church to deal finally with Satan *(Matthew 16:18-19, Romans 16:20)*. He is going to use the Church to rule and reign with Him for eternity *(Revelation 20:6)*. He is going to use the Church to bring back mankind into the right relationship to God in fellowship and priestly function *(I Peter 2:5-9, I John 1:3)*. He is going to use His Church to fulfill His desire for multiplicity of seed and sinless offspring *(Revelation 12)*. When we realize this, it makes the process of God's dealings in our lives so precious and exciting. He is preparing us by His Spirit for eternity.

An obvious question that must be answered then is what is the relationship of the Jewish nation to this eternal purpose? The next chapter will deal more specifically with this question, but the only way we can see this is by looking at God's purpose as a unit from beginning to end. God has always been concerned with the same final product. He has moved through stages in the realization of the purpose. Israel was a part of the process but not the end in itself.

When God began in Genesis in the process of redemption the most important part of His plan was the bringing forth of the seed and the preparation of the world for that coming seed, the Messiah. The promises made in Genesis were for the whole world, not one nation. The promises were for all in Adam.

From the beginning Satan's chief desire was to frustrate and bring to naught the purposes of God especially since God pronounced his doom in declaring that his head (the seat of authority) was going to be crushed *(Genesis 3:15)*. From the birth of the first manchild, Cain, Satan has been seeking to devour, pervert and destroy man, so that he could in some way keep the seed of the woman from being manifested.

Satan came against the first manchild Cain, and won him and used him to kill the second son Abel. Satan thought he had destroyed God's plan but God brought in a substitute seed, "Seth". Satan's main preoccupation was to corrupt the race of men so that this deliverer would never come. As the world was filled with people Satan was quite successful in perverting the whole race of man *(Genesis 6)* except for one godly man and his family. To preserve the seed from corruption, God destroyed the wicked world of man and saved the righteous Noah to begin anew on a cleansed earth.

Soon after Noah's new beginning, Satan was able to fill the heart of Ham in an attempt to pervert the seed line again. As time progressed, the world again fell deeper into sin. One sin led to another sin and soon idolatry and false religion spread, culminating in the tower of Babel. God again responded by intervening and destroying the attempts of the enemy. Continually man's weakness to keep himself pure was exposed by the devices of his greatest and most powerful enemy, Satan.

In order to preserve man from Satan and preserve the seed line to Messiah, God called a man named Abraham. He called him out of idolatry and separated him from the world of his day. He prepared Him as the father of a nation, a nation that He would use as His vessel to bring forth the Messiah.

To save the nation by a virgin-born mediator, God called one nation and separated them from the other nations. He chose them by His sovereign grace and made them a special and peculiar people. He built a hedge of protection around them which was to be a schoolmaster or guardian for them, to make sure that they got where they were supposed to go. He hedged them in with the law that they might be able to keep themselves pure until the Messiah would come who would be the light of the world.

While Israel was under the law, God made them a showcase of divine principle and government, and the stranger was invited to come and join himself to the true God. Israel was the "church in the wilderness". *(Acts 7:38)*. They were to be the nation of priests that mediated God's principles to the world and were instrumental in preparing the world for the coming seed. In many respects Israel as a nation failed to understand and fulfill their ministry to the world. But the law did not fail. The law did preserve a seed line from Abraham, through David, and up to Mary, from whom the Messiah would come. And from that line,

Jesus the Christ was born. He was born as the "Consolation of *Israel*" but also the "Light of the *World*".

With the coming of Christ, the need or purpose for the hedge was no longer there, so the hedge or guardian was removed. Christ came, and in its place He established the church which until His second coming would be the instrument through which God would carry out His purpose. God's desire was that all of natural Israel would become part of Spiritual Israel, the church *(Galatians 6:16)*. Many of them did *(Acts 6:7)*, but most people had been so caught up with the schoolmaster they missed the One to whom it pointed.

We have to see that in all of God's dealings with man His desire has been not for one nation or one race only, but it involved the bringing together of all nations into ONE BODY — THE BODY OF CHRIST!!

God's purpose involved the nation of Israel but not Israel alone.

God's purpose was not merely to bless the nations through their connection with the chosen nation, Israel, because that was not something that was hid in ages past *(Genesis 12:3)*. That was something that was taken for granted in the Old Testament age *(Genesis 22:18; 26:4; Deuteronomy 32:8, Psalm 18:49)*. Paul, however, was able to say that whatever this purpose was, it is something that is now revealed. God's purpose was to raise up one many-membered body out of all nations, Jew and Gentile, that would fulfill the demands of the Father's heart. In the New Covenant something takes place between Jew and Gentile that is exciting in Paul's mind. He uses some significant terminology to describe the new relationship of the Jew and Gentile in the new covenant, including the following:

1. One Body *(I Corinthians 12:13, Ephesians 2:16; 4:4)*.
2. Abraham's Seed *(Galatians 3:27-29)*.
3. Children of Promise *(Galatians 4:28)*.
4. Fellowheirs *(Ephesians 3:6)*.
5. The New Man *(Colossians 3:10-11)*.

Paul unfolds this purpose in detail in *Ephesians 2:11-22*. An outline of this passage reveals the following truths:

1. Paul Describes The Former Condition Of The Gentiles:

*Gentiles In The Flesh
 *Uncircumcision
  *Without Christ
   *Aliens From the Commonwealth Of Israel
    *Strangers From the Covenants Of Promise
     *Having No Hope
      *Without God In The World
       *Far Off
        *Enmity From God and Man

2. Paul Describes The Present Condition Of The Gentiles:

*BUT NOW
 *In Christ Jesus
  *Made Nigh By The Blood Of Christ
   *At Peace With God And Man
    *Made One With The Jew
     *Middle Wall of Partition Broken Down
      *Enmity Abolished
       *One New Man
        *Both Reconciled Unto God In One Body
         *Preaching of Peace To Those Which Were Far
          *Both Have Access To The Father

3. Paul Describes The New Relationship That Results:

*No More Strangers And Foreigners
*Fellow Citizens With The Saints
*Of The Household of God
*Jew and Gentile Fitly Framed Together

There is now no distinction in Christ between the Jew and Gentile. When Christ came, all those Jews who did not believe were cut off the tree of God, while all those Gentiles that believed were grafted into the tree of God which is above all a tree of *faith*. The visible expression of that tree is the Church, the one new man, the household of faith and the temple of God. Hence, in order for the eternal purposes of God to be realized it necessitated the "mysterious" coming together of both Jew and Gentile into one. Both the believing Jew and the believing Gentile are fitly framed and perfectly joined together into one new man. Any unbelieving Jew who now turns to Christ becomes part of the Church. Any unbelieving Gentile who now turns to Christ becomes part of the Church. Once in the Church they become "fitly framed together". To maintain any national, racial or natural distinction in the one new man is to divide the Body of Christ, for in Christ there is neither Jew or Gentile, bond or free.

What makes all of this so exciting is that it changes our whole perspective on what God is doing in the Church. The Church is not an accident, it is not a second thought; it is not a parenthetical invention; it is not a substitute for something else that is more important; it is not a 'fill in', it is at the very center of God's will and it is the very instrument that God will use to accomplish His eternal purpose. When we realize this, we know that we are not just "killing time" but God is presently moving in our hearts to conform us to His image.

Chapter 3
THE CHURCH AND THE KINGDOM

When we realize that the Church is at the very center of God's will and purpose, and that God has only had but one eternal purpose that He has been working toward for all eternity, it must cause us to re-evaluate much of our thinking in the realm of dispensational truth. At the center of this debate is the whole question of the relationship of the Church to the Kingdom of God. In understanding what is going on, it is absolutely essential for us to understand the distinction between, and the relationship of, the Church and the Kingdom. We need to be able to answer questions that are being raised by many today. Some of these questions include: "Is the Church equal to the Kingdom? Is the Church Gentile and the Kingdom Jewish? Is the Kingdom past, present or future? Is the Kingdom material or is it spiritual?"

Many of our concepts in regard to the nature of the kingdom and its relationship to the Church are based on sandy soil. We want to make sure that what we believe is what the Bible teaches because we know that if the tree is not of God's planting it will be plucked up and destroyed. Many of our concepts regarding the kingdom of God are put forth to defend a system of eschatology or to defend a system of biblical interpretation. Because of this there are times when we find a twisting and arranging of the Scripture to confirm a pre-conceived conclusion that we have made. Whatever our understanding of these areas we should never have to twist the Word of God to make it fit into our system. If our system of biblical interpretation is correct, all the Scriptures should fit beautifully together, and they should all teach and affirm the same thing. Too often we do not allow the Scripture to speak for itself but when we read or study it, we do it through glasses that have been colored by our traditions. God is challenging us in our day to approach the Scripture in these areas objectively and let it speak for itself. The summary of any doctrine or teaching consists of all the Scriptures dealing with that subject in the Bible. This kind of approach is needed in regard to the biblical teaching concerning the kingdom of God.

A. THE KINGDOM DEFINED

The word "Kingdom" occurs about 160 times in the New Testament and means, in its simplest form, "royal reign". If God is a king He must have a realm or domain in which He rules. The kingdom of God in its broadest sense is that realm over which God reigns. It is the domain of God under God's rule. When we pray for His kingdom to come we want the rule and reign of the King to be recognized in the earth *(Matthew 6:9-10)*.

B. THE KINGDOM OF GOD AND THE KINGDOM OF HEAVEN

In defining terminology it is very important to see that the Scripture often times uses different terminology for the same thing. In the New Testament it is clear that the terms "Kingdom of God" and "Kingdom of Heaven" are such terms. Careful examinations of the following cross references will show this to be the case:

KINGDOM OF HEAVEN	KINGDOM OF GOD
Matthew 4:17 *"The **kingdom of heaven** is at hand"* *Matthew 5:3* *"Theirs is the **kingdom of heaven**"*	*Mark 1:14* *"the gospel of the **kingdom of God**"* *Luke 6:20* *"Yours is the **kingdom of God**"*

KINGDOM OF HEAVEN	KINGDOM OF GOD
Matthew 10:7 *"Preach, saying the* **kingdom of heaven"**	*Luke 9:2* *"to preach the* **kingdom of God."**
Matthew 11:11 *"He that is least in the* **kingdom of heaven"**	*Luke 7:28* *"He that is least in* **the kingdom of God"**
Matthew 13:11 *"to know the mysteries of the* **kingdom of heaven"**	*Luke 8:10* *"to know the mysteries of the* **kingdom of God"**
Matthew 13:31 *"the* **kingdom of heaven** *is like to a grain"*	*Luke 13: 18-19* **"kingdom of God** *. . . is like a grain"*
Matthew 19:14 *"of such is the* **kingdom of heaven."**	*Mark 10:14* *"of such is the* **kingdom of God"**

It is interesting to note that the term "kingdom of heaven" is most common to the Gospel of Matthew which is recognized as the Gospel to the Jew. Perhaps Matthew chose this term over the "kingdom of God" to combat the idea that the kingdom which was right at hand was an earthly, physical kingdom. Matthew does however at times use both and in at least one case he himself uses the terms interchangeably. In *Matthew 19:23-24*, it says:

> *"Then said Jesus unto his disciples, Verily I say unto you, that a rich man shall hardly enter into the* **kingdom of heaven.** *And again I say unto you, It is easier for a camel to go through the eye of a needle than for a rich man to enter into the* **kingdom of God."**

On the basis of this evidence we can only draw the conclusion that there is really no distinction made in the New Testament between the terms "kingdom of God" and "kingdom of Heaven".

C. THE EXTENT OF THE KINGDOM

The kingdom of God is an everlasting kingdom. It extends from eternity to eternity and it covers all. God's throne is in the heavens and everything has to answer to Him.

> *"All thy works shall praise thee, O Lord; and thy saints shall bless thee. They shall speak of the glory of the kingdom, and talk of thy power. Thy kingdom is an everlasting kingdom, and thy dominion endureth throughout all generations."*

Psalms 145:10-13

> *"The Lord hath prepared his throne in the heavens; and his kingdom ruleth over all."*

Psalms 103:19

> *"The Lord shall reign forever and ever."*

Exodus 15:18

D. THE KINGDOM OF GOD IN EARTH

In relationship to the earth and to time, God is also to be seen as the king of all. The kingdom is the Lord's and *"He is the governor among the nations"* (Psalm 22:28-29). When God made the earth and the universe of worlds it was all under His authority as the king of all, yet He chose, in keeping with His eternal purpose, to share His rule with His creation. God delegated a measure of authority to man and gave rulership and dominion into the hands of man *(Genesis 1:28)*. Since the creation of man, God has chosen human instruments through whom He would exercise His rulership in the earth. Because the kingdom is the Lord's, he can give rulership and deliver the kingdom into the hands of whomever He will *(II Samuel 16:8; I Kings 2:15)*. God is most concerned about fulfilling His original goal and purpose. Therefore He will rule through whatever instrument is best fitted to His purpose. *The instrument that God uses to demonstrate His kingdom in the earth may change, but His purpose remains the same.* We must remember that the kingdom of God relative to time must be seen in two main divisions *(Matthew 6:10)*. There is the kingdom of God in heaven, which God himself rules in glory, and there is the kingdom of God in the earth, which God Himself rules through human channels. In the history of man and God's dealing with man God has used various channels to demonstrate His kingdom in relation to the earth, but all of them have centered around the central purpose of God.

E. INSTRUMENTS OF THE KINGDOM

Although God's kingdom is everlasting in its extent relative to heaven, it has stages in its demonstration relative to the earth and man. God only has one kingdom, but He has used various instruments or channels for the demonstration of that kingdom in the earth.

1. The kingdom in the earth was given to Adam and Eve *(Genesis 1:26-28)*.
Adam and Eve were to have dominion in the earth and subdue all their enemies. Had they not failed through sin God would have used them as an instrument to fulfill His eternal purpose.

2. The kingdom in the earth was given to the patriarchs *(Genesis 9:1-2; 12:1-3)*.
These men that God singled out were to be the representatives of God's kingdom in the earth, and they were to minister the authority of God's kingdom to all. They too failed to accomplish all that they were called to do.

3. God raised up the nation of Israel through whom he would rule. Israel
became the instrument by which God would continue to carry out His purpose in the whole earth. Israel was to be a nation under God, bringing God's rule to the rest of the earth *(Exodus 19:2-6; Deuteronomy 7:6-8; Numbers 24:7)*. Israel continued to be God's instrument in the earth through whom He manifested His rule and carried out His purpose through the theocracy, the Kingship of Saul *(I Samuel 10:16,25)*, David *(I Chronicles 10:14)*, Solomon *(I Kings 1:46)* and even in the divided kingdom of Israel *(I Kings 11:31-35; I Kings 21:7; Ezekiel 16:13)*. Israel too, failed to measure up to their full potential and fell miserably short of the fulfillment of God's purpose.

4. Because of Israel's backslidden condition, God, at times, even used the Gentile world as an instrument or channel through which to accomplish His purpose. While Israel was in captivity, God no longer used them as the instrument in the earth. During this time God used the Gentile nations and kings to administrate His kingdom and to do his bidding *(II Chronicles 36:22-23)*.

5. When Jesus came on the scene as the last Adam He came as the only hope through whom the purpose of God could be realized. While He was on the earth He was the channel through whom God exercised His rulership in the earth. Jesus was the perfect expression of what Adam was intended to be and yet in Himself Christ could not fulfill God's original purpose. All he could do was provide a way by which the purpose could be accomplished. Jesus came as the King of the kingdom. He came to usher in the kingdom of God, He came with power and authority to build His Church.

6. The present instrument through whom God is demonstrating his rule in the earth is the Church *(Matthew 21:43; Ephesians 3:10)*. Not only is this the *present* instrument and channel through whom God is working, it is the *final* instrument through which the purposes of God *will* be realized. In the Church God is going to see man come to maturity and full stature. It is the Church that will be used to bruise Satan and storm the gates of the enemy *(Romans 16:20; Matthew 16:18)*. It will be the Church which will become that bride for the Son. It will be the Church that will ultimately satisfy the heart of the Father. There is no other instrument or channel that God will use to fulfill His purposes before the return of the Lord because the Church will not fail. The Church will not fail, because of the difference that the atonement makes in the instrument and man's ability to be what God has designed him to be.

F. THE CHURCH AND THE KINGDOM IN THE NEW TESTAMENT

When we understand that God has used various instruments throughout history for the expression of His Kingdom in the earth it is not difficult for us to understand the relationship of the Church to the Kingdom. The inauguration of the Church by Christ in the first century was to be the initiation of a new phase in the operation of the Kingdom relative to the earth. This is why John the Baptist was able to declare, *"Repent ye, for the Kingdom of heaven is at hand" (Matthew 3:2).* In what sense is this true? In what sense could he say that the kingdom is nigh and yet he himself already be in the kingdom? He could say this because John's ministry was transitional to this new phase or instrument of God's kingdom in the earth *(Luke 16:16; Matthew 21:43).*

Some of the clearest teaching on the relationship of the Church and the Kingdom in the New Testament is given to us by Jesus Himself. Even though Jesus only mentions the Church twice in the Gospels yet He made it very clear that the object of His ministry was to build His Church. When we understand this much of Jesus's teaching on the Kingdom, it clarifies the relationship that exists between the two.

1. Jesus preached the gospel of the Kingdom *(Matthew 4:23; 9:35; Mark 1:14).* Jesus
is preparing the world for the Church and so the gospel of the Kingdom is the subject He preaches to accomplish that purpose. In fact, even after His death, burial and resurrection as the Church's birthday is drawing near, He is still teaching the things pertaining to the Kingdom of God *(Acts 1:3).*

2. Jesus taught that the Kingdom of God was at hand *(Matthew 4:17; Mark 1:15).*
Jesus was not taken by surprise when He was crucified by the Jews, but all that happened was according to God's foreknowledge. When Jesus came preaching that the Kingdom was at hand, he knew full well that the Church was the next thing on God's prophetic timetable.

3. Jesus taught that His ministry ushered in the Kingdom of God *(Matthew 12:24-28; Luke 11:20).* Did Jesus know that He was coming as the Head of the Church, that He was to be the first born among many brethren? He certainly did! And all of His teaching was perfectly compatible with that vision.

4. Jesus instructed His disciples to preach the gospel of the Kingdom *(Matthew 10:7; Luke 9:2,60; 10:9-11).* The disciples carried the same message that Christ did. Not only did they preach the gospel of the Kingdom while Jesus was with them but they continued throughout the book of Acts to preach and teach the gospel of the Kingdom *(Acts 8:12; 14:22; 19:8; 20:25).* In fact, right up to the last verse of the book of Acts they were preaching the Kingdom *(Acts 28:23,31).*

5. Jesus taught His disciples to pray that God's Kingdom would come *(Matthew 6:10; Luke 11:2).* They were praying that God's government would be again established in earth even as it is in heaven. The Church is the instrument through which that government came *(Matthew 18:15-20).*

6. Jesus declared His intention of building a Church to which He gave the keys of the Kingdom *(Matthew 16:19).* Christ makes it very clear in this passage that the Church is entrusted with the administration of the Kingdom in the earth. Keys in scripture are often connected with government and authority. Here the keys of the Kingdom are given to the Church.

7. Jesus declared that He would come in His Kingdom before some standing there had tasted death *(Matthew 16:28; Mark 9:1; Luke 9:27).* What did He mean by this? Was he referring to the transfiguration? Perhaps He was referring to the inception of the Church on the day of Pentecost *(John 14:18).*

8. Jesus declared that the Kingdom had been taken from the Jews and

given to a nation *(Matthew 21:43).* That chosen nation is specifically identified later in the epistles as being the Church *(I Peter 2:5-9).*

9. Prior to His crucifixion, Jesus said that He would not eat with the disciples again until He did it in the Kingdom *(Matthew 26:29; Mark 14:28; Luke 22:16,18).* Yet after His resurrection we find Him eating with them *(John 21:13; Acts 1:4; Acts 10:41).* The Lord continues to eat and drink with us as we commune with Him around the Lord's Table that we observe in His presence in the Church *(I Corinthians 11).* The Lord communes with us spiritually as we open our hearts to Him *(Romans 3:20).* Perhaps the greatest time of feasting with the Lord will occur in the great marriage supper. Does not all of that suggest a vital connection between the Kingdom and the Church?

10. Jesus declared that His Kingdom was presently spiritual and not natural *(Luke 17:20-21).* It is a spiritual Kingdom that is not of this world system *(John 18:36).* It is a spiritual Kingdom that belongs to those with spiritual qualities *(Matthew 5:3; Luke 6:20; Matthew 5:10).* It is a spiritual Kingdom that is entered through a spiritual experience, not natural rites *(Matthew 5:20; 7:21; 19:14-24; 21:31; 23:13-14; Mark 12:32-34; Luke 9:62; John 3:1-5).* It is a spiritual Kingdom where greatness is determined on the basis of spiritual qualities *(Matthew 5:19; 11:11; 18:1-4).* It is a spiritual kingdom built on the royal law of love, a spiritual reality *(Mark 12:32-34).* It is a spiritual Kingdom that consists of the faithful, not just the natural seed *(Matthew 8:11; Luke 13:28-29).* Jesus could even turn to the Jewish leaders of the day and tell them that even though they had certain natural qualifications they were still outside of the Kingdom *(Mark 4:11).*

11. Jesus taught that we were to seek first the Kingdom *(Matthew 6:33; Luke 21:31).* This is true for every believer today. We can't seek that Kingdom apart from an identification with God's seat of authority in the earth, the Church.

12. Jesus declared that this gospel of the Kingdom was to be preached in all the world *(Matthew 24:14).* Is not this the commission given by Jesus to the church? *(Mark 16:15).* Is there more than one gospel? Is there a difference between the Gospel of the Kingdom and the gospel of Christ? There are many phrases used to describe the gospel in the New Testament. There is:

a. The Gospel of Jesus Christ *(Mark 1:1)*
b. The Gospel of His Son *(Romans 1:9)*
c. The Gospel of God *(Romans 1:1)*
d. The Gospel of the Kingdom *(Matthew 24:14)*
e. The Gospel of the Grace of God *(Acts 20:24)*
f. The Everlasting Gospel *(Revelation 14:6)*
g. The Glorious Gospel *(I Timothy 1:11)*
h. The Gospel of the Circumcision *(Galatians 2:7)*
i. The Gospel of the Uncircumcision *(Galatians 2:7)*

There are many titles for the gospel but Paul makes it eminently clear that there is only ONE gospel *(Galatians 1:6-9).* There is only one way of approach for both Jew and Gentile.

The disciples were commanded by Christ to go into all the world and preach the gospel *(Mark 16:15),* and in response to this command they went out and preached the gospel of the Kingdom *(Acts 8:5,12; 20:24-25; 28:23,31).*

In addition to the teaching of Jesus we have other implications that the Kingdom and the Church are joined. John who was a pillar in the Church considered himself to be in the Kingdom *(Revelation 1:9).* Paul, the master builder of the New Testament Church, considered himself to be a laborer in the Kingdom of God *(Colossians 4:11)* and taught that we are now in the Kingdom by new birth *(Galatians 1:13; I Thessalonians 2:12; Hebrews 12:28).*

Does all this mean that the Church and the Kingdom are identical? No! The term "church" is not synonymous with the terms "Kingdom of God" or "Kingdom of heaven". The terms cannot be used interchangably in the New Testament. The Kingdom is greater than the Church. Try substituting "church" for "Kingdom" in the Lord's prayer and it will become evident that the terms are not identical. The church is the visible expression of the kingdom of God in the earth, but God's Kingdom is greater than the Church. God's rule under Christ includes the angels and the universe of worlds, but the Church at the present time is that instrument in the earth through which God is demonstrating His Kingship. The Church is the Kingdom in mystery form. The manifest form of the Kingdom on earth is yet to come.

> "The mystery form extends from Pentecost to the return of Christ, when the visible will replace the invisible, and Christ will no longer reign through the Holy Spirit but will reign in person Himself."

The Kingdom is all inclusive. It includes the angels while the Church only includes the redeemed. The Church is in the Kingdom of God and it is God's instrument in the earth for the expression of God's Kingdom.

G. ENTRANCE INTO THE KINGDOM

In Duewel's book on *Ecclesiology* there is an excellent discussion on entrance into the Kingdom. He says:

> "For the Christian, God's Kingdom begins as a personal experience of righteousness, peace and joy in the Holy Ghost (Romans 14:17). It is God's personal reign over the life of the Christian; it is the acceptance of Jesus as Lord. The root of the evil of the world is the rejection by sinners of this reign of God over their lives, the rejection of God's will and plan, the rejection of the Lordship of Christ. God brought His kingdom near in the person of Christ, and man was called to repent because of the nearness of that kingdom (Matthew 3:2; Mark 1:15). Man cannot create the Kingdom by his own efforts. God must bring it near by taking the initiative Himself. The message of the Gospel is that God did take this initiative. Those who accept Christ as Lord become children of the kingdom (Matthew 13:38), the born again ones who can see and enter the kingdom of God (John 3:3, 5-7), the members of Christ's church. As they seek first the kingdom (Matthew 6:33) putting God's interests first in their own souls and in their own lives, they form a part of the blessed society of those with like spiritual life and like spiritual interests. They fulfill the royal law of the kingdom of supreme love to God and love for the neighbor like that for one's self (Mark 12:30; James 2:8)."

(Ecclesiology, Duewel, pg. 11-12.)

Chapter 4
THE NATURE OF THE CHURCH

Where do we get our idea of what the Church is to be? Do we get our views from what unbelievers expect of us? Do we get our ideas from what various religious commentators suggest? Is our concept of what the Church is to be shaped by traditions? Or do we get our understanding of the Church from what God says? Whatever view we have in regard to the church will shape how we relate to the present world. We must be sure that the traditional views that we have held are really those views which God sets forth.

"Therefore brethren stand fast, and hold the traditions which ye have been taught, whether by word or by our epistle."

II Thessalonians 2:15

A. THE WORD DEFINED

In order for us to understand the true nature of the Church we have to understand the meaning and usage of the word "church". The word "church" comes from the Greek word "ekklesia". This word in its simplest definition means "the called out ones".

In the secular Greek society the word was used commonly and it referred to an assembly of free citizens who were called out from their homes and/or places of business to assemble together to give consideration to matters of public interest. The word is used this way a couple of times in the New Testament. When Paul and his company had stirred up the local god-makers in Ephesus the citizens of Ephesus had such an assembly in an attempt to deal with the problem, and this assembly is referred to by the word usually translated "church" *(Acts 19:32,39,41)*.

When Jesus refers to a church or assembly He is not introducing a totally new concept. God had his "called out ones" in the Old Testament as well. In fact Stephen referred to the children of Israel as the "church in the wilderness" *(Acts 7:38)*. In the Old Testament, Israel was the called out company and is often referred to as the "Kahal Jehovah" (i.e. the called and assembled people of God). Whenever the Israelites were summoned from their dwelling and gathered unto the Lord they were referred to as the called out ones, the congregation or the assembly *(Numbers 10:7; 20:10; I Kings 8:14; I Chronicles 29:20; Psalm 40:9; Psalm 107:32; 149:1)*. It is interesting that when the Septuagint translates the Hebrew term "Kahal" it uses the term "ekklesia". Israel's twelve tribes encamped around the Tabernacle's four sides according to a careful plan. When the trumpet was blown, they assembled before the door of the Tabernacle as the people of God, as the "called out ones", to receive His instructions, commands or blessings.

In the New Testament the word "ekklesia" is used 114 times and 110 times it definitely refers to the "called out ones" of Jesus Christ. Jesus Himself introduces this usage when He refers to "His Church" *(Matthew 16:18)*. The personal pronoun "My" differentiates this company from all other groups of people. This is not just any gathering or assembly this is "His" gathering and assembly. It includes those who have been called out from their place of habitation in this world, who have separated themselves unto God unto the door of the New Testament Tabernacle, Jesus Christ Himself! They are the free citizens of the heavenly community summoned by the trumpet of the gospel to assemble themselves together for worship and fellowship *(Philippians 3:14; I Corinthians 1:24-26; II Peter 1:10)*.

It is important for us to understand that the word "church" is never used to refer to a building or a house of worship. In our English usage it is often used of a building, but this usage is foreign to the New Testament concept of the Church. It is unfortunate that the King James translators have rendered *Acts 19:37* as "robbers of churches". The Greek word in this passage is not "ekklesia" but it is the word that comes from the word usually translated "temple". The Church is the people of God that are builded together into a spiritual building for God's habitation *(Ephesians 2:20-22)*. The Church meets in a building or house but it is not a material building itself *(Romans 16:5)*. The people of God are a spiritual house and if we make the mistake of thinking of the Church as a natural building we will become building worshippers. We will be much like the religious leaders of Jesus' day who admired the stones and materials out of which their natural buildings were constructed *(Mark 13:1; Matthew 24:1-2)*. The tragedy is that we can have the view that the Church is a building and miss the true Church. We can put all our energies into glorifying a natural facility and miss the responsibility that we have before God to give our energies and time to the edification of the people of God who, after all, are the true spiritual house that God is indwelling *(Hebrews 3:6)*. The actual building that the people of God meet in is only an auditorium or "sheepshed". We have to be very careful that we put the emphasis where God does. The mistake could cause us to hold the material building (sheepshed) above the spiritual building (the sheep).

It is also important for us to realize that this word "church" in the New Testament is never used to refer to a sect, a denomination, or an organization. In our day we talk of "the church" or "our church" indicating a form of ecclesiastical system, but this concept is also foreign to the New Testament. The Church is "His" church. He is the central authority to whom all New Testament churches must relate. The Church on earth is bigger than any one denomination, sect or organization. By making this mistake we can make God's Church narrower than it really is and exclude ourselves from a vital participation with part of Christ.

B. THE OLD TESTAMENT CONNECTION

As was seen earlier there is a vital connection that exists between the Old Testament Church or "called out ones" and the New Testament Church or "called out ones". God only has one purpose toward which he is building. The Church of the Old Testament is foundational and preparatory to the Church of the New Testament. The Church of the Old Testament and New Testament are pictured by Paul as an olive tree whose roots comprise the fathers of faith in the Old Testament *(Romans 11; Galatians 5:7)*. God only has one tree. It is a tree of faith rooted in men of faith. Faith and trust in God are seen as the criterion for entrance into and security in that tree of faith. The Church of the Old Testament and the Church of the New Testament must be seen as both part of the same plan. What God called the nation of Israel to be in the Old Testament He called the church to be in the New Testament. Israel had one destination—to bring us to Christ and the Church *(Galatians 3:24)*. The Church has one destination—the new Jerusalem, the city of God. The gates of that city are the twelve tribes of Israel but the foundations are the twelve apostles of the Lamb (see *Ephesians 2:20-22*). The Old Testament Church looked forward to Christ, but the New Testament Church is built on Christ.

As a nation Israel failed to fulfill God's eternal purpose, but its failure was not complete, God has always had a remnant of faith-righteous individuals from Adam to the present. His remnant has been a faithful instrument in His hands and has been covered by His covenant. Israel was to be God's instrument in the earth through whom God would demonstrate His purpose and through whom He would bring forth Christ. When Christ came, He came to build the Church which was the new instrument or vehicle which God would use to carry on and fulfill His divine and ultimate purpose. Many of those who belonged to natural Israel flowed into the new Spiritual Israel of God *(Acts 6:7)*. However, many of the natural seed of Israel rejected the Messiah and eliminated themselves from the tree of faith *(Romans 11:20)*. Some of the natural Israel of God were never even a part of God's tree of faith in the Old Testament *(Luke 3:8-9; John 8:39,44; Jeremiah 9:25-26)*.

As Christ comes and establishes the Church, the Church becomes all that Israel was to be, so much so that the exact same terminology is used of the Church in the New Testament as was used of the Church in the Old Testament. Notice the following chart:

TERM USED	O.T. CHURCH	N.T. CHURCH
A Chosen People	*Deuteronomy 10:15*	*I Peter 2:9*
A Holy Nation	*Exodus 19:6*	*I Peter 2:9*
The People of God	*Psalm 100:3*	*II Corinthians 6:16*
A Priesthood	*Exodus 19:6*	*I Peter 2:9*
God's Treasure	*Exodus 19:5*	*Matthew 13:44*
The Bride or Wife	*Isaiah 54:6; 62:5*	*II Corinthians 11:2-3*

TERM USED	O.T. CHURCH	N.T. CHURCH
God's Vineyard	*Isaiah 5:7*	*Matthew 20:1; I Corinthians 3:9*
God's Inheritance	*Isaiah 19:25*	*I Peter 5:3*
Israel	*Isaiah 44:6*	*Galatians 6:16*
God's Flock	*Jeremiah 23:3*	*I Peter 5:2*
A House	*Ezekial 18:31*	*I Timothy 3:15*
A Light	*Isaiah 60:1,3*	*Matthew 5:14*
God's Witness	*Isaiah 43:10*	*Acts 1:8*
A Church	*Acts 7:38*	*Galatians 1:13*

The great mystery hidden for ages but preached by the apostles in the New Testament was that the Jew and the Gentile were now made one *(Ephesians 2:14; 3:5-6)*; in one body; one building; built upon the foundation laid by the Old Testament prophets and the New Testament apostles; Christ being the Chief Cornerstone *(Ephesians 2:20-22)*; and that the old and new were built into one habitation of God through the Spirit. There is but one foundation with the prophets of the old dispensation and the apostles of the new dispensation together forming the basis for the new spiritual and true Israel, the Church of Jesus Christ!

It must be remembered that there have always been tares in the Kingdom. In the Church in the Old Testament, natural Israel, there were those who had been circumcised externally but had not had the circumcision of the heart *(Jeremiah 9:25-26)*. The same is true in the Church in the New Testament, spiritual Israel. There are those who are Christians in name only. But that does not alter the fact that there has been a true Church in every generation which has consisted of the faith righteous.

C. TWO ASPECTS OF THE CHURCH

There are two primary ways in which the term "church" is used in the New Testament. Jesus Himself used the term "church" twice and each time He used it in a unique sense. An understanding of these two senses is foundational to an appreciation and understanding of all subsequent usages. The first usage is introduced by Jesus in *Matthew 16:18* where He says *"upon this rock I will build my Church"*. When Jesus used this term in this passage He was not referring to any particular locality or group of believers, He was designating the Church in its broadest sense. He was referring to that which is heavenly, eternal, comprehensive and still in the process of construction. In this Church is included that company of believers in Christ in all ages, living and dead, who are distinct from the world by virtue of their calling from and separation unto God *(Ephesians 1:22; 3:10; 3:21; 5:25-32)*. In its broadest sense we could say that it even includes those of the human race who are even as yet unborn but who in their lifetime will be numbered among the redeemed by virtue of their responsiveness to the calling of God to salvation. This Church involves a mystical union of all believers of all ages into a spiritual body for the habitation of the Spirit, with Jesus Christ as its head. It is not a union that can presently be seen in the visible sense, but it is an invisible reality in the eyes of God.

The second usage of the word "church" is initiated by Christ in His only other reference to the term "church" in the New Testament in *Matthew 18:17*. In this context Jesus is discussing disciplinary procedures. He is dealing here with a specific group of people that make up a local, earthly, definable, restricted body consisting of professed Christians voluntarily associated together around the name of the Lord Jesus Christ. Out of the 114 uses of the word "church" in the New Testament it is interesting that 96 references are clearly to what we shall call "the local church". The local church is the present, visible earthly expression in time of the body of Christ. Local churches are New Testament organizations of groups of believers in given localities, which are marked out by confession of faith, discipline of life, obedience in baptism, gathered to the person of Jesus Christ, having gifted ministries and keeping the memorial of the Lord. They are always spoken of as complete units within themselves which may voluntarily co-operate and fellowship with other local bodies.

"The same word designates at one and the same time the universal church and the local assembly. Even broader expressions like "the church of God" or "the temple of God" refer sometimes to one, sometimes to the other *(I Co. 15:9 and I Ti. 3:5; II Co. 6:16 and I Co. 3:16)*. The local church is only a small part, a fraction, of the universal church. In the ancient world when each group of Roman citizens gathered, wherever it might be, it was a *Conventus Civium Romanorum*, a voice of Rome. This group had no meaning apart from Rome and her various functions. Each Roman citizen arriving in a city where such a group existed, automatically and without ceremony, became a member of that assembly. Geographically these groups could be several thousands of miles from Rome; in spirit they were a part of Rome. "That is the true idea of the Church; each local church is only a part, a miniature of the great general Church."[1]

D. JESUS ON THE NATURE OF THE CHURCH

Jesus only referred to the Church in specific terms on two occasions and yet in those two places He implied a great deal about what the nature of the Church was to be. In *Matthew 16:15-19* we find these words:

"He saith unto them, but whom say ye that I am? And Simon Peter answered and said, Thou art the Christ, the Son of the living God. And Jesus answered and said unto him, Blessed art thou, Simon Bar-jona; for flesh and blood hath not revealed it unto thee, but my Father which is in heaven. And I say also unto thee, that thou art Peter, and upon this rock I will build my church; and the gates of hell shall not prevail against it."

In *Matthew 18:15-20* it says:

"Moreover if thy brother shall trespass against thee go and tell him his fault between thee and him alone: if he shall hear thee, thou hast gained thy brother. But if he will not hear thee, then take one or two more, that in the mouth of two or three witnesses every word may be established. And if he shall neglect to hear the church, let him be unto thee as a heathen man and a publican. Verily I say unto you, Whatsoever ye shall bind on earth shall be bound in heaven; and whatsoever ye shall loose on earth shall be loosed in heaven. Again I say unto you, that if two of you shall agree on earth as touching any thing that they shall ask, it shall be done for them of my Father which is in heaven. For where two or three are gathered together in my name, there am I in the midst of them."

Out of these two portions of Scripture many things concerning the nature of the Church can be gleaned. The main truths that Jesus tells us concerning the Church that He was going to build are (1) that God Himself is the architect of the Church, (2) that Jesus Christ is the builder of the Church, (3) that Jesus Christ is the owner of the Church, (4) that Jesus Christ commissioned the Church, (5) that the Church is a living and spiritual organization, (6) that the Church will be holy unto the Lord, (7) that the Church will be a unified church, (8) that the Church will be a victorious church and (9) that the Church has a local expression. Let us look at these concepts a little more closely.

1. God Himself is the Architect of the Church of Jesus Christ.
Being the architect, it must be remembered that God had the *idea* for the church. This is not something that man conceived, it was something that God determined in His own mind before there ever was a man *(Ephesians 1:9; 3:10-11)*. Man is always seeking credit for that which God produces. We can have confidence that the Church is a "better idea" simply because it has its origin in the mind of God.

Being the architect, it is also true that God has the *plan, pattern* or *blueprint* for the Church. God did not conceive a beautiful idea and then turn it over to the ingenuity of man to come up with a plan to make it work *(Hebrews 8:5)*. As men we must be willing to concede that if God has an idea or a goal, He also has a pattern, a blueprint or a design by which He will insure that His idea or goal will be reached. If the Lord is going to build a Church, it is basic that He as a wise master builder build it according to the divine blueprint or design.

---

[1]William Barclay, New Testament Wordbook.

Being the architect, God only has *one* pattern for the church. We know that God has firmly established in heaven, a pattern for all things. *(Hebrews 9:23)*. There is one blueprint, and all the laborers must build according to this blueprint. As laborers together with God we need to make sure that the pattern and the blueprint that we are following is truly the pattern and blueprint of God's making.

There are several sources from which we can get a pattern. First of all, we can get our pattern from the *world.* Israel had a basic weakness in that at times in their history they looked to the world for a pattern. They looked to all the other nations that were not established under the government of God and they desired to pattern themselves after them. They rejected God's pattern of theocracy for the world's plan of monarchy. They paid for their mistake. The world's ways will not produce heavenly results. This is a challenge for the people of God today. Are we seeking methods of building God's house that are successful business practices of this world but are not sanctified by God? Do we look at those who have had successful business endeavors, and in an attempt to be successful in man's eyes, copy their ways? Have we been willing to use only God-ordained means to achieve God-ordained results? The pattern of the world can never bring forth life, and even as with Saul, it is doomed to end in tragic failure.

Secondly, we can get our pattern from the *religious traditions* of the past. Traditions in themselves are not bad. There are good traditions to which we are to hold fast *(II Thessalonians 2:15; 3:6)*, but there are also bad traditions. Traditions are bad if they keep us from obeying the Word of God. What happens when the Word of God says something but our tradition says something else? Someone has once said that the seven last words of any church are, "We never did it that way before". When the Church becomes so crystalized that it can no longer respond to the direction of the Head, it is a dying, paralysed Church.

Thirdly, our pattern can come from the *mind of regenerate man.* Sometimes we actually believe that just because we have been born-again, every thought, idea or program that comes into our sanctified minds must be from God. And so we feel that as Christians, as long as we are sincere, we will not go wrong. This is a form of deception that Satan would have us believe, because he knows that if he can divert the Church from God's pattern, the church will lose its effectiveness in the battle against him. Sincerity is no substitute for obedience to the God ordained plan, and it will never produce the same results. A nurse can be absolutely sincere in ministering a certain toxic drug, but the effect is going to be bad no matter how sincere she is.

Our pattern has to come from God. God is a God of order and He has a plan and pattern for everything he does. Right from the very first chapter of the Bible we are impressed with the fact that God never does anything promiscuously. He had an order in creation, He had a pattern for the first man *(Genesis 1:26);* and He had an exacting pattern for worship (Leviticus). Even in the children of Israel's conquest of the promised land God had an order.

Over and over we are made to realize that God is very detailed and exact about how He wants things done. He knows that "there are many devices in a man's heart; nevertheless the counsel of the Lord, that shall stand" *(Proverbs 19:21)*. Many churches have good intentions but they are not experiencing the blessing of God in these days. Why is one church seemingly blessed while another is not experiencing blessing? Does not the Bible teach that God is no respector of persons? It is true that God is not a respector of persons, *but* He is a respector of principles. If we are going to be successful in these days we are going to have to be like David and be willing to seek the Lord after the due order *(I Chronicles 15:13)*. David had good intentions, he had a love for the presence of God, but what he was doing was not producing life in his people. It was his responsibility to stop what he was doing and seek after the biblical pattern. This is what God wants of us, because God has a pattern.

God has had a pattern for every structure that He ever commanded to be built. He had a pattern for the ark of Noah *(Genesis 6:14-15)*. He left nothing to the mind of man. God was the only one who knew all that had to go into the ark. He was the only one capable of providing the pattern. God provided the pattern for the tabernacle of Moses *(Exodus 25:9, 40; Numbers 8:4)*, the temple of Solomon *(I Chronicles 28:11-19)*, Ezekiel's Temple *(Ezekiel 43:10-11)*, the City of God *(Revelation 21:15)*. Is not God much more concerned about the New Testament Temple of God, the Church *(I Corinthians 3:10)*?

Everything in the structure has to measure up to the pattern if we expect God to fill that structure with His glory. The glory of God can only fill that which is built according to the pattern. All of the biblical structures were to be places where God's glory dwelt. God's glory would never have filled the Tabernacle of Moses if Moses had tampered with the divine pattern *(Exodus 40:33-34)*. God's glory never would have flooded the sanctuary in the Temple of Solomon had not Solomon been exacting about strict adherence to the divine blueprint *(II Chronicles 5:1-14)*. So also, the Church will never be filled with all the fulness of God, unless we are concerned about the pattern of God *(Ephesians 3:17-21)*.

This truth is declared throughout the entire Bible. The pattern of God cannot be violated if we are to experience the blessing of God. Cain tried to offer God his own ideas about worship, the end result of which was banishment from the presence of God *(Genesis 4:1-8)*. Nadab and Abihu tried to offer strange fire on the altar of incense and they found out that God is concerned over the pattern *(Leviticus 10)*. Uzziah thought he could approach God his own way and he died a leper as a result *(II Chronicles 26:16-20)*. If the Church is to maintain the presence of the Lord they must determine that they will accept the pattern of the Word as their pattern. God only promises to bless and fill that which is made according to the pattern *(Mark 16:20)*.

As the people of God we need to be honest with ourselves. Do we believe what we believe because the Word says it, or because it causes no problems? God wants us to step out in faith. He is not interested in our excuses for not following His pattern. The plan and pattern of God is never out of date. The style of church architecture may change throughout the centuries, but God's plan for the Church has not changed. God's plan is as applicable today as it was in the Church of the first century. God's plan cannot be improved upon by man. The foundation and the basic structure of every local church should be the same worldwide, even as the framework of every human being is the same. There will be differences of personality and expression, but God has one basic pattern for all churches everywhere in the world!

2. Jesus Christ Himself is the Builder of the Church.
When Jesus spoke of the Church in Matthew 16 He indicated to the disciples that it was something that He was going to build. Jesus had a desire, mission and calling to build the Church. He did not say that man would build it for Him. He did not just give the blueprint to man and tell him to do the best he could. He would not leave such an important task up to the strength and mind of man. There is too much at stake for God to trust the whole project in the hands of finite creatures. It is a beautiful thing, however, that God has called us to be co-laborers together with Him. He has called us to be helpers in the greatest mission ever, but we must ever keep in mind that He is the master builder. We must look to him as the source and not to our own strength. We can devise programs to get people to join our churches, but if the Lord has not added them they are not His Church. All of our labors apart from the Lord are futile *(Psalm 127:1)*.

3. Jesus Christ is the owner of the Church.
Jesus said that this Church that He would build would belong to Him. The Church belongs to Him because He designed it, built it and purchased it with His own blood *(Acts 20:28)*. The Lord has never relinquished His claim to the Church, in fact He calls it by His Name *(Romans 16:16)*. The Church is the Church of God *(I Corinthians 1:2)* and the Church of Christ *(Romans 16:16)*. Men have been entrusted with the administration of the affairs of the Church, but it does not belong to them *(I Corinthians 4:1)*. Because of this, man will be held accountable for what he has done with this trust.

4. Jesus Christ commissioned the Church.
In Matthew 16 Jesus gives to the Church, represented in the twelve, the power to bind and loose. This authority was confirmed to them in *Matthew 18:18*. This authority was foundational to the commission that Christ gave to the Church upon H's departure *(Matthew 28:19-20; John 20:21; Acts 1:8)*. The Church is the one institution that the Lord has set in the earth by which He will carry out His program. It is interesting that He did not say He was building a hospital, or an orphanage, or a social center. Not that any of these structures is wrong in itself, but God is building a Church because He knows that a Church in proper New Testament order, which is fulfilling that to which it has been commissioned, will meet the needs for which all these other human agencies are designed. The Church is commissioned by God because it is the instrument of God in the earth to fulfill the mission of God.

It is clear from Jesus' own words that the Church is a divine institution in the fullest sense. It is purposed by God, built by God, authored by God, owned by God, headed by God, sanctified by God, indwelt by God, and appointed to service by God. The Church has a divine origin, a divine existence and a divine function.

5. The Church is a living and spiritual organism.
In the context of *Matthew 16:16-18*, Jesus also implies that the Church is more than an organization, it is an organism. An organism is

something that has structure and life, while an organization implies only structure. A machine has organization in that it is composed of an orderly arrangement of many parts, but it is not an organism because it has no life.

Peter's confession of faith in Jesus Christ as the Son of the *living* God makes the Church something that has life. The Church is an organism made up of those who have had a spiritual experience and possess spiritual life. There is no evidence that anyone ever became a member of a New Testament Church until they had experienced that new birth which comes through faith in the Lord Jesus Christ. In addition to the fact that the Church is comprised only of those who have spiritual life and are indwelt by God, it also in a corporate sense is the dwelling place of the Spirit of God *(I Corinthians 3:16-17; Matthew 18:19-20)*.

6. The Church will be holy unto the Lord.
Nowhere in the New Testament do we read of a defeated, failing and battered bride. Jesus presents a picture of the Church in Matthew 18 that is concerned about sin in the camp and is willing and eager to purge out leavening influences. The best descriptive New Testament words regarding the church are "glorious" and "holy" *(Ephesians 5:23-32)*. The New Testament Church may be called holy for various reasons. Among the more important of these are the following:

a. The Church is holy because it is the unique, special possession of a thrice holy God *(I Peter 2:9)*.

b. The Church is holy because it is separated from the world *(John 15:19; 17:14-16; II Corinthians 6:17)*.
The Church is not separated from the world because it refuses to have any contact with the world, but it is separate from the world in spirit and life while carrying on its ministry in the midst of the world.

c. The Church is holy because it is consecrated unto God *(Ephesians 5:27; Colossians 1:22; Romans 12:1; James 4:7)*.
It is consecrated to God for His indwelling, for His fellowship, for His service and for His glory *(Psalms 93:5)*.

d. The Church is holy because it is cleansed from sin *(Ephesians 5:26; Hebrews 13:12; II Corinthians 7:1; I Thessalonians 5:23-24; I John 1:7-9; Titus 3:5, 2:14)*.
Impurities are to be purged out from the individual as well as the corporate life *(I Corinthians 5:7)*.

e. The Church is holy because she is to marry Christ.
The Son of God is going to have a worthy bride. God cannot violate His own word in relation to His Son. Jesus, the Son of God, cannot be unequally yoked *(II Corinthians 6:14)*. God is preparing the bride who is to be a holy, pure, chaste virgin, who is unspotted by the world and sin. The bride for the son is to be without blemish, spot, wrinkle, or any such thing *(Ephesians 5:27)*.

Because the Church is holy in the eyes of God those who are members of His Church are referred to commonly as "saints" or "holy ones". This is what we are called to be. Sometimes in actual experience we may fall far short of this and yet in the atonement we must believe that God has provided the means for victory over sin. The Church to date has never been the glorious, holy, undefiled, wrinkle free or mature body that God desires. It has been at times a very poor example of what the grace of God can produce. The historic church has been but a pale reflection of its Lord, and a very imperfect instrument for the fulfillment of God's purposes. Its sins are many. It has betrayed Christ, trifled with false gods, stooped to compromise, left the sheep unfed, and in so many ways failed to fulfill the sacred trust committed to its charge.

But God will have such a Church that will be a powerful instrument in His hands. His Word has declared it. The failings and shortcomings of man will not disannul it. God will have a people that will come to the measure of the stature of the fulness of Christ *(Ephesians 4:11-16)*.

7. The Church will be a unified Church.
Jesus declared in *Matthew 18:19* that the church would be a place that would be characterized by agreement among its constituency. The Amplified New Testament renders this passage in the following manner:

> *"Again I tell you, if two of you on earth agree (harmonize together, together make a symphony)*

about — anything and everything — whatever they shall ask, it will come to pass and be done for them by My Father in heaven."

Matthew 18:19 Amplified Bible

The church is a complex organism that has a tremendous unity in the midst of diversity. Unity does not mean uniformity. Uniformity implies a loss of identity and individuality. In the unity that exists in the church we maintain individuality, personality, unique expression and a variety of function, and yet we come into a corporate identification where we forfeit our rights to act independently of the rest of the members. This relationship is seen in various New Testament pictures of the church;

The church is **ONE** body with **MANY** members.
The church is **ONE** temple with **MANY** stones.
The church is **ONE** flock with **MANY** sheep.
The church is **ONE** nation with **MANY** citizens.
The church is **ONE** vine with **MANY** branches.
The church is **ONE** family with **MANY** brothers and sisters.
The church is **ONE** army with **MANY** soldiers.

This kind of unity exists nowhere else in the world, and is the source of tremendous power in the Church. It is this unity that will be a witness to the whole world of the truth of the Gospel *(John 17:20-24)*. It is the unity of the people of God that will be their defence in the days of storm. It is this kind of unity that is foundational to all that God desires to do through His people.

The Church of Jesus Christ will experience two kinds of unity, and the first is foundational and must precede the second, or it can lead to division. First, God desires there to be a **unity of the Spirit** *(Ephesians 4:3)*. This is the kind of unity that is created in each member of the body of Christ the moment he is born into that body. Yet it must be pointed out that it is also a relationship that must be cultivated and maintained, for Paul tells us that we are "to endeavor, to make an effort, to labour, to be diligent, to be prompt to: keep the unity of the Spirit in the bond of peace." The only way we can give ourselves to this goal of unity is to keep before us a picture of the Body of Christ as God sees it. God is calling His body to unity in these days so that His glorious purpose might be fulfilled through it. If any church body is going to be effective, it is going to have to be unified.

Second, God desires to establish a **unity of the faith.** Paul tells us that Christ gives ministries in the Church to help adjust the saints to do the work of serving, but also to establish the unity of the faith *(Ephesians 4:13)*. Paul writes as if he firmly believed that the day would come when there would be a unity of faith. This involves a doctrinal unity. This was somewhat of a lofty dream for Paul because it was not the reality even in his own day that we sometimes think. Paul knew that he differed doctrinally from others *(Galatians 2:6-12; Acts 15:7; II Peter 3:15-16)*. Yet Paul knew that as they gave themselves to maintaining the unity of the Spirit in the bond of peace, that the day would come when they would experience the unity of the faith.

A beautiful demonstration of this principle is found in Acts 15. Here many were gathered with various doctrinal viewpoints. Many of the viewpoints were very strong and yet because they were all committed to each other in the Spirit of God they were submitted to the Word of God. Before that day was over, as they endeavored to maintain the unity of the Spirit in the bond of peace, they all came to the unity of the faith.

The Church can only become one as it follows after the one Head, Christ *(Ephesians 4:13)*. The foundation of this unity in the church is in its relationship to God. The Church is one because its God and Father is *one*, because its loyalty is to *one* Lord, because it is indwelt by *one* Holy Spirit.

Jesus prayed that the church might be one. If ever anyone prayed according to the will of God it was Jesus. If anyone's prayer will ever be answered it will be the prayer of the only begotten Son of God. He prayed that the people of God would be one even as He was one with the Father *(John 17:11,21)*. The Father and the Son have a two fold unity. There is the unity of the Spirit in that in essence, nature, and substance, they are one. This we experience when we are born of one Spirit and become partakers of the divine nature. There was also a unity of doctrine *(John 7:16; 8:26; 12:49-50)*, in purpose *(Matthew 26:39; John 4:34; 5:30; 5:38; 16:10; 17:4)*, in love *(John 3:35; 5:20; 15:9-10; 17:23-24,26)*, and in work *(John 4:34; 5:19; 8:29; 14:10-11)*. God desires this kind of unity in the Church as well.

Paul prayed often for the unity of the Church. He desired to see unity in many areas. He wanted unity:

a) of mind *(Romans 15:5-6; Philippians 1:27; 2:2; 4:2)*,

b) of fellowship *(Romans 15:7; I Corinthians 1:10-15; 3:3-8)*,
c) of love *(Philippians 2:2)*,
d) of doctrine *(Ephesians 4:13-14; Galatians 1:8-9; II Timothy 1:5-9)*,
e) of witness *(Romans 15:6; Philippians 1:27)* and
f) of Spirit *(Ephesians 4:3)*.

If ever the body of Christ needed to seek unity it is today, for Christ is coming for a united Church.

8. The Church Will Be A Victorious Church.
Many times we think of the Church as an anemic force in society. But that was not the type of Church that Jesus said He would build. In *Matthew 16:18-19* He tells us of a Church that would march against the very gates of hell and be successful. Satan would like to keep us believing that we are powerless against the forces of darkness, for in doing so his seat of authority is secure. But the Church that Jesus is building is a Church that has been commissioned by God, empowered by God and is operating with divine authority. The Church that Jesus is building cannot be overcome by Satan's wisdom or power. This Church is on the move as the army of the Lord. This Church, not Satan, is the most powerful force in the world today. This Church is the instrument of the kingdom of light at work destroying the works of darkness. The Church does not only have a system of defense, but it has a powerful offense that God expects to be in full operation.

God gave to the Church the keys of the Kingdom *(Matthew 18:15-20)*. God gave to the Church the power to bind and loose *(Matthew 18:18)*. And God will use the Church as the army of the Lord to deal the death blow to Satan *(Romans 16:20; Ephesians 1:20-23)*. The Church for too long has fled before the serpent like Moses did when in reality God has given us the power to tread upon serpents!

9. The Church Has A Local Expression.
Jesus taught us a great deal about the nature of the local expression of the Church that He was building. In *Matthew 18:15-22*, where he deals with an example of an actual body, he implies the following:

a. The Church is composed of brothers.
b. The Church is involved in areas of discipline.
c. The Church is an area of local government.
d. The Church is a defined body from which one could be expelled.
e. The Church is a place of fellowship in faith and prayer.
f. The Church is a place where Christ promises to be in the midst.
g. The Church is a gathering identified with the Name of Christ.
h. To be disciplined by the Church is to be disciplined by Christ.
i. The authority of the Church is based on unity.
j. One person cannot make up a church.
k. Until the Church is completed, there is going to be a great need for love, patience and a lot of forgiveness.

Most of these concepts will be dealt with in later chapters, but it is amazing that Jesus says so much in such a short passage. Jesus is not only interested in our becoming identified with the body of Christ worldwide, but He is also very much interested in our becoming identified with its local expression for our own protection, well-being and growth.

E. THE CHURCH UNFOLDS.

In Jesus' teaching we have the foundation on which the New Testament Church is built. On the day of Pentecost that Church was inaugurated. In the years that followed, the Church and man's concept of the Church grew and matured as the early leaders faced problems, crises and opposition. As the Church developed the local expression of the Church became more easily definable. This Church can be seen in direct relation to what Jesus taught about the Church. In the books of Acts we see the local Church as:

1. A congregation or assembly of people in a given locality *(Acts 8:1)*.
2. An assembly of believers in Christ *(Acts 5:14)*.
3. A place of teaching and discipline *(Acts 11:26)*.

4. A complete unity in itself with corporate authority *(Acts 15:22)*.
5. Built by Christ Himself *(Acts 2:47)*.
6. Part of Christ Himself *(Acts 5:14)*.
7. A place where the Lord joins people, not man *(Acts 5:13)*.
8. Disciplined by Christ Himself *(Acts 5:5)*.
9. Structured, having men ordained in positions of authority to exercise leadership, discipline and oversight *(Acts 14:23; 20:17-28)*.
10. A place of manifold ministry *(Acts 13:1; 15:4)*.
11. Joined in voluntary fellowship with other local churches *(Acts 15:3-4)*.
12. A place established in the faith *(Acts 16:5)*.
13. A place from which ministry was sent out *(Acts 13:1-4)*.

The whole thrust of the New Testament is the Local Church. Each book of the New Testament demonstrates how God uses the Local Church to bring His people to maturity and completion. Nowhere in the New Testament do we have an alternative plan suggested. God wants us to emphasize what He emphasizes and get excited about what He is excited about.

Chapter 5
THE CHURCH — GOD'S PECULIAR PEOPLE

"And to make all men see what is the fellowship of the mystery, which from the beginning of the world hath been hid in God, who created all things by Jesus Christ:
To the intent that now unto the principalities and powers in heavenly places might be known by the church the manifold wisdom of God.
According to the eternal purpose which he purposed in Christ Jesus our Lord:"

Ephesians 3:9-11

In *Ephesians 3:10* Paul refers to the fact that the manifold wisdom of God is going to be unfolded and demonstrated by the instrument of the Church. The word "manifold" here is a Greek word that occurs no other place in the New Testament. This word means "very many sided, much varied, having great variety or diversity". The wisdom which God is revealing through the Church is very many sided, much varied, having great variety or diversity. In some respects it could be referred to as a precious diamond with many facets. In order to get a true picture of a many faceted diamond you need to look at it from many different angles. In order to get a true picture of what God is doing through the Church we must also look at it from many different sides.

God's wisdom is so complex as it comes to the mind of man that God has had to employ the visual method of teaching that we might get a true glimpse of what He has in mind. In order to give us greater understanding of the Church and the mystery of God, God has given us various pictures and metaphors of the Church in the Bible. No one picture can give us a full understanding. God has given over 70 different names and titles to the Church. Each of these declares to us another facet of divine truth relative to the Church. It is only as we examine all of these individual pictures can we have a complete understanding of the whole. Each of these individual pictures tells us something unique about the nature of the Church and what God plans to do through the Church.

The Church is likened to many things including:

1. The Branch of the Lord's Planting *(Isaiah 60:21)*.
2. The City of the Living God *(Hebrews 12:22)*.
3. The Church of the Firstborn *(Hebrews 12:23)*.
4. The Flock of God *(Ezekial 34:15; I Peter 5:2)*.
5. A Golden Candlestick *(Revelation 1:20)*.
6. God's Husbandry *(I Corinthians 3:9)*.
7. God's Heritage *(Joel 3:2; I Peter 5:3)*.
8. Heavenly Jerusalem *(Galatians 4:26; Hebrews 12:22)*.
9. An Inheritance *(Psalm 78:71; Isaiah 19:25)*.
10. The Israel of God *(Galatians 6:16)*.
11. Mount Zion *(Hebrews 12:22)*.
12. The Mountain of the Lord's House *(Isaiah 2:2)*.
13. The Pillar and Ground of Truth *(I Timothy 3:15)*.
14. A Pleasant Portion *(Jeremiah 12:10)*.
15. A Vineyard *(Jeremiah 12:10; Matthew 21:41)*.
16. Bride of Christ *(Revelation 21:9)*.
17. Congregation of Saints *(Psalm 149:1; 89:5)*.
18. General Assembly *(Hebrews 12:23)*.

Each of these pictures could be examined individually to see the distinct contribution that each one of these makes to the whole concept of what God is doing through the Church, but we are going to give ourselves to several of the main New Testament pictures of the Church that seem to be emphasized to a greater degree throughout the whole Bible. As we examine these including:

God's Peculiar People
God's Temple or Building

32

God's Family or Household
And The Body of Christ,
we can expect to glean and untold some of the truths that God has concealed in these pictures for us.

GOD'S PECULIAR PEOPLE

"Ye also, as lively stones, are built up a spiritual house, a holy priesthood, to offer up spiritual sacrifices, acceptable to God by Jesus Christ.

Wherefore also it is contained in the Scripture, Behold, I lay in Sion a chief corner stone, elect, precious: and he that believeth on Him will not be confounded.

Unto you therefore which believe he is precious, but unto them which be disobedient, the stone which the builders disallowed, the same is made the head of the corner.

And a stone of stumbling, and a rock of offense, even to them which stumble at the word, being disobedient whereunto also they were appointed.

But ye are a chosen generation, a royal priesthood, a holy nation, a peculiar people: that ye should show forth the praise of Him who hath called you out of darkness into his marvelous light:

Which in time past were not a people, but are now the people of God; which had not obtained mercy, but now have obtained mercy."

I Peter 2:5-10.

The Church of Jesus Christ is called "a peculiar people." At first glance a lot of people would agree because they know some Christians who are really "strange" or "odd". But when God calls the Church a "peculiar" people, He does not mean that the Church is something "odd, eccentric or funny". This word is not used in a negative sense in the Bible but it is used in a positive sense. The word peculiar here refers to "a special, precious, private possession". It is something that is exclusively individual that is set apart because of its special value from all other things. When we see it in this sense, it is not undesirable to be called God's peculiar people. In fact, it is a great honor and a place of distinction. As the Church of Jesus Christ we are a special people, a precious people, a people of special value, and a people that are set apart from all others by God for a unique and special purpose.

As we examine God's dealing with man we find that God has dealt with two groups of people in a special way. The first group or nation that God dealt with as a peculiar people was the nation of Israel. The second group or nation that God has dealt with as a unique possession is the Church, the New Testament Israel of God. God has only called two groups of people *"My People"*. In Exodus when God sees the children of Israel in cruel bondage and their cry comes up to Him He distinguishes them as being His unique and private possession by calling them His people. Israel was called to be distinct and separate from all the other nations. Israel was forbidden to integrate with other people or to learn their ways, because they were God's people. Unfortunately, Israel did not maintain the separation to which God had called them *(Hebrews 2:3)*. They ended up following after the ways of other nations. In the New Testament this place of unique possession is given to the Church *(Hebrews 8:10; I Peter 2:9-10)*. The Church, too, has the challenge that this title evokes. It, too, is challenged to remain separate from all other nations and to keep itself from all other gods. In the Church's sometimes dark history there has been much compromise with the nations round about, but the Church that Christ will meet as a bride will be separate from sin and decked in fine linen.

In addition to the appellation "My People", God has only called two groups of people the *"children of God"*. God is a loving Father. As a Father He has a family that He is in the process of bringing to maturity. This family is made up of children who are peculiar in that they have a different heritage than those around them. Heredity does make a difference. The children of Israel were different because they had a different father, not Abraham but God. In the Old Testament dispensation it was possible to have Abraham as your father and not be the children of God *(John 8:39, 44)*. It was also possible not to have Abraham as your father and still to be a child of God *(Matthew 1:5)*. The qualifications in the Old Testament were not natural but they were spiritual *(Hebrews 11; Romans 9:6-8; 11:20)*. In the New Testament, the Church fills this place as the *"children of God"* *(Romans 8:16)*. The qualifications remain the same. We all become the children of God by faith in Jesus Christ. Natural heritage is not important, but spiritual heritage is very important. Because of our spiritual heritage we become the "called out", separated, unique, chosen children of God.

separated, unique, chosen children of God.

In addition to the title "children of God", God has only called two groups of people "peculiar". In the Old Testament God referred to Israel as a peculiar people *(Deuteronomy 14:2; 26:18; Psalm 135:4).*

"Now therefore, if ye will obey my voice indeed, and keep my covenant then ye shall be a peculiar treasure unto me above all people: for all the earth is mine:
And ye shall be unto me a kingdom of priests, and a holy nation. These are the words which thou shalt speak unto the children of Israel."

Exodus 19:5-6

Again in the New Testament this distinction is given to the Church *(I Peter 2:9; Matthew 13:44).* treasure in the field

GOD'S TITLE APPLIED	TO ISRAEL	TO THE CHURCH
MY PEOPLE	*Exodus 6:6-7; 3:7; 5:1*	*Hebrews 8:10; I Peter 2:9-10*
CHILDREN OF GOD	*Isaiah 63:8*	*Romans 8:16*
PECULIAR PEOPLE	*Exodus 19:5-6*	*I Peter 2:9*

There are many similarities between how God dealt with Israel and how He dealt with the Church as His peculiar people *(I Corinthians 10:1-11).* They were both objects of sovereign grace *(Deuteronomy 6:6-10; Ephesians 1:3-6,11; 2:3-9);* they were both called out of bondage *(Ephesians 2:1-3);* they both experienced passover *(Exodus 12; I Corinthians 5:7);* and they were both to be distinct from the nations *(Numbers 23:9; Exodus 11:7; Leviticus 20:26; John 15:18-19; 17:14-17; I Corinthians 4:13; II Corinthians 6:14-18).*

Israel was given several things which separated it from other nations which should serve as examples to the Church. Israel was given geographical isolation, dietary regulations, an order of worship, a mode of dress and marital laws. All of these were to serve to keep them distinct and totally separated unto the Lord and the purposes of God. Let us examine these five areas a little more closely and see some of the implications that these distinctions have for us in the New Testament Church.

A. GEOGRAPHICAL ISOLATION

When God called Israel out of Egypt He led them to a land flowing with milk and honey. In this land they were to be totally separated from all of the wicked influences of the nations around Him. They were to cast out all the nations before them including their gods and evil customs. Unfortunately Israel did not drive out all of the inhabitants as God has instructed. The story of the book of Joshua is one of incomplete conquest. As a result these nations became a snare to the peculiar people and they lost that which made them peculiar. As a result they were finally vomited out of the land because of their pollutions and idolatries.

When God called the New Testament people of God out of the Egypt of this world He called us to a new land, not a natural land, but a spiritual land flowing with the milk and honey of the word of God. This land, too, is to be an isolated country which owes its spiritual loyalty to the King of heaven *(Philipians 3:20; Galatians 3:1).* Unfortunately there are many believers who have not left it all behind. There are many believers who want to be the peculiar people and have the privilege of the people of God but who have not driven out all of the idols in their hearts. Just as with Israel, these things easily ensnare them, and they soon lose the very land that they once possessed, they lose the distinction of being a "peculiar people".

B. DIETARY REGULATIONS

In addition to geographical isolation God gave the children of Israel dietary laws in great detail distinguishing between clean and unclean. There were certain types of animals and creatures which God commanded them not to eat. There is much debate today as to whether or not these regulations are to be maintained today, but, whatever the case, one thing is very clear, God wants His people to know that one principle: "what you eat affects what you are". The people of God were to separate themselves from all that was unclean or they themselves would become defiled in the sight of God.

God has given dietary regulations to the Church as well. These are not natural regulations dealing with a natural diet, although there are some of these here as well (Acts 15:20), but spiritual regulations dealing with our spiritual diet. God is concerned about what we eat spiritually. God has instructed us not to touch the unclean thing (II Corinthians 6:17). This means that we must be very concerned about what is going into our minds through the doors of our senses. What kind of things are we watching? What kind of things are we reading? What kind of things are we hearing? On what kind of things are we thinking and meditating? If it is anything other than the milk, meat, honey, and bread of God's choosing, the Word of God, it will not produce that which is pleasing to God. Everything we eat spiritually will produce something, but only the Word of God has the power to change us into the image of God. It is on the Word of God that we are to meditate day and night!

C. AN ORDER OF WORSHIP.

God also separated Israel from the other nations in terms of their worship. They were not given the liberty to worship what they wanted or in the way they wanted. They were to destroy all false forms of worship and be separated unto God alone. Worship is important with God. It is not a side issue, because God knows how true worship is vitally connected to the ultimate purpose of God. God's plan for us is to become like Him. The worship of God is a means by which God is going to bring about that change, because we become like what we worship (Psalm 106:19-20; II Corinthians 3:18). God was, therefore, very exacting about how He wanted Israel to worship. They were not to do as the heathen or to copy their ways (Leviticus 17:5-6). The precious, private possession of God, the people of God, were to have their eye single. They were to worship the Lord their God with all of their mind, soul, heart and strength. That leaves no room for anything else.

God is just as concerned about the New Testament worship of the people of God. God is searching for those who will worship Him in *spirit* and *truth* (John 4:24). He has set us apart and has consecrated us to be worshippers. This is part of our high calling as priests unto God. As priests, we too need to pay attention to the particulars of worship that we offer unto the Lord.

D. A MODE OF DRESS

As God's special people the Israelites in the Old Testament were also distinguished from those around them by the way in which they were to dress. The Lord gave many specific instructions concerning how an Israelite was to be attired (Deuteronomy 22:11-12; Numbers 15:38,40). When an Israelite was going anywhere he could easily be recognized because His garments were made according to the divine prescription.

The New Testament Church is also to be distinctive in its dress not only in the natural sense (I Timothy 2:9-11; I Peter 3:3-4), but it is also to be distinct because it has its spiritual garments in order. God has given the believer many garments that he is to wear that will distinguish him from those around him in the world. Oftentimes true believers cannot be easily identified because they have on the wrong garments. Every believer is to be clothed with the garments of salvation (Isaiah 61:10), the robe of righteousness (Isaiah 61:10) and the garment of praise (Isaiah 61:3). Without these we are not able to be identified as the peculiar people of the Lord.

E. MARITAL LAWS

In the Church in the wilderness God expressly forbid the children of Israel to intermarry with the heathen nations (Deuteronomy 7:2-4; 22:10). God knew that if their affections were divided it would lead to compromise, and Israel would no longer be the showplace that God intended for it to be. This is demonstrated in the life of Solomon, who married many wives who served strange gods. As his heart was turned to them he was led to compromise in building places of false worship.

The Church of Jesus Christ, too, is forbidden to intermarry with the world *(II Corinthians 6:14-17)*, not only naturally, but spiritually. If anyone loves the world and the things of the world he is the enemy of God. The two concepts are diametrically opposed. Friendship with the world is enmity against God. The world has nothing to contribute to the plan and purpose of God. It can only detract from, divert from, and draw us away from, God's best for us.

God has called His people to a very high calling. It is a tremendous privilege to be considered by God as His "peculiar people". God looks at His people as a special treasure, as a personal, private possession, as the apple of His eye; but they will never be that fully if they do not maintain the areas that make them "peculiar". They must maintain their isolation from the world, they must maintain their spiritual diet, they must maintain true spiritual worship, they must maintain the garments that make them distinct, and they must maintain their affections solely unto the Lord. As they do, they will continue to be and to become what God intends for them to be — God's peculiar people.

Chapter 6
THE CHURCH — THE TEMPLE OF GOD

In the last chapter we saw that because the Church and God's purposes in Church are such complicated concepts for the human mind to fully understand, God has given to man visual pictures by which He can better communicate His mind to man. We looked briefly at one such visual picture and saw the Church of Jesus Christ as God's peculiar people. Another picture that God has given to us of the Church, is the Temple, Building, or House of God.

> *"But if I tarry long, that thou mayest know how thou oughtest to behave thyself in the house of God, which is the church of the living God, the pillar and ground of the truth."*
>
> *I Timothy 3:15*

> *"For we are laborers together with God: ye are God's husbandry, ye are God's building."*
>
> *I Corinthians 3:9*

> *"But Christ as a son over his own house; whose house are we, if we hold fast the confidence and the rejoicing of the hope firm unto the end."*
>
> *Hebrews 3:9*

> *"In whom all the building fitly framed together groweth unto a holy temple in the Lord: In whom ye also are builded together for a habitation of God through the Spirit."*
>
> *Ephesians 2:21-22*

This picture that God gives us is to help us better understand the purpose and nature of the Church. It is an exciting picture that begins all the way back in the garden of Eden. Right from the creation of man as a special, unique being from the hand of God, God has had a desire to dwell in the midst of His people. This desire is first seen in the warm relationship that existed between God and the first human beings in the garden of Eden before the terrible breach that was caused by the fall *(Genesis 1:3)*. Even after the fall of man into sin God continued to demonstrate this desire in His relationship to the patriaches and His provision through the altars of stone *(Genesis 8:20; Exodus 20:24-25)*. With the coming of Moses and the formation of Israel as a nation God was more specific about that desire. While Moses was on Mt. Sinai God gave him specific instruction for a tabernacle in the wilderness.

> *"And let them make me a sanctuary; that I may dwell among them."*
>
> *Exodus 25:8*

In God's dealings with man His presence went from *"tent to tent, and from one tabernacle to another"* *(I Chronicles 17:5)*, but one thing that remained the same was His desire to dwell in the midst of His covenant people. God continued in the Old Testament to make provision in the Tabernacle of David *(I Chronicles 15)*, and the Temple of Solomon *(I Kings 8:8,13)*. All of these prepared the way for God's greatest expression of this desire, the incarnation. When Jesus came among us He came as the Tabernacle of God. John declares that the Word was made flesh and dwelt or tabernacled among us *(John 1:14)*. Jesus declared that He was the Temple of God *(John 2:19-21)*, but Jesus came to build another house, the Church, which would also be the Temple of God. The Church is the present provision of God for His dwelling among His covenant people *(Matthew 18:20; 28:20)*. The Church will one day give place to the New Jerusalem where we will experience the highest expression of God's dwelling among men.

> *"Then I saw a new heaven and a new earth; for the first heaven and the first earth had passed away, and the sea was no more. And I saw the holy city, new Jerusalem, coming down out of the heaven from God, prepared as a bride adorned for her husband; and I heard a loud voice*

from the throne saying, "Behold the dwelling of God is with men. He will be with them and they shall be his people, and God himself will be with them."

Revelation 21:1-3

One thing that must be noticed in each of these dwelling places that was provided by God as a means by which He could dwell with man is that God's dwelling with man has always been on His terms and according to His pattern. David had a tremendous desire to see God's presence once again in the midst of Israel. God's desire was to be in the center of His people as well, but when David tried to make it work according to an approach other than the God-ordained approach it brought death to the camp *(II Samuel 6:1-9)*. As we look at the Church as the Temple of God and desire His presence to be in the midst, we, too, must experience the power of God's presence. The pattern must begin from the ground level.

A. THE FOUNDATION IN THE CHURCH.

Every house or building is grounded on some kind of foundation. The Scripture basically refers to two kinds of foundations. There is the foundation that man lays and the foundation that God lays. The foundation that man lays is in God's mind, equivalent to no foundation at all *(Luke 6:49)*, it is in the shifting dust *(Job 4:18-19)* and will be overflown with the flood *(Job 22:15-16)*. The foundation that God lays is a sure and everlasting foundation *(II Timothy 2:19; Proverbs 10:25)*. This is the only kind of foundation that will stand the tests of time.

God wants to lay a sure foundation in His New Testament Temple, the Church. A sure foundation is very costly, but it will enable the building to stand inspite of the storms that may come. The structure that God is building will stand strong through any test because of the foundation upon which it is built. What is the foundation of the New Testament Church? There are four main views as to the foundation of the Church based on *Matthew 16:16-18*.

"And Simon Peter answered and said, Thou art the Christ the Son of the living God.
And Jesus answered and said unto him, Blessed art thou, Simon Barjona: for flesh and blood hath not revealed it unto thee, but my Father which is in heaven. And I say also unto thee, that thou art Peter, and upon this rock I will build my church: and the gates of hell shall not prevail against it."

Matthew 16:16-18

The four views are as follows:

1. The confession that Peter made is the foundation of the Church.
2. Peter is the foundation of the Church.
3. All of the apostles are the foundation of the Church (Peter being the representative of the group).
4. Christ is the rock foundation of the Church.

The first three of these views have a measure of truth to them but the fourth one is the emphasis of the scripture. It is true that the confession that Peter made was to be the foundation for the faith of the Church. The fact of Christ's sonship is foundational to any acceptance of Christ as our Saviour. This message was central to the preaching and teaching of the apostles in the establishment of the New Testament Church *(Acts 9:20)*. It is this profession in the New Testament that qualifies one to become a part of the Church *(Acts 8:36-37; Romans 10:9-10; I Corinthians 12:3; I John 4:15)*. It is the message of the deity of Christ that becomes a stumbling-block to many but to others it becomes a stepping-stone to life and victory. The Church is built on a confession but it is the confession of Christ, the rock of our Salvation.

It is also true that Peter was the first living stone to make this confession of faith. Peter was a representative of many who would follow with a similar confession of faith. Jesus was not singling out Peter here as an authority or as a foundation. No doubt Peter was going to have the privileged role of opening the door of faith to the Jews *(Acts 2)* and opening the door of faith to the Gentiles *(Acts 10)*, but Jesus was not setting Peter up above the others. At least the apostles did not interpret Jesus this way, for later they were still arguing about which of them would be greatest *(Luke 22:24)*. Peter himself did not interpret Jesus this way for he himself pointed to another foundation in his epistle *(I Peter 2:4-9)*. The authority that Jesus gave to Peter in *Matthew 16,* He gave to the whole Church in *Matthew 18.* Hence Peter is only a representative or a type of the whole.

It must also be remembered that all of the twelve apostles in the New Testament have a distinctive place in relationship to the foundation of the Church *(Ephesians 2:20)*. It was their teaching that was going to root and ground the Church *(Acts 2:42)*, but what did they teach? What principles did they establish? The apostles in the New Testament Church laid down the first principles of the doctrine of Christ *(Hebrews 6:1-2)*. They were faithful in the beginning stages of laying the foundation, and because of that their names will be in the foundation of the Holy City *(Revelation 21:14)*.

The central teaching of the Word of God in regard to the rock foundation is clear. Jesus Christ, Himself is the rock foundation. Every other figurative use of the Greek word for "rock" used in the New Testament is clearly a reference to Christ *(Romans 9:33; I Corinthians 10:4; I Peter 2:7-8)*. Paul clearly states that Christ is the only foundation that can be laid *(I Corinthians 3:9-11)*.

The Old Testament clearly confirms this teaching in typology. All of the houses of God constructed in the Old Testament pointed to the establishment of the New Testament house of God, the Church. In the foundation of every house builded in the Old Testament there is an illusion to Christ. In *Genesis 28,* Jacob named the place of his vision *"the House of God"*. That place was founded on a rock that was anointed with oil *(Acts 10:38)*. In *Exodus 26:19* we find that the Tabernacle of Moses was grounded in sockets of silver, redemption metal. The silver provided for this was atonement money. The temple of Solomon was also built on a piece of ground purchased with silver *(II Samuel 24:15-25)*, but even more significant is the fact that it was built on the site where Abraham had offered up his son Isaac as a type of the death, burial and resurrection of the Lord Jesus Christ *(Genesis 22)*. All of these foundations pointed to Christ the rock foundation of the New Testament Church.

In addition to the types in the Old Testament we find that th symbolic use of the word "rock" throughout the Old Testament indicates a consistent application to the divine person of God *(Psalm 18:2; 31:2-3; 28:1; 62:7; 89:26; etc.)* God is our rock and He brings stability to His people. If the Church is built on anything but Christ it is doomed to fall. We are living in a day when everything that can be shaken will be shaken. We are living in a time when kingdoms are rising and falling. If we are built on Christ, if we are rooted and built up in Him, we will not be shaken nor will we fall, because Jesus Christ is the same yesterday, today and forever *(Hebrews 13:8)!*

B. THE CORNERSTONE.

The word "cornerstone" in the scripture has basically two meanings. The most common Old Testament usage of the word refers to the "stone of the corner". In this sense the term is used as a symbol of stability and faith.[1] In the Old Testament it usually means the foundation stone *(Job 38:6)*. In the architecture of the day this was a very large stone that was placed at the foundation of a wall to bind two walls together.[1] This stone was very important because it would not only give stability to the structure but it would give alignment to the adjoining walls. For this reason particular care would have to be used in the selection and preparation of this stone for its place in the structure.

Christ is the head of the corner. He is the most perfect stone *(Isaiah 28:16)*, who is the beginning or the first stone of the building (firstborn). Christ is the tried stone to whom the whole building is to be aligned *(Ephesians 2:20)*. Christ is the one who has broken down the middle wall of partition separating Jew and Gentile and has reconciled both walls into one becoming the head of the corner. Both walls must be perfectly aligned unto Him if they are going to have stability. Both walls have to be fitly framed together if there is going to be a suitable building for the habitation of God through the Spirit *(Ephesians 2:21)*.

The other meaning of the word "cornerstone" has in it the idea of the "head of a corner". In this sense it refers to the "final stone" in a building which was usually set over the gate. This is most likely the thought used in *I Peter 2:6.* In Roman architecture that was the keystone.[2] It was the last stone to be placed which gave strength, stability to the whole. It was the final stone that completed the work and bound the whole thing together.

---

[1]IDB E.M. Good "Cornerstone" page 700 Volume 1
[2]Kittel Volume 1 Joachim Jeremios " $\alpha \varkappa \rho o \gamma \omega \nu \iota \alpha \iota o s$ " pg. 792

Christ is also the capstone, the keystone or the headstone in the temple of God. Christ is the first and the last, the beginning and the ending, the Alpha and Omega *(Revelation 1:11)*. Christ is the author and the finisher of our faith *(Hebrews 12:2)*. Christ is the one who will bring completion to the Temple of God and it is by Him that all things consist *(Colossians 1:17; 2:9)*.

C. THE MATERIALS

Every building has to have materials from which it is constructed. The building that God is erecting in these days is no different. God also has to have materials with which to work. Most materials come to us in raw form. They must be prepared and tooled upon before they are fit to put into a building. So it is with the material that God is using. The Temple that God is building is to be made up of stones, living stones *(I Peter 2:5)*. These stones have to be dug out of the quarry of this world *(Isaiah 51:1-2)* and cut and shaped by the hand of the Lord before they are ready to be built into the house of the Lord *(I Kings 5:17-18; 6-7)*. When the preparatory work is done the stones can be laid on the proper foundation and fitly framed together with other stones in the building of God *(Ephesians 2:21-22)*.

The temple is composed of individuals whose lives have to be builded out of solid materials *(I Corinthians 3:9-16)*. The temple that God is building is going to have to stand the test of fire *(Numbers 31:21-23; Job 23:10; I Peter 1:7)*. Each individual building block must be composed of materials that can pass through the fire unburned and purified. As building blocks, our lives can be composed of wood, hay and stubble. All of these things spring from the cursed earth, are produced by the sweat and self-effort of man, and are perishable. Fire reduces all of these things to ashes. God wants our lives to be composed of gold, silver and precious stones. These are all things that are produced by God under pressure, and will not only go through the fire unharmed, but will actually become more precious when they do. These are imperishable qualities that will pass the test of time.

God wants to take all of these building blocks or stones, tool them and build them into a building suitable for His habitation. The New Testament word to describe this process is "edification". God wants the stones to be edified or built up. This sounds like an obvious statement but it runs contrary to the emphasis of many churches today. Many are looking for a tremendous increase in numbers and they feel that when they have big numbers on their rolls that the house will be built. This is not exactly the way God looks at it. To understand God's viewpoint we have to understand the difference between *multiplication* and *edification.* God wants both. The first leads to the second. But if multiplication is emphasized over edification God will never have what He is after.

There is a difference between a church being multiplied and a church being edified. God desires for the Church to multiply because in doing so there is a gathering of raw materials with which to build the desired structure. One of the beautiful characteristics of the early church is that there was rapid multiplication *(Acts 12:24; 6:1; 7:17)*. Evangelism is the gathering of the stones for the building. This work is to be done primarily in the quarry of this world in our day to day encounters with people. This work is extremely important and cannot be over emphasized, however, many churches today center their whole message on evangelism, the gathering of stones. God wants us to see from His perspective and from an understanding of His purposes. A pile of stones does not make a building. Many are glorying over their huge piles of stone, but at present they do not have the end product for which God is searching. God wants all the stones He can get, but He wants the stones to be fitly framed together. He wants the stones to be edified or built up into a temple suitable for His habitation.

The word "edify" means "to be built up, to be placed, to be put in order, or to be arranged." This is the assembling process that must follow the gathering of the stones. This operation takes place at the temple site and involves the building of the stones into a structure. It is the fitting of each stone into its proper place of function and its proper place of relationship with the other stones in the building. God desires that the churches be at rest and that they be edified *(Acts 9:31; Hebrews 10:25)*. It is only as they are built together that they will become all that God has intended for them. This is why the Word of God places such a premium on the edification of His people *(I Corinthians 14)*. God wants us to govern our actions on the basis of that which edifies and builds up.

There are many things that God uses to build up His people into the temple of God. As the people of God we are instructed to seek to excel to the edifying of the Church *(I Corinthians 14:12)*. To do this we need to give ourselves to and emphasize those things which build. God's Word gives us ten things that edify the people of God:

1. The Word of God *(Acts 20:32).*
2. The Five-fold ministry *(Ephesians 4:11-12).*
3. Body Ministry *(I Corinthians 14:26).*
4. Spiritual Sacrifices *(I Peter 2:5).*
5. Being rooted and built up in Christ *(Colossians 2:7).*
6. Praying in the Spirit *(Jude 20; I Corinthians 14:2-5).*
7. Love *(I Corinthians 8:1).*
8. Right Communication *(Ephesians 4:29; Colossians 4:6).*
9. Harmony and Peace *(Romans 14:19).*
10. Seeking to please our neighbor *(Romans 15:2).*

God wants to bring multiplication, but multiplication must lead to edification or the building of God will never be completed. God is looking for a building that grows and increases with the increase of God. He is challenging us to get our lives in tune with the program of God. He is interested in a glorious house.

D. THE WORKMAN

Not only is Christ the foundation for this building that is going up but He is also the master builder. Christ declared that He was building a house *(Matthew 16:16-18; Ephesians 2:10; Hebrews 3:1-6).* This is the only thing that gives us confidence that the house is going to be built *(Psalm 127:1-2).* Jesus has everything at His disposal and is very aware of the details, cost, sacrifice, and time involved, but as the master builder Christ is not building alone. He has enlisted the help of others. He has called upon others to be co-laborers together with Him *(I Corinthians 3:9).*

Initially God used the Old Testament prophets and the New Testament apostles to do the groundwork and lay the foundation for the House of the Lord. Since then God has sub-contracted much of the work to the governmental ministries that He has set into the Church including the apostle, prophet, evangelist, pastor and teacher *(Ephesians 4:11-16).* Each of these ministries is used by God to build up the body of Christ. Each of these ministries is necessary in the building process *(I Corinthians 3:9-10).* Even as in a natural building plumbers, electricians, masons, carpenters and carpet layers are necessary, each one having their own particular function and contribution to the whole, so it is with the five ministries that God has given to build His house. No one ministry can do it all. Each one is inter-dependent on the others. All of these ministries together are given the responsibility of equipping the saints to do the work of the ministry that the whole might be built up and strengthened *(Ephesians 4:12).*

In addition to the five-fold ministry God has given the responsibility to every believer to be involved in the work of building up the House of God. Every member is to contribute that specialized talent or ability which God has given to him that the whole might receive the benefit *(I Corinthians 12; Romans 12:1-8; I Peter 4:10-11).*

E. THE PRIESTHOOD

There is much more involved in the Church, however, if it is to measure up to the privilege of being the Temple of God. The building of the Temple itself is great, for it is a building like no other building. It is a building with living stones that grow! The fact that God wants to fill this Temple with His fulness is exciting for in His presence is fulness of joy. In every other temple in Scripture, however, there was more involved than just a building and the presence of God although these were indispensible. Every other temple in the Old Testament had a *priesthood* and *sacrifices.*

> *"Ye also, as lively stones, are built up a spiritual house, an holy priesthood, to offer up spiritual sacrifices, acceptable to God by Jesus Christ."*
>
> *I Peter 2:15*

In the Old testament, under the law, God gave a priesthood to the Children of Israel. God has always desired to have a righteous nation in priestly fellowship with Himself. This was His purpose in calling Israel, that they might be a nation of priests. In fact, He offered to Israel exactly what He was later to give to the Church.

"Now therefore, if ye will obey My voice indeed, and keep My covenant, then ye shall be a peculiar treasure unto Me above all people: for all the earth is Mine: and ye shall be unto Me a kingdom of priests, and an holy nation."

Exodus 19:5-6

Because of the disobedience of the Children of Israel, however, God did not make Israel a kingdom of priests. They did not fulfill the conditions of this promise. Instead God gave them an inferior priesthood as a tutor and a governor to bring them to Christ in whom they could once again become heirs to this same promise. God gave to Israel the Aaronic priesthood. Instead of having the whole nation be a kingdom of priests, God singled out the tribe of Levi to act as priests and handle the holy things. This Aaronic priesthood was not God's ideal. In fact, it was a substitute for the ideal. It actually became a shadow of the priesthood that God desired to give.

The priesthood of which God desires us to become partakers is described for us in *Hebrews 5-7.* This priesthood has a High Priest, the Lord Jesus Christ *(Hebrews 2:17; 4:14; 6:20).* Just the fact that there is a High Priest implies that there are other priests in the priesthood, or the designation HIGH Priest would be superfluous. This priesthood is the Melchizedek Priesthood. This is the priesthood that was offered to Israel, God's chosen people *(Exodus 19:5-7).* Because they failed to enter into this priesthood, it was taken from them and given to another, the Lord Jesus Christ *(Psalms 110:1-2).* What they forfeited on the basis of disobedience, Jesus inherited on the basis of His perfect obedience *(Hebrews 5:8-9).* As we stand in Him, therefore, we can become partakers of this everlasting priesthood.

It is not our purpose at this time to give a detailed analysis of this priesthood, for it is a lengthy study. Yet, it is beneficial at this point to look at a few key verses in regard to this priesthood and its implications.

"If therefore perfection were by the Levitical priesthood, (for under it the people received the law) what further need was there that another priest should rise after the order of Melchisedec, and not be called after the order of Aaron? For the priesthood being changed, there is made of necessity a change also of the law. For He of whom these things are spoken pertaineth to another tribe, of which no man gave attendance at the altar. For it is evident that our Lord sprang out of Judah; of which tribe Moses spake nothing concerning priesthood. And it is far more evident: for that after the similitude of Melchisedec there ariseth another priest, who is made, not after the law of a carnal commandment, but after the power of an endless life. For he testifieth, Thou art a priest forever after the order of Melchisedec."

Hebrews 7:11-17

"For every high priest taken from among me is ordained for men in things pertaining to God, that he may offer both gifts and sacrifices for sins."

Hebrews 5:1

F. THE SACRIFICES

In *Hebrews 5:1* we just learned that a priest is ordained to offer gifts and sacrifices *(Hebrews 8:3).* Christ as our High Priest has offered such gifts and sacrifices, but we, as kings and priests unto God also have sacrifices to offer. Priestly fellowship is always grounded on the basis of sacrifice. This principle holds true in both the Old and New Testaments. When the patriarchs desired to meet with God, they always sacrificed. They built an altar unto God, knowing that if they were to have His presence, they must sacrifice. Jacob built an altar; Abraham built an altar; Elijah built an altar on Carmel. In all of these cases, God never failed to meet with these individuals who approached on the basis of sacrifice. God never denies or changes His principles. We too must prepare an altar of sacrifice to meet with God—not a literal altar to sacrifice a literal animal, but we are priests born to offer "spiritual sacrifices" unto the Lord. In Christ we become partakers of that ROYAL PRIESTHOOD *"to offer up spiritual sacrifices, acceptable to God by Jesus Christ" (I Peter 2:5).*

There are many sacrifices that the New Testament priest is ordained to offer. These include the following:

1. Ourselves

— The New Testament teaches that we are to yield ourselves to God *(Romans 6:13).* God wants to use all of our members as instruments of His glory. Each day we need to yield our members afresh to this tremendously high calling. In the Old Testament we have a picture of this in Solomon who had a scaffold built that was the exact size of the Brazen Altar on which all of the Tabernacle sacrifices offered. He placed this scaffold in the midst of the court, stood upon it, *"Kneeled down before all the congregation of Israel, and spread his hands toward heaven" (II Chronicles 6:13).* Solomon was actually presenting himself a living sacrifice. God desires for us to present ourselves upon the altar as a living sacrifice.

> *"I beseech you therefore, brethren, by the mercies of God, that ye present your bodies a living sacrifice, holy, acceptable unto God, which is your reasonable service. And be not conformed to this world; but be ye transformed by the renewing of your mind, that ye may prove what is that good, and acceptable, and perfect, will of God.*
>
> *Romans 12:1-2*

Part of this sacrifice involves cutting ourselves off from the world system. How do we present ourselves holy and acceptable unto God?! By not being conformed to this world system. This means we will have to sacrifice and give up our worldly desires and let God transplant His perfect desires in us, giving us the desires of our heart *(Psalms 37:4).*

This sacrifice needs to be a daily offering of ourselves afresh. As we offer ourselves, spirit, soul and body, God promises to use us for His glory.

2. Our Time

—Paul tells us of the importance of redeeming the time *(Ephesians 5:16; Colossians 4:5).* God has given us time that we might give it back to Him. He has given it to us as a trust and a stewardship and, therefore, holds us accountable for our use of it. This sacrifice grows more and more essential as the days of His coming draw near. Every hour that passes brings us that much closer to that day when time shall be no more. God desires that we sacrifice our time for His use.

3. Our Substance

— Everything that we own belongs to God. What do we have that was not given to us? In the Old Testament the Children of Israel were obligated to give tithes unto God. In the New Testament we are called to a higher law; we are obliged to put all that we have at His disposal. God promises to take care of our needs so we can communicate or give as He desires. The Philippian Christians were willing to offer such sacrifices to God which, Paul says, were pleasing to God *(Philippians 4:18).* He says that such a sacrifice was an odor of sweet savour. The sweet savour offerings of the Old Testament were those offerings that were given not from compulsion, but voluntarily of the giver's own free will. God desires us to give of our substance in like manner. He desires us to give of our own free will without a specific command. This sacrifice pleases God.

This sacrifice involves two different aspects. There is the giving of our substance to the storehouse, and there is the communicating of our substance to those of our brethren who are in need. Even in the Old Testament God gave instruction for how the Israelites were to care for the needy in their midst *(Deuteronomy 15:7-18),* and He gives strict warning to those who build up their own barns and neglect the needs of those around them *(Deuteronomy 8:11-12; Luke 12:15-31).* God is interested in our money. How we spend our money is a good indication of where our heart is *(Matthew 6:21).* If you want to know how you are doing in regard to this spiritual sacrifice, read your check stubs.

> *"Do not forget or neglect to do kindness and good, to be generous and distribute and contribute to the needs (of the Church as embodiment and proof of fellowship), for such sacrifices are well-pleasing to God."*
>
> *Hebrews 13:16*

4. Our Good Works — Faith without works is dead *(James 2:20)*. God wants us to do good *(Hebrews 13:16)*. He has called us to a life of faith, but a life of faith will produce the fruit of faith—obedience. A vital, living faith will always bring forth good works. These do not gain salvation for us, but they are something that we can offer to God on the basis of what He has done for us. Our righteousness is to exceed that of the scribes and pharisees *(Matthew 5:20)*, because we have been empowered by God in a way that the scribes and pharisees were not. You will know the people of God by their fruit *(Matthew 7:16)*.

5. Our Fruit — God desires for us to declare His glory to the ends of the earth. As we give ourselves, our time, our substance and our works to Him, there is bound to be fruit from the earth *(Isaiah 66:19-20)*. We have the privilege as priests unto God to offer these back to God as an offering acceptable unto Him.

> *"That I should be the minister of Jesus Christ to the Gentiles, ministering the gospel of God, that the offering up of the Gentiles might be acceptable, being sanctified by the Holy Ghost."*
>
> Romans ~~14:16~~ 15:16

6. Sacrifice of Joy — There is a difference between the joy of the Lord and a naturally joyful and exhuberant spirit. Some people are naturally happy and outgoing. This type of joy involves no real sacrifice. There are times, however, when we are not of this disposition. There are times when it is very difficult to enter into the aspect of praise that involves the expression of joy. At these times joy becomes a sacrifice. As a priest unto God we have the privilege of offering this sacrifice of joy to God. As we learn to place our confidence in the Word and promises of God we will come to a place where we will be able to rejoice even in times of distress *(II Corinthians 4:8-10)*. Naturally speaking there may be nothing to cause one to rejoice, but we will still lift our voice in joyous shouts of praise. A more literal rendering of this sacrifice as it is used in the Hebrew would be a "sacrifice of shouting". This would seem to imply that this sacrifice involves more than just an inner expression of joy, but it involves a life of Christian victory.

> *"And now shall mine head be lifted up above mine enemies round about me: therefore will I offer in His tabernacle sacrifices of joy; I will sing, yea, I will sing praises unto the Lord."*
>
> Psalms 27:6

Because of the testimony that the people of God carry in these last days, the time is coming when men will revile us and speak evil of us. They will persecute the truth in their ignorance. In that day, we are not to be sad or worry, but we are to *"leap for joy"* *(Luke 6:22-23)*. For us to do this will involve our ability to offer the sacrifice of joy unto God. This sacrifice of joy which can only spring from a heart of faith will actually produce joy. This joy will be the strength of the people of God *(Nehemiah 8:10)*, and a tremendous testimony to the uttermost parts of the earth.

7. Sacrifice of Thanksgiving — Even under the law age God instituted the sacrifice of thanksgiving *(Leviticus 7:12)*. It is so easy to be thankful when we feel we have something for which we should be thankful. But to give God the sacrifice of thanksgiving is to give thanks for everything. It is this sacrifice that will cause us to lift up our hands and our voices and thank God in even the most adverse of circumstances realizing that God is in control of all the affairs of our life and that all of His dealings with us are to lead us into green pastures and beside still waters. Many times this will involve much sacrifice on our part, but this sacrifice is pleasing to God.

Jonah was in the most terrible of circumstances *(Jonah 2:9)*. He was in the belly of a fish where the natural eye could see nothing for which to be thankful, no cause for thanksgiving. But even here, something of God in Jonah was greater than Jonah's natural flesh and circumstances, and Jonah refused to let his spirit be bound. In chapter 2 of Jonah's account we find Jonah trying everything to no avail. He repented, he cried unto God, he confessed that he was not "observing lying vanities", but in verse 9, when he sacrificed to God with a voice of thanksgiving, immediately the fish became ill. A thankful prophet was too much for the fish.

The secret to the sacrifice of thanksgiving involves the hearing ear and the believing heart. *"Faith cometh by hearing" (Romans 10:17).* When we sacrifice with the voice of thanksgiving, our ears hear what our mouth declares. This confession produces faith in the heart. It is this faith which causes our deliverance. It is the faith of a people who have learned to give thanks in every situation that will cause the world to believe.

> *"And let them sacrifice the sacrifices of thanksgiving, and declare His works with rejoicing."*
>
> *Psalms 107:22*

> *"I will offer to thee the sacrifices of thanksgiving, and call upon the name of the Lord."*
>
> *Psalms 116:17*

8. Sacrifice of Praise

— A blessing is something which you receive when you come into the House of God, but the "sacrifice" of praise is something that you bring with you. It is something that we offer to the Lord not on the basis of our circumstances or our feelings, but on the basis of our revelation of God and His greatness, and our desire to please Him and obey His Word *(Jeremiah 17:26).*

> *"The voice of joy, and the voice of gladness, the voice of the bridegroom, and the voice of the bride, the voice of them that shall say, Praise the Lord of hosts: for the Lord is good; for His mercy endureth forever: and of them that shall bring the sacrifice of praise into the House of the Lord."*
>
> *Jeremiah 33:11*

> *"By Him therefore let us offer the sacrifice of praise to God continually, that is, the fruit of our lips giving thanks to his name . . . for with such sacrifices God is well pleased."*
>
> *Hebrews 13:15,16b*

As a Royal Priesthood we have the privilege of being both priest and offering even as Christ offered himself. As kings and priests unto God part of our ministry involves service at the Altar of Incense *(Revelation 5:10; 8:3-4).* Prayer and praise are the spiritual sacrifices that are offered at the Altar of Incense. It is here that God comes down and meets with His people *(Exodus 29:42).*

The apostle Paul understood this principle of praise. Paul had his hands and feet in stocks, yet he would not allow his spirit to be bound *(Acts 16:25).* In the midst of adverse circumstances he offered to God the sacrifice of praise. It was in this atmosphere of praise that God brought deliverance.

The Scripture indicates that God, who is holy, inhabits or lives in the praises of His people. If we desire God to come down and dwell in the midst of His people, it is our responsibility to offer the sacrifice of praise continually which will create the atmosphere in which God chooses to dwell. People often wonder if perhaps God has forsaken them in a particular situation, but often times their attitude is far from one of praise. As we begin to enter into this sacrifice of praise in every situation we will begin to experience something of the abiding presence of God.

9. A Broken and a Contrite Heart

— God is never as interested in external sacrifices as He is in a heart that is rightly related to Him. If the heart relationship is right, none of the other sacrifices will be a problem. But if the heart relationship is not right, all the other sacrifices will be mere forms. It is at this point that our righteousness exceeds that of the scribes and pharisees. It is from this heart condition that WORSHIP springs forth. True worship can only ascend from a heart that has been broken before God. It can only come from the lips of one who realizes his own unworthiness and, at the same time, beholds the magnificence of God. God desires people to worship Him in spirit and in truth *(John 4:24).* A broken and a contrite heart can produce nothing else.

> *"The sacrifices of God are a broken spirit: a broken and a contrite heart, O God, Thou wilt not despise."*
>
> *Psalms 51:17*

We have seen at least nine spiritual sacrifices that we are to offer to God. The first five have to do with the area of the physical and material realms. God wants us to sacrifice our possessions and offer them for His unconditional use. The next three deal with the area of the mind, will and emotions. They are attitudes that God wants us to offer to Him. God wants all of our affections to be centered in Him. The last sacrifice has to do with the center of all sacrifices, the spirit realm. God wants to possess us spirit, soul and body (see diagram).

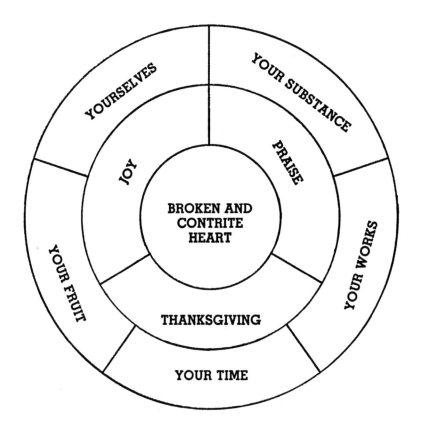

SPIRITUAL SACRIFICES

This picture of the Church as the Temple of the living God, helps us to understand better God's purpose for the Church, that the people of God might be fitly framed together that He might fill us with the fulness of Himself.

"And to know the love of Christ, which passeth knowledge, that ye might be filled with all the fulness of God.
Now unto him that is able to do exceeding abundantly above all that ye ask or think, according to the power that worketh in us.
Unto him be glory in the church by Christ Jesus throughout all ages, world without end."

Ephesians 3:19-21

Chapter 7
THE CHURCH — THE FAMILY OF GOD

In spite of the tremendous wealth of truth contained in the pictures of the Church as the Peculiar People and the Temple of God, no one picture is adequate to give a totally exhaustive view of what God is doing in and through the Church. To these pictures God adds an extremely valuable revelation of truth by referring to the Church as the family of God *(Ephesians 3:14-15; Galatians 6:10)*. As with all of the pictures God has given to us, this picture helps us to better understand some of the purpose, nature and function of the Church. This picture is given us by God so that we might better understand (1) the relationships in the family, (2) the membership in the family, (3) the automony of the family, (4) the covering of the family, (5) the discipline in the family, (6) the commitment of the family.

A. THE RELATIONSHIPS IN THE FAMILY.

God has given us various things in natural creation and in society that we might better understand spiritual things. When God made man in family relationships he wanted us to better understand something of a spiritual relationship that exists in the family of God. All of the relationships that exist in the natural family point to relationships in the spiritual family of God, the Church.

1. In the Church we have but one father. God is our Father *(Psalm 68:5; 89:26; Isaiah 64:8; Matthew 5:16)*. As a true father God is faithful to fulfill all of the responsibilities of a father to His children. As a true father God has provided the *seed* that has brought about our birth into the family of God *(I Peter 1:23)*. That seed is the incorruptible seed of the Word of God. As a true father God has provided an inheritance for His offspring. He has laid up for their future *(Acts 26:18; Ephesians 1:11)*. As a true father God is responsible to discipline us when we need it. God will not fail to keep His obligations as father in the family of God.

2. In the Church we have an elder brother, the Lord Jesus Christ *(Hebrews 2:14-17)*. Christ is the unique son over his own house *(Hebrews 3:6)*. He is the firstborn *(Romans 8:29)* and pattern son in the family *(I Peter 2:21)*. He is our kinsman redeemer who has paid the price to restore our lost inheritance. He is our example, the one who has gone before us and the one on whom we can rely as we go through all of life's problems.

3. In the Church all true believers are the children of the family. If God is a father then He must have a family. In a natural family, there is only one normal way to become a part of the family. This is equally true with the spiritual family of God. If we are to be part of the family of God we must be born into the family by the process of the new birth *(John 1:12-13; 3:3; I Peter 1:23)*. As members of the family we are all partakers of the same blood *(John 6:53)*, we all take on the family name *(Ephesians 3:14-15)* and we all bear the family resemblance or image *(Ephesians 4:13; I Corinthians 15:49)*. As children of the family we must fulfill all the duties and responsibilities of children which are outlined in the Word of God. Children are to be the servants of the house giving honor to, and rendering obedience to, the father *(Exodus 20:12; Proverbs 23:22)*. As Christians we must show this kind of respect, and loyalty to our Heavenly Father.

4. In the Church we enter into a place of permanent relationship. As members of the Body of Christ we have many beautiful new relationships with our Heavenly Father and His Son, with mothers and fathers in the Lord, and with the many brothers and sisters with whom we have been called. It should be noted, however, that these are *permanent* relationships even as in a natural family. Just as in a natural family you are not able to choose those with whom you will share family privileges so in the Church we have no say as to whom God will call as members of the body. Just as in a natural family those who become members of the family come into permanent identification with their brothers and sisters, so in the Church we must realize that we are going to be permanently related to each other.

In times of trouble it is most important to remember this. When natural family members have problems and strife among themselves they realize the absolute need of reaching a resolve because they realize that they are going to have to live together as a family. In the Church it is important for us to see the need of settling all differences with others who make up the family of God. We are going to be living together for eternity, so to avoid years of grief and turmoil we would be wise to learn how to live together now. God is not going to throw anyone out of the family to accommodate individuals who refuse to change and adjust. On the contrary, God has, right next to us in the family, the people that we need the most to expose our weaknesses, adjust our character and sand down the rough edges. God will make sure that no one goes anywhere until His purpose is accomplished.

B. MEMBERSHIP IN THE FAMILY

To every natural family there is a defined membership. God has, in a natural sense, placed every child in the world under a set of parents which are to oversee the growth and development of that child. The Bible teaches that it is God's purpose to set the solitary into families (Psalm 68:6). In the realm of the Spirit, God has done this by providing local assemblies which are visible, local expressions of the invisible, corporate, world-wide family of God. God has established local churches wherein He has placed His government to be our visible link to the invisible whole. As such, membership is a matter of concern to God.

Many today do not feel that it is scriptural for a Church to have a defined membership. They feel that to number the people is to be guilty of a similar sin to that of David when he numbered the people against God's wishes. They feel that numbering has bred an over-emphasis on numbers and hindered the genuine care and concern over individuals in the church.

Most of these fears spring from hearts of genuine concern and love for God's people. Yet there is another side to the question of membership when we look at it in connection with the Church as part of the family of God. True pastoral care, nurturing, admonition and discipline can never be truly effective where there are no committed relationships. The Early Church was lacking one of the modern problems that every church has to face today. This is the problem of a splintered Church. In the days of Paul, because they were breaking ground with the gospel there was only one church in any given community. If you were a Christian living in a certain locality, you were automatically part of the local church of that locality. There was no other group with whom you could identify. Today in any given locality you have the choice of attending many different local assemblies. If you are not able to get along in one you can move to another. If you do not like the discipline in the one you are in, you can find one that will leave you alone. For this reason we have many nomadic uncommitted, "tumble-weed" Christians, who blow in and out without warning or accountability. This becomes a great distress to anyone who would seek to give pastoral care to such an individual, and it becomes a stumbling block to the maturing of that individual in the Body of Christ.

For this reason the question of membership needs to be reconsidered. God has given us some guidelines that can be of tremendous help to us in arriving at a conclusion.

1. Church membership is implied by the numbering and accounting in the Early Church. God is concerned about numbers. The numbering and accounting of those added to the Lord and to the Church indicates that God is not against the concept of numbering (Acts 2:41; 6:7).

2. Church membership is implied in other New Testament terminology.

When Paul was speaking to the Corinthians and giving them guidelines for their meetings together he talked about times when the whole church came together (I Corinthians 14:23). If there was no defined membership there would be no one group that could be specified as "the whole church". The New Testament also speaks of the gathering together of groups of believers (Acts 14:27; Hebrews 10:25; Acts 20:7). This was not in a general sense. This gathering together was with a defined group of people. In addition to this there are many New Testament phrases that imply that the churches were a distinct body. Phrases such as, "brethren, among you, in the midst of you, one of you, anyone of you, and one another" seem to indicate that there was some knowledge of who was a part of them and who was not.

> "*All of these presuppose a definite group in which people know each other, where they can distinguish those who are 'among them' from those who 'are without', where they can admonish one another, care for one another, encourage one another, etc.*"[1]

The whole concept of body ministry implies that we know who the members of the body are. We cannot serve, exhort, lay down our lives for or wash one another's feet if we do not know and have a committed relationship to each other.

3. Church membership is based on certain conditions and is therefore exclusive.
The very definition of the word "ekklesia" implies that membership is not open to all. The "ekklesia" in the Greek culture consisted of only those who were citizens of that city. In the Old Testament the "called out ones" consisted only of those who were circumcised according to the law of Moses. This is why the Judaizers felt that this was such an important issue (*Acts 15:1*).

No-one becomes a member of the New Testament Church of Jesus Christ by signing up, taking a pledge or subscribing to a particular set of doctrines. There is only one thing that qualifies you as a member of the Church. You are a member of the universal Church by being rightly related to the Lord Jesus Christ, the head of the Church. Jesus Himself often speaks of the things that gain one's entrance into the Kingdom of God. All of the qualifications that are listed are spiritual including repentance (*Matthew 3:2*), humility and sacrifice (*Matthew 19:14-24*), faith (*Mark 1:14-15*), the new birth (*John 3:1-5*), obedience (*Matthew 7:21*) and endurance (*Luke 9:62*). The accepting of the unregenerated as Church members is totally incompatible with all of the teaching of the New Testament.[2]

Even though membership in the New Testament Church is meant to be exclusive, Church attendance is certainly to be open to all (*James 2:2-4*). Visitors are to be encouraged and ministered to by those who are members of the family. God's desire is that all would be joined to the family of God and separated from the world. Just as the natural family is to be open, and a place of refuge and hospitality to the weary and the wayfarer, so the New Testament Church is to be a place of refuge to the spiritually weary.

4. Church membership is not to be seen as a matter of choice.
The Church in our day is plagued by those who answer to no one in their spiritual life. This is not God's way. God has not designed this in the natural family. Every child born into the world has a natural place. He has no particular choice about his placement. God does the choosing according to His own purpose and will. So it is in relationship to the Household of Faith. God's will is to place the solitary into families. In the New Testament all those who were members of the universal Church were also members of the local Church, the visible expression of the universal Church. Whenever they were not identified with the local Church it was because they had been disciplined by the leadership. It was the most serious form of judgment to not be allowed to identify with the local Church (*Matthew 18:17*). Alan Stibbs in his book *God's Church* puts it this way, "Any idea . . . of enjoying salvation or being a Christian in isolation is foreign to the New Testament writings."

Over and over again in the New Testament we are made aware of the fact that fellowship with Christ precludes fellowship with His Body (*I John 1:3,6-7; I Corinthians 1:9*). If we reject those whom Christ has sent, we reject Christ. If we persecute those who belong to Christ we persecute Christ. If we refuse to join ourselves to the Church we are refusing to join ourselves to Christ. If we have a low level of commitment to Christ's seat of authority in the earth, we have a low level of commitment to Christ. Christ desires obedience, humility, submission and loyalty from those who bear His name.

5. Church membership should be recorded.
Both the Old and New Testaments refer to books where names of God's people were kept for records. In the Old Testament the genealogical records are a constant reminder to us that God is concerned about individuals. Before any of the Levites could minister in the priestly offices they had to be numbered before the Lord (*Numbers 3*). In fact, after the restoration of God's people from Babylonian captivity, no priest was allowed to minister who was not

[1]Kuen, *I Will Build My Church*, pg. 129
[2]Kuen, Alfred R. *I Will Build My Church*, see pgs. 127-150 for an excellent discussion of accepting the unregenerate as members.

registered in the book *(Ezra 2:62-63)*. In the New Testament Paul's letters reflect a stability of membership in the various salutations that he gives listing specific names of individuals.[3]

God has given the leadership of the Church the responsibility to care for His people as shepherds over the flock of God. It would be virtually impossible to take proper care of God's sheep if no-one knew where they were or where they really belonged. Jesus who is the Good Shepherd declares this same principle:

> *"To him the porter openeth; and the sheep hear his voice: and he calleth his own sheep by name, and leadeth them out. And when he putteth forth his own sheep, he goeth before them, and the sheep follow him: for they know his voice. And a stranger will they not follow, but will flee from him: for they know not the voice of strangers. I am the good shepherd, and know my sheep, and am known of mine."*
>
> *John 10:3-5,14.*

6. Church membership should be transferred. This is primarily a matter of practical consideration although it seems to be a practice that was common in the New Testament. Often times those going from one church to another would carry a letter of commendation *(Acts 18:27; Romans 16:1; Colossians 4:10; II Corinthians 3:1-2)* or a personal introduction from another member *(Acts 9:27)*. This would be of tremendous benefit to the receiving Church. For a pastor who has a desire to truly feed and tend the flock of God such a letter could break through a lot of initial barriers.

C. THE AUTONOMY OF THE FAMILY

In a normal society every family is to be an autonomous social unit. The word "autonomous" simply means "having the right or power of self-government; undertaken or carried on without outside control". This does not mean that a family answers to no-one, but that the normal family has the means of its own government, the means of its own support, and the means for perpetual propagation. No one family has the right or responsibility to exercise authority over another family in these fundamental areas. The Church in its local expression (and it must be remembered that the local expression should be a true representation of the universal expression) is to be autonomous in the sense that it is self-governing, self-supporting and self-propagating.

1. The Local Church is to be self-governing. God has placed in the New Testament Local Church the provision for its own government. The issue of government is one that has divided many churches and yet we must realize that God does have a pattern for this area of Church life. God has given a pattern for government that cannot be ignored if we are to experience the kind of "family life" that God wants for us. In the Church God refers to "those that rule" or "he that ruleth", or "them that have the rule" *(I Tim. 5:17; Rom. 12:8; Hebrews 13:17,24)*. The word rule means "to be over, to superintend, to preside over, to care for, and to give attention to." Certainly it must be remembered that to be a "ruler" in the House of the Lord you must meet certain qualifications, but the important thing to see is that God has made provision for government in every local Church even as He has made provision for government in every family.

There are many forms of government that God could have designed and prescribed for the Church. He could have established a *dictatorship* or one man rule. This is what Israel desired when they looked to the nations of the world for a pattern. Many natural families operate this way with a male dictatorship, but that is not a government of God's choosing. The problem is that when the one man fails or falls, the whole family, church or nation suffers the consequences.

God could also have inaugurated a *democracy* or rule by the majority. Many churches are established this way, but no sensible family would work on this basis. In most families the children out number the parents or could we say the immature outnumber the mature. If the decisions of the family were made on the basis of a democracy then they would be made by those with little or no experience in life who have not yet been able to develop good judgment. The same is true in the Church. If we function in the Church on the basis of democracy it is going to be the immature and those who spiritual sensitivity and divine vision are as yet undeveloped who will control the Church. In any growing Church those who have been in the Church for a shorter time will outnumber those who are more mature, and therefore decisions would be made by those unskilled in the Word. Just as in the natural family small children rarely know what is good for them and could invariably make unwise decisions, so also sheep do not always know the ways of the Lord, the Word of the Lord, the statutes of the Lord, the commandments, precepts and judgments of the Lord so that they can render wise judgments. Many times those who are immature in their faith lack spiritual insight and vision into the purpose of God. For these reasons God's government for the family and the Church is not a democracy. The word "Laodicea" means "judgment by the people". Rule by the people would tend to cause a lukewarmness because of the lack of vision in those with ruling power. Democracy may be a good form of government in society but it could only work in the Church if the majority of those in the Church were sensitive, responsive and obedient to the Word of the Lord. This kind of sensitivity comes only with maturity as a Christian.

Another form of government that God could have ordained is external human control, headquarters control or *central control*. It is interesting in the New Testament Church that we have no such development. The Church of Antioch never exercised authority over the Churches that Paul founded even though Paul worked out of the Church at Antioch. Jerusalem never exercised authority over Antioch even though Barnabas, one of the leaders of the Church at Jerusalem, had a large part in the establishment of the Antioch Church. Many have suggested that Acts 15 is an evidence that Jerusalem was the headquarters of the New Testament Church. However, it is clear from a careful study of the context and background of this account that this was simply a case of taking an issue back to its source (something we should also do as individuals). The problem was the Judiazers and their source was the Jerusalem Church, therefore dealing with this subject at any other location would have been unbiblical and futile. In the natural family the authority is self-contained. No family has dominion over another family in terms of family policy, discipline, expenditure and vision. God ministers to families as individuals, leads them individually and imparts a unique vision and expression to each. God does this as well with each local church. God's government for the family and the Church is not central control. We repel this concept in the family as has been reported in communistic countries where the state or central authority monitors and controls the individual family relationships yet we have taken a different attitude toward this form of government in the Church. In this case the decision-making body is totally removed from the scene and has no criterion on which to base effective judgment.

Another form of government that is quite popular is control by a *deacon board*. Most often these deacons are elected by popular vote and may or may not qualify under the scriptural qualifications of a deacon. These "deacons" are often times successful businessmen or men of renown among the congregation who serve on the controling board of the Church. This board chooses or deposes pastors, makes decisions about properties, and controls the vision and direction of the Church. It is interesting that the word "deacon" means servant and no where in the New Testament do we ever find deacons in government in the Church. In fact, when the qualifications for the office of a deacon are given in *I Timothy 3:5* and *12* there is no mention of the function of ruling in relation to the house of the Lord as there is with elders. The main danger of a deacon board is that it can tie the hands of the spiritual leadership appointed by God and it can be directed by men with knowledge and skill in the world of business but not necessarily having the same skill with relation to the Word of God. It follows that much decision making is on the basis of the wisdom of the world and not the higher wisdom of God which is often at odds with the world's ways.

God has not left us without direction in the area of Church government. He has not left man to do that which is right in his own eyes. Even as God has clearly established the principles of government in the natural family, He has also given clear insight and direction in the government which He would have in His Church. God's form of government in His house is *plurality*. Every home has plurality of leadership in the parents of the children. The fact that they are the parents gives them the authority to make decisions that affect all the family members. In the Church, God's form of government is also plurality. Every local Church that has had time to come to stability should have plurality of leadership. Those who have been given the responsibility of rulership and government in the house of the Lord are the elders (*I Timothy 5:17; Hebrews 13:17,24*). All of the Churches in the New Testament eventually had plurality of eldership (*Ja. 5:14; Acts 21:18; I Tim. 5:17; I Peter 5:1; Phil. 1:1*). These are mature ministries that God has raised up in the various churches who meet strict spiritual, domestic and moral qualifications. These are ministries who have demonstrated their maturity and who have a father's burden for the local church to which they belong. These are ministries who have had time to know the ways of the Lord and are called by God to shepherd His people. These are ministries who are sensitive to the voice of God and have demonstrated Spirit-ruled and Spirit-led lives that the qualifications for this office demand *(I Tim. 3:1-7; Titus 1:5-9)*. This is God's form of Government, a Theocracy. God rules the Church because God rules in the lives of His anointed and appointed servants.

Under God's form of government the New Testament Local Church can be said to be self-governing. It looks to no outside authority, no special group functioning outside or above the local church to effect decisions. The Local Church is the final court of appeal for disputes between believers *(Matthew 18:15-17)*, for questions of doctrine *(Acts 15)* and for the discipline of moral conduct *(I Cor. 5:1-5)*.

2. The Local Church is self-supporting. God has given principles of finance to the Church that make it possible for every New Testament Local Church to be self-supporting. In the natural family in a normal society every family should be able to care for its own needs. This does not mean that in times of crisis one family will not rush to the assistance of another family as the churches of Galatia sent aid to the Jerusalem church in a time of famine. But it does mean that there were no regular systematic, legal or imposed financial links between Local Churches in New Testament times. No New Testament Local Church sent a part of its income to any outside governing body. No outside governing body sent funds to establish new works, and when one body did send relief funds to another it in no way gave them the right to dictate to that church as a result. Funds were exchanged with no strings attached. The Local Church of the New Testament depended on no heirarchy for financial support, nor did it have to go to the government for any special financial grants. Each Church grew and with it grew the financial base to fulfill God's unique call.

To understand God's financial plan for the Local Church better it is necessary to be familiar with God's financial system in the Old Testament. This does not mean that the New Testament Church must follow all of the Mosaic admonitions in regard to finance but it is significant that there is only one financial system that God ever gave to any nation in the world and that is the system of the tithe that God gave to the nation of Israel.

The concept of the tithe was not new with the Mosaic system. Long before Moses' ascent to Mt. Sinai, Abraham had offered tithes to Melchizedek, priest of the Most High God *(Genesis 14:18-20)*. Jacob also in a time of consecration to the Lord had vowed to give God a tenth *(Genesis 28:22)*. But it is with Moses that God gives detailed definition to what He desired for His people in regard to the tithe. God was very concerned about the plan of giving in the nation of Israel. God prescribed certain offerings, sacrifices, freewill offerings and tithes that constituted His plan for their giving.

The principal area of tithing in Israel's economy was referred to as the "Lord's tithe" *(Lev. 27:30-33)*. This tithe consisted of ten percent of all their increase before anything else was taken out *(Numbers 18:21-24)*.

In Israel's history the tithe was not always maintained because the people themselves were not always stable in their personal relationship to God. When Israel backslid the neglect in the area of tithing was usually one of the first symptoms of their spiritual condition. In these times it was not uncommon for the Levites to have to go to work at regular jobs *(Neh. 13:10-12; Mal. 1:7-14)*. When God's people did not honor God in their tithing it released the devourer and calamity ate up whatever they would withhold. *(Mal. 3:7-12)*. However, it is equally important to note that whenever there was spiritual revival in Israel there was also a restoration of the system of tithing *(II Chronicles 31:5-12)*.

In the Old Testament tithing was only the beginning of their giving. Beyond the tithes were free will offerings that were entirely up to the individuals. The individual, however, had no choice when it came to the tithe and no decision as to the use of his tithe.

To understand our present relationship to the tithe we must first understand Jesus' relationship to the law. We know that the law and the Prophets were until John and after that the kingdom of God was preached and every man presses into it. Jesus came as the king of the kingdom. As the king He was also the law-giver. In Matthew 5 Jesus fulfills this ministry and even as Moses had received the law in Mt. Sinai in the Old Testament. Jesus now sets Himself on a Mountain and lays down principles or laws that will govern the Kingdom under His rule and authority. In every case He begins from the law of Moses, moves to the principle behind the law, magnifies the law and makes it honorable *(Is. 42:21)*. He later summarizes the whole of the Mosaic law into the command to love God and love your neighbor *(Matthew 22:36-40)*. This commandment of Jesus does not make the Mosaic law any weaker, in fact, it makes it much more difficult. Jesus summarizes the Mosaic Law into one higher law, the law of love. When we fulfill the higher law of love we automatically fulfill the Mosaic Law. If the royal law of love does not allow me to hate my brother, it certainly more than covers the Mosaic admonition against killing my brother.

In the New Testament Jesus seems to take this same attitude toward tithing. First of all, He confirms the truth contained in the Mosaic law by supporting and fulfilling it *(Matthew 23:23; Luke 20:25)*. He then teaches on principles of giving which stand behind the law *(Mark 12:41-44; Luke 6:38)*. Finally, He institutes a higher law to cover the principles of New Covenant giving. He teaches us that all that we have belongs to God, and that it is more blessed to give than to receive *(Acts 20:35)*.

For this reason the Epistles never explicitly command tithing. We do, however, find an outline of the higher law that is prescribed by God. Before the law, tithing was done voluntarily. Under the law, tithing was compulsory. In the New Covenant tithing is to be done willingly. The net result is the same, the difference is that a higher law motivated by love has been introduced. The New Testament principles of giving reflect this higher law. Giving of our substance unto the Lord begins by giving ourselves to the Lord *(II Corinthians 8:5; Romans 12:1-2)*. Once we have done that we are free to fulfill the New Testament requirements, giving:

generously *(II Corinthians 8:2; 9:6)*,
willingly *(II Corinthians 8:3,12)*,
proportionately *(II Corinthians 8:14-15; 9:6)*,
lovingly *(II Corinthians 8:24; I Corinthians 13:3)*,
cheerfully *(II Corinthians 9:7)*,
systematically *(II Corinthians 9:7)*,
thankfully *(II Corinthians 9:11-12)*,
sacrificially *(Hebrews 13:16; Mark 12:44)*
as unto the Lord *(Matthew 25:40)*.

Tithing is God's cure for coveteousness, which is the root of all evil *(Ephesians 4:28; I Timothy 6:10)*.

Any New Testament church that follows these basic New Testament principles of giving will never have a financial problem. They will have plenty for salaries, missions and all of the other regular functions of the church. In addition, their members will begin to experience the blessings of God on their lives in a new and exciting way. Any church that fails to teach biblical principles of giving to their members is robbing their people of the blessing of God that can only come when God's principles are followed *(Malachi 3:6-12)*. This includes small missions that are established in poor countries. Whenever a poverty-stricken people is deprived of biblical teaching concerning giving it is being deprived of the very means that God uses to bless His people financially. We are hurting them and not helping them.

3. The local Church is self-propagating.
It is the responsibility of every New Testament local Church to adhere to God's first command to man and His first command to the Church to be fruitful and multiply and fill up the earth *(Genesis 1:28)* and to go into all the world and preach the Gospel to every creature *(Mark 16:15)*. Reproduction is part of the normal family process. It is an abnormal condition when this reproduction does not take place. Not only is it the responsibility of the parents to have children, but it is also their responsibility to raise those children that they too can be heads of households themselves one day.

If the Church is to be successful in this aspect of its responsibility, the church must be a training center for those that are born in its house. Even as each father of each family is held responsible by God for the training and establishing of his offspring, so each local Church is responsible for the training and equipping of its own spiritual offspring. God never gave Israel permission to send their children to Egypt or any other place for their learning or training. In fact, He absolutely forbade it!

It is only as the Church accepts a vision for the training and equipping of its constituency, will there be a surfacing of ministry and a thrusting out into the harvest field. For this reason each local Church should support and maintain Christian education for its young people. Each local church should support and maintain a training program for prospective ministries. And each local Church should encourage and be willing to make sacrifices to fulfill the commission set before the Church. Often times this will mean sacrificing their very best for the furtherance of the Gospel of Christ *(Acts 13:3)*.

D. THE COVERING AND PROTECTION OF THE FAMILY.

There are many today who are seeing that the day of the Lord is at hand. There are many in the land today who feel that a John the Baptist-type ministry is coming forth in the land to prepare the way of the Lord. There is no question that we are living in unusual days. We are seeing great pressures coming upon the earth and tremendous challenges in this atomic-computer age. We are living in days where it is easy to understand Scriptures which speak of a day of great shaking when everything that can be shaken will be shaken. If our trust is in horses or chariots, if our trust is in military might, if our trust is in economic security, if our trust is in a superior political system, if our trust is in natural resources, then we are living in days where that trust is being tested.

The Word of God teaches us that the days prior to the coming of the Lord will be times of great pressure. These days will be similar to the days of Noah where violence and immorality abounded. These days will be similar to the days of Lot marked by perversion of every sort. These days will be characterized by tremendous deception and departing from the faith. In fact, if we could use one word to describe the days preceding the coming of the Lord it would have to be the word "deception." Jesus in His own discourse concerning the second coming warns us of this time and time again. In *Matthew 24* He tells us to *"take heed that no man deceive you" (vs. 4)*. He tells us that many false ministries will rise and using great signs and wonders they will deceive and deceive and deceive and *"if it were possible they shall deceive the very elect" (vs. 24)*.

This sounds like a very gloomy picture. Yet the people of God who are walking in the ways of God need not be fearful. The Day of the Lord is referred to by Joel as *"the great and terrible day of the Lord" (Joel 2:31)*. He refers to it as *"a day of darkness and of gloominess, a day of clouds and of thick darkness" (Joel 2:2)*. Yet, he also sees it as a day that is *"like the morning spread upon the mountains" (Joel 2:2)*. How can the day of the Lord be both dreadful and great at the same time? It is dreadful because it is a day of wrath and vengence upon the wickedness of the earth. It is great because it is also going to be a time of great preservation and salvation for the people of God. Even though wickedness will abound in the world, we know that righteousness will also abound among God's people. While the enemy is going to come in like a flood, we know that our God is going to raise up a standard against him. While storms may rage in the world, God is going to provide a covert from the storm and a hiding place for His people. There is a beautiful summary of this in *Isaiah 4:2-6:*

> *"In that day the Branch of the Lord will be beautiful and glorious, and the fruit of the earth will be the pride and the adornment of the survivors of Israel. And it will come about that he who is left in Zion and remains in Jerusalem will be called holy—everyone who is recorded for life in Jerusalem. When the Lord has washed away the filth of the daughters of Zion, and purged the bloodshed of Jerusalem from her midst, by the spirit of judgment and the spirit of burning. And the Lord will create upon every dwelling place of Mount Zion, and upon her assemblies, a cloud and smoke by day, and the shining of a flaming fire by night: for upon all the glory shall be a defence. And there shall be a tabernacle for a shadow in the daytime from the heat, and for a place of refuge, and for a covert from storm and from rain. (NAS)*

God tells us that upon every dwelling place (natural family) and upon every assembly (spiritual family) the glory shall be for a defence as "a covering." God has promised protection and covering to His people. He has promised to be a wall of fire around about them. He has promised to give His angels charge over them in time of danger and pressure. God wants to separate or put a difference between His people even as He put *"a division between Israel in the days of plagues" (Exodus 8:22-23)*, BUT if God's people are *going to be protected and covered in these days they are going to have to be in the place where God says they are to be; they must be rightly related to the family of God, the CHURCH.*

God has given us many examples throughout the Word of God for our admonition and exhortation in days of pressure. We need to pay close attention to these examples because they are God's warning to us. The family is a place of covering and protection.

1. This is seen in the days of flooding. Our day is characterized by the days of Noah. We are seeing a flooding of filth across the land and thousands of people are being swept away in the tides and undercurrents of it. Every form of media is being used to flood the earth with a permissive spirit. Satan knows that his days are numbered and he, too, is looking for one great final harvest, the tares coming to full fruit. In the days of Noah, however, God warned his people of the coming desolation and the people of God responded by faith and prepared a vessel that would be their ark of safety *(Hebrews 11:7)*. For this family of God in the days of Noah, God provided a place of refuge, a covert and a hiding place. It was the only safe place for the family to be. All outside of the ark were washed away in the flood waters that swept over the earth. Only those who identified with the family, who entered into the one door and who accepted and entered into the provision of God were spared from the judgments which came upon the whole earth. What a tremendous warning to the people of God! It is not good enough to be only right in our thinking, we must be right in our placement!

2. This is seen in the days of plagues. Our days are characterized by the days of the Exodus. All of the plagues that came upon the Egyptians as a means of judgment are prophetic of plagues that are to come upon the earth in the last days and correspond to judgments in the book of Revelation. During the time of plagues in the book of Exodus God worked a special miracle in behalf of His people. God put a division between His people and all the Egyptians.

> *"But on that day I will set apart the land of Goshen, where My people are living, so that no swarms of insects will be there, in order that you may know that I, the Lord, am inthe midst of the land. And I will put a division between My people and your people. Tomorrow this sign will occur."*

> *Exodus 8:22-23*

The word "division" in the Hebrew means "a redemption." God has severed us from Egypt by the redemptive blood of Jesus Christ. Moreover, if the Israelites were going to experience the benefit of the "redemption" they had to be in the place of God's provision. When there were flies in Egypt there were no flies *in Goshen*. When there was darkness in Egypt there was light *in Goshen*. God did His sovereign part by separating Goshen, but the Israelites had to do their part by staying in the place of God's provision, Goshen. The name Goshen means "drawing near." *They had to stay near to the Lord in the place of the Lord to experience the provision of the Lord.*

If an Israelite would have ventured out of Goshen, throwing off his identification with the people of God during the time of plagues, he would in no way be immune to the plagues. He did not have a personal light over him, the light was in Goshen.

This principle is seen more dramatically in the last plague, the death of the firstborn. In this plague God used the picture of the family. Each family that was spared by this plague had to follow strict guidelines laid down by God. To be an Israelite was not enough to spare you. To be circumcised according to the Abrahamic Covenant was not enough to spare you. You had to follow God's instruction. You had to have partaken of the passover lamb and sprinkled the blood of the lamb on the doorposts of your house, but beyond that, *you had to stay in the house.*

> *"Then Moses called for all the elders of Israel, and said to them, 'Go and take for yourselves lambs according to your families, and slay the Passover lamb. And you shall take a bunch of hyssop and dip it in the blood which is in the basin, and apply some of the blood that is in the basin to the lintel and the two doorposts; and none of you shall go outside the door of his house until morning. For the Lord will pass through to smite the Egyptians; and when He sees the blood on the lintel and on the two doorposts, the Lord will pass over the door and will not allow the destroyer to come in to your houses to smite you."*

> *Exodus 12:21-23*

God's promise to the Israelites if they followed this admonition was that He Himself would form or become a covering over the door of their houses so that the angel of death or the destroying angel could not enter in and bring death to the family. This covering and protection only helped them, however, if they did not *"go out at the door of his house until the morning."* To go out of the place of God's provision in a time of judgment would be foolish. As soon as they would leave the house they would be susceptible to the work of the destroying angel *(Psalm 78:49)*.

3. This is seen in the days of shaking. Certainly we are living in days when the strongholds of man and the walls of man's strength are crumbling before our eyes even as did the walls of

Jericho. Praise the Lord that it is a day when the people of God are possessing their inheritance as well, even as did the Israelites at Jericho. In the days of the conquest of Jericho God has given us another picture of salvation and deliverance in connection with the family. This is the preservation of Rahab's family. When the spies came to search out the land and it was apparent that God was about to judge the land, Rahab, a woman of faith, befriended the spies and made a special request. She requested with much wisdom that her family be saved *(Joshua 2:4, 9-14)*. The spies granted her request upon certain conditions. First of all, she had to have the sign of blood, in the scarlet thread, in the window. This identified her as belonging to the Lord. In addition they gave her another condition:

> *"Behold, when we come into the land, you tie this cord of scarlet thread in the window through which you let us down, and gather to yourself into the house your father, and your mother and your brothers and all your father's household. And it shall come about that anyone who goes out of the doors of your house into the street, his blood shall be on his own head, and we shall be free; but anyone who is with you in the house, his blood shall be on our head, if a hand is laid on him."*

> *Joshua 2:18-19*

This condition was, that when she gathered her household in the time of judgment, that if they were to experience the protection and provision of the Lord, they would have to remain inside the door of the house and identify with the family which was distinguished by the scarlet thread. If they chose to go outside, it didn't matter how close they were naturally related to Rahab, their blood would be upon their own heads. No protection or provision could be guaranteed. This, too, is a tremendous warning to those of us who are seeking to be immune to that shaking that is coming upon the earth when everything that can be shaken will be shaken. It must have been quite a sight for the people to see death and destruction all around except for one family, one house with a scarlet thread in the window, emerging from the rubble safe and secure.

This message of preservation and protection is seen in every ark in the Bible. That which was outside of the ark was destroyed by the judgments of the day. That which was on the inside was preserved. The ark of Noah was an ark of salvation to Noah and his family. Anyone who chose not to accept the ark as God's provision, and stayed without the door, perished and was swept away. The ark of Moses preserved a godly remnant in a time when many other babies were being martyred and experiencing death. The same waters that were death to some brought the others to life. The difference was the ark. Even as the ark of Noah had been built according to God's word by the faith of God's people, so the local Church today is being established according to the work and pattern of God by the faith of God's people. It, too, is God's prescribed place of refuge and safety.

The third ark in the Bible that is a beautiful picture of Christ and the Church is the Ark of the Covenant. This ark portrays the head of the body, Christ, as the mercy seat covering of the box or body of the ark. Over the whole thing are the outstretched wings of the two cherubims. In this ark, too, is the message of preservation. One picture of preservation is seen in connection with the golden pot of manna that was to be kept inside the ark *(Exodus 16:33)*. It is interesting that when the manna was given by God, if you gathered more than God instructed or tried to keep it longer than God directed, the manna always bred worms *(Exodus 16:20)*. But the manna that was placed under the shelter of the wings, under the blood-stained mercy seat, in the ark of God's provision never saw corruption, did not breed worms and did not stink. It was in the right place. It experienced preservation.

God is showing us that in our day, a day of judgment, a day of wickedness, a day of perversion and a day of deception, that He has provided a place of covering and protection. When we submit to God's authority in our lives, through humility and the acceptance of God's provision, we will be covered and protected from the fiery darts of the enemy, and we will not be deceived in days of moral, religious, political and natural upheaval. But if we choose, through pride and stubbornness, to reject the message and provision of God, and to step out from under the canopy of God in these days because of our rebellion, our blood will be upon our own hands. God promises no protection.

Jesus made it clear to Satan, who was tempting Him to step out of submission to the will and direction of the Father, that He could not expect the safety and protection of the promises in God's Word if He did so. Satan told Jesus to cast Himself down and God's angels would protect Him and bear Him up. But Jesus knew that unless He met God's conditions for protection, to expect protection is foolish. In fact, to expect protection when we are not in the place of protection is presumptuous. Jesus knew that it would be tempting God to claim a promise of Scripture without meeting the conditions of that Scripture *(Matthew 4:5-7)*. The promise of protection that Satan quoted to Jesus was conditional. God only promises that kind of protection to those who fear Him and come under the shadow of His wings in submission and obedience.

"The angel of the Lord encamps around those who fear Him, and rescues them."

Psalm 34:7

"He who dwells in the shelter of the Most High will abide in the shadow of the Almighty. I will say to the Lord, 'My refuge and my fortress, My God, in whom I trust!' For it is He who delivers you from the snare of the trapper, And from the deadly pestilence. He will cover you with His pinions, and under His wings you may seek refuge; His faithfulness is a shield and bulwark. You will not be afraid of the terror by night, or of the arrow that flies by day; of the pestilence that stalks in darkness, or of the destruction that lays waste at noon. A thousand may fall at your side, and ten thousand at your right hand; but it shall not approach you, you will only look on with your eyes, and see the recompense of the wicked. For you have made the Lord, my refuge, even the Most High, your dwelling place. No evil will befall you. Nor will any plague come near your tent. For He will give His angels charge concerning you to guard you in all your ways. They will bear you up in their hands, lest you strike your foot against a stone. You will tread upon the lion and cobra, the young lion and the serpent you will trample down. Because he has loved Me, therefore I will deliver him; I will set him securely on high, because he has known My name. He will call upon Me, and I will answer him; I will be with him in trouble; I will rescue him, and honor him. With a long life I will satisfy him, and let him behold My salvation."

Psalm 91:1-16

This concept of protection can be illustrated by the following diagram:

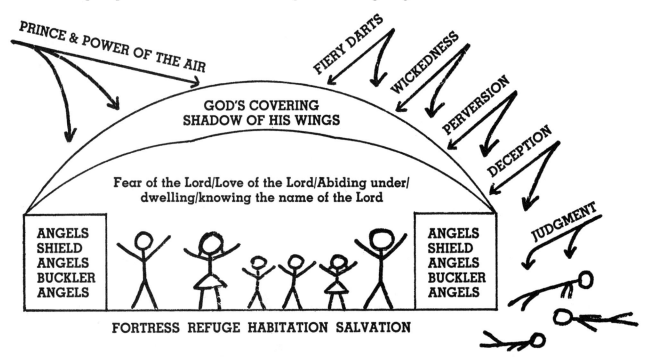

Right relationship with God brings covering and protection. Satan has to keep his hands off any that are properly related to the family.

E. THE DISCIPLINE OF THE FAMILY

There are tremendous benefits involved in belonging to the family of God. It is the greatest family in the universe. It is in the context of the family of God that we are going to come to fruitfulness and maturity. One means God uses to produce this maturity in us is discipline. Many natural families vary in terms of discipline and it is not difficult to see the different results in the fruitfulness and maturity of the children produced in those homes. There is only one right way of discipline and that is God's way of discipline. Only God's means of discipline will achieve the desired results. Families in which there is no discipline administered are chaotic and the children produced are generally rebellious. Discipline in the family is necessary because none of us is born into the family with a natural desire for, or knowledge of the right ways of God. Man naturally tends to be egocentric in all of his pursuits. If God's people are ever going to be matured, discipline is absolutely essential. God is very fair in His discipline, as can be seen in His use of it in the following ways:

1. Discipline is to be administered where there is a persistent following after the wrong ways of God *(Matthew 18:15-20).* When a man or woman claims to have Jesus as his Lord, but will not follow the ways of God, his confession must be challenged.

2. Discipline is to be exercised where there is danger of harm to the rest of the family of God *(I Corinthians 5:1-13; II Thessalonians 3:6-15; II Timothy 2:17-18; Titus 3:9,11).* Paul clearly taught that a little leaven leaveneth the whole lump. When problems go unchecked, others who are likeminded will tend to err from the faith as well. Problems unchallenged will never "work themselves out." God wants unhealthy situations that affect body life dealt with in a positive way.

3. Discipline is always administered with a view to restoration *(Galatians 6:1; Revelation 3:19; Hebrews 12:5-11; II Corinthians 2:5-11).* God does not want any to perish but He would have all come to the knowledge of the truth. For this reason He has to discipline. Most people do not come to the knowledge of the truth without some kind of external stimulus (i.e. discipline).

4. Discipline has degrees *(Matthew 18:15-20).* God in His mercy never disciplines severely unless an individual has been given warning or instruction in the mouth of two or three witnesses. God gives to every individual a chance to repent and change at an early stage. But if we fail to respond to a voice, He may have to use a switch. If we fail to respond to the switch, He may have to use a bigger stick. God cannot make us obey Him but He has ways of making us more willing to respond. God has given us a natural progression in New Testament Church discipline involving four stages, (a) go to the brother alone, (b) take two or three others, (c) tell it to the Church and, finally, (d) expel him from the fellowship. God is gracious and full of mercy but that does not preclude the fact that He desires truth in the inward parts. God will continue to discipline until He gets the desired response.

The fourth step in this process which is the most extreme is more severe than most of us realize. When we understand that the Church is a place of covering and protection that is respected by God and Satan alike, we realize that to be removed from that place immediately opens one up to the attacks and deceptions of the enemy. This act of excommunication was so severe in Paul's mind, that when referring to it, he indicated that what they were doing was in effect delivering *"such an one unto Satan for the destruction of the flesh" (I Corinthians 5:5).* He talked about Hymenaeus and Alexander whom he had *"delivered unto Satan, that they may learn not to blaspheme" (I Timothy 1:20).* Even this drastic measure, however, is administered with the view to restoration that *"the spirit might be saved in the day of Jesus Christ" (I Corinthians 5:5).* What a great day of rejoicing when the Corinthian believers were able to receive the repentant son back into the doors of the assembly *(II Corinthians 2:5-11).*

F. THE COMMITMENT OF THE FAMILY

Every natural family is a place of commitment. It is a place where God, not man, sets people in *(Psalm 68:1-6).* A family cannot operate without a commitment from its membership. When God places you in a family He knows what He is doing. You might not understand it all, but God's ways are sometimes past finding out. When a person is committed to a body of believers, to a local assembly, it means he is:

1. Committed to a specific place (family).
2. Committed to the vision of the leadership in that family.
3. Committed in terms of time and energy to that family.
4. Committed to the meeting times (meal times) of that family.
5. Committed in terms of financial support of that family.
6. Committed in a special way to the membership of that family.
7. Committed to bearing the burdens of that family.

Every general commitment to Christ and His Church must manifest itself in a specific commitment to a place or it is a false commitment. To say you are committed to what God is doing in a general way and not identify with a local Church in a specific way is to dwell carelessly and it could lead to deception. For a child to do this in the natural, to say that he belonged to the great family of mankind but he refused to identify with a specific natural family would seem almost ridiculous. Yet, how many of God's people desiring to identify with the universal body of Christ and family of God have refused to identify and commit themselves to a specific local assembly?

God has not established the local Church family just because He had nothing else to do for 2,000 years. God wants us to see His three-fold purpose in establishing His Church into families.

1. God desires to develop character in us. To do this, God plants us in context with other believers or family members. These are just the ones we need to help balance our deficiencies and to rub off any rough edges in our character. If a tree is going to be strong and bring forth fruit (something God has called all of us to be and do), then it cannot be continually transplanted. Someone who moves when discipline comes will never experience the life change that the discipline was meant to produce.

2. God desires to develop ministry in us. Just as the natural family is the proving ground for all church leadership (I Timothy 3:4), so is the local church the proving ground for all other ministry we may have in and beyond the body of Christ (Acts 16:1-2). If we are not under authority in a local setting and of good report among the brethren, God cannot use us mightily nor develop us fully. One qualification that God places on church leadership is that they are not to be novices (I Timothy 3:6). The word "novice" in the Greek means "newly planted." If we are only newly planted in a body we cannot expect God to use us in a great way. God tells us as a safeguard that we are to know those that labor among us (I Thessalonians 5:12). If we never stay in one place long enough to be known or to be truly planted, God will never sanction and bring forth our ministry as we would like. There are many, many people who think that they are called to "go" into the fields who are not willing to "be" witnesses and examples where they are. That is not God's way.

3. God desires to edify or build up the Body of Christ. We lose our effectiveness to build others up when we are unknown among people. A stranger who exhorts does not have the same effect as a brother who exhorts. God wants every member to be able to contribute effectively to the edification of the whole body (Ephesians 4:16).

God has given us this picture of the family that we might be better able to understand some of God's purposes for the Church. God desires that we should be joint heirs with Him in His glory (Romans 8:17; Hebrews 2:10). He desires that we grow up and become mature sons of God (Romans 8:23; Ephesians 4:13-15). It is in the context of His family that all of this is going to take place. Praise God!

Chapter 8
THE CHURCH — THE BODY OF CHRIST

Saul was a man who had a real passion and zeal for God. When he was convinced of a truth he was an unshakable rock in relation to that truth. If he believed something was true he would give it every ounce of his strength and energy. Even if it meant coming violently against opposition to that truth, he was prepared to do it. He was a man of firm convictions who had been raised with a high regard for the Word of God. There was only one problem. Not everything that Saul thought to be truth, was truth. Because of this, Saul became a persecutor of the truth in the name of truth. This is the tragic story of the man we find dragging Christians off to prison for their faith in the early pages of the book of Acts. What happened to this persecutor of Christianity that made such a difference in the way his life turned out? What would it take for such a man to make so complete an about-face in his life? He received a revelation from the Lord. The Lord arrested him, blinded him and gave him a revelation of Himself that Saul/Paul would never forget as long as he lived.

It happened in Saul's experience when he was on the road to Damascus with letters of authority from the high priest which gave him the right to arrest anyone who claimed to be a follower of Jesus *(Acts 9:1-3)*. While he was traveling, suddenly a bright light shone round about him and he fell to the earth. As Saul was laying there in the dirt, fallen before a manifestation of the glory of the Lord, Jesus gave him a revelation that would take three days of blindness, several years in Arabia and Tarsus and many more years of ministry to understand fully. Jesus said, *"Saul, Saul, why persecutest thou Me?"* Saul found out that when you persecute Christians or followers of Christ, you persecute Christ Himself. Here Saul received his first revelation of the Church as the Body of Christ, a revelation that was to infiltrate every aspect of his life and theology.

The truth of the Church as the Body of Christ was not a "new revelation" for Jesus had on occasion made strong allusions to it *(Matthew 25:34-40)*. But for Saul, his eyes were opened in a new way. In fact, as we look at the whole of Scripture, we see that God has progressively revealed this picture of the body throughout His dealings with man.

The first man that God created was a prophetic type *(Romans 5:14)* of Him who was to come. When God prepared the body of the first man, Adam, He was very careful and exacting in everything that He did. He left nothing to chance but He made man with His own hands personally. God was so careful about this creation because He had great plans for man. This first man or first Adam, was going to be a shadow of what God would do in a later man.

This first man that God made had a *very intricate, many-membered body made of earth (Genesis 2:7)*. There were many different organs, muscles, ligaments, bones and appendages, and all had their own particular use and function in relationship to the rest of the body. This first body was an undefiled body (sin had not yet corrupted it) that was incapable of sickness, disease or death. It was a body that was absolutely free from sin. It was a body that was full of life and of the Spirit of God. It was truly a body made in the image of God *(Genesis 1:26-27)*.

What a marvelous type this first Adam was of the last Adam, the Lord Jesus Christ. Even as Adam had a body that was specially prepared by God, so our Jesus had a prepared body when He became incarnate *(Hebrews 10:5)*. Jesus' also had a *very intricate many-membered body made of earth (Galatians 4:4; Hebrews 2:14)*. Jesus had a body that was totally undefiled by sin *(Hebrews 4:15)*, and hence it was totally incapable of sickness, disease and death. This is why Jesus could touch the unclean and never become unclean Himself *(Matthew 9:35)*. This is why He passed through the crowds when people tried to sieze Him or kill Him. Jesus was incapable of death unless He chose to lay His own life down *(John 10:18)* and until He took our sin upon Himself and became sin *(II Corinthians 5:21)*. The body of Jesus was full of life and of the Spirit of God *(John 6:63; Luke 4:14,18)*, and He was made in the image of God *(Hebrews 1:3; Colossians 1:15)*.

The body of Jesus, however, is not the last man that interests God. Jesus is called the last Adam but not the last man *(I Corinthians 15:45-47)*. Jesus is referred to as the Second Man, The Second Man because there is a THIRD man in God's progressive plan. The third man that is prophesied by the first two is the Body of Christ—The Church which is made up of Christ who is the head, and all those who are in Christ as the Body.

62

"For He Himself is our peace, who made both groups into one, and broke down the barrier of the dividing wall, by abolishing in His flesh the enmity, which is the Law of commandments contained in ordinances, that in Himself He might make the two into one new man, thus establishing peace and might reconcile them both in one body to God through the cross, by it having put to death the enmity. And He came and preached peace to you who were far away, and peace to those who were near; for through Him we both have our access in one Spirit to the Father."

Ephesians 2:14-18

The Church or the Body of Christ is also a *very intricate, many-membered body made of earth.* Because of Christ's atoning work in behalf of this body it is going to be a body free from sickness, disease and death *(Matthew 8:17; I Corinthians 15:25-26).* It is to be full of life and of the Spirit of God and in God's plan it is to be conformed to the image of the Son of God who is made in the image of God *(Ephesians 4:12-16; Colossians 3:10).*

"And we know that God causes all things to work together for good to those who love God, to those who are called according to His purpose. For whom He foreknew, He also predestined to become conformed to the image of His Son, that He might be the first-born among many brethren; and whom He predestined, these He also called; and whom He called, these He also justified; and whom He justified, these He also glorified."

Romans 8:28-30

A. THE STRUCTURE OF THE BODY

The Church as the Body of Christ has only one head, but it has many members. *The one and only head of the Body of Christ is the Lord Jesus Christ.*

"And He put all things in subjection under His feet, and gave Him as head over all things to the church, which is His body, the fulness of Him who fills all in all."

Ephesians 1:22-23

Jesus Christ is the head and hence sovereign authority in the Church *(Ephesians 5:24,28-31; Colossians 2:18-19).* As the authority, He is to give all the directives to the body. He is to guide and control the body. In the natural, if you have a body that does a lot of things without the administration of the head it is considered spastic, yet how many members of the Body of Christ do not give the Head its rightful place of authority in their lives and churches.

"Let no one keep defrauding you of your prize by delighting in self-abasement and the worship of the angels, taking his stand on visions he has seen, inflated without cause by his fleshly mind, and not holding fast to the head, from whom the entire body, being supplied and held together by the joints and ligaments, grows with a growth which is from God."

Colossians 2:18-19

Only as members of the body are in subjection to the Head and respond to His commands can the body function healthily and properly. The proper response of the body then would be basically two-fold. The body should only do those things that are directed by the Head, and it should do all that the Head has directed. Failure of the body to respond to the impulses of the Head indicates that the nerve involved has been severed or deadened and a condition of *paralysis* has entered in. A Church that does not respond to the head is a paralyzed Church.

Jesus talked about a Church like this in the Book of Revelation. The Church of Sardis was a Church that had the name of one who lived yet it was really dead *(Revelation 3:1).* How many Churches today bear the Name of Christ, the One who lives and yet they themselves are dead. The only way for a dead Church to come alive is to come back to Jesus, the Head, who is the Resurrection and the Life.

The life source of the body is the Head *(Colossians 1:18; 2:11-13).* The life of the body is nothing less than the risen life of the Lord Jesus Christ *(Colossians 3:4)*. Every body will die rapidly it if is severed from its head *(I Corinthians 15:45)*. This is so obvious in the natural, but it is just as great a reality in the spiritual Body of Christ. Christ is the sustainer of life to the Body of Christ.

> *"He also head of the body, the church; and He is the beginning, the first-born from the dead; so that He Himself might come to have first place in everything. For it was the Father's good pleasure for all the fulness to dwell in Him."*
>
> *Colossians 1:18-19*

Once the Head is given His correct place as the source of life, the fulness that is in the Head can flow to the rest of this body which is made up of many members *(I Corinthians 12:20)*. From the human body we can learn a great deal about the relationship of the members in the spiritual Body of Christ.

1. Each member is vitally connected to the other members through the bloodstream.
In the human body the blood stream connects every member, servicing every cell in the body, cleansing and purifying as it flows from member to member. This is a beautiful picture of how the blood of Christ unites the people of God into one people and one body. It is the line of scarlet that connects us all. It is the blood of Christ that brings us together *(Ephesians 2:13)*. It is the flowing blood of Christ released by the unity and fellowship of God's people that cleanses and purifies its membership *(I John 1:7)*. It is the blood of Christ that makes us members one of another.

2. Each member is activated by the breath of God.
Apart from the breath of God every man is a lifeless mass of protoplasm *(Genesis 2:7)*. God originally gave man breath, and any living being today must continue to breathe or it will soon die *(James 2:26)*. In the human body the breath or oxygen is carried to every cell by the bloodstream and it activates the energy resources of the body. A body without proper breathing and oxygen will soon build up toxins, become numb and eventually die. Jesus said that the words which He spoke were Spirit and life *(John 6:63)*. It is the Word of God and the Spirit of God which activate, motivate and energize the members of the Body of Christ. Any Church that does not allow for the full expression of the Word of God and the full release of the Spirit of God is choking itself and cutting itself off from the source of its own life.

3. Each member must function at the direction of the Head.
Not only is there a corporate responsibility of a people to listen and respond to the directions of the Head, each individual member must also be "plugged in" to the source of life if it is going to realize any usefulness or purpose in relation to God's purposes. Each member has its own unique function *(I Corinthians 12:27)* and is accountable to the Head for the demonstration of that service.

4. Each member is totally dependent upon the other members
(I Corinthians 10:17). Every member of the body is unique and special in its function, but the only way it can properly function is to be rightly related to the whole. The message of the Body of Christ is that no-one is useful alone and no-one can survive alone. As soon as you sever the hand from the body it withers and dies. Eventually it will return to the dust from which it came. So many individuals today are trying to function apart from any ties or identification with the Body of Christ. They are independent and they pride themselves in their independence. How amusing to picture a hand cut off from the body, declaring its independence. Soon it will realize that in its position of independence from the body it has gone from a well-watered place to a dry land *(Psalm 68:6)*. The members of a body only have right function if they are linked to each other in proper placement. They have no ministry or function alone. Every member of the body is mutually dependent on each other member, and absolutely dependent upon the Head. Perhaps to be called an "Independent Local Church" is not a title in which to boast. Perhaps we should realize that we are all "Dependent Local Churches."

5. Each member has a unique and important place of function
(Romans 12:4-5). As much as some researchers would like to have us believe that there are certain organs or

appendages in the human body which render no service and have no function, it seems difficult to believe that God who does all things well would waste energy creating things which have no purpose to fulfill. Just because the scientists may not as yet have discovered the function of certain members, it does not mean that those members have no function. The truth is never dependent upon our understanding of it. If the scientists research long enough perhaps they will one day discover that function. The same is true of the Body of Christ. We may not always immediately recognize the function of every member, but God has declared that all have a purpose and function that is vital to the success of the whole *(Romans 12:4-5)*.

Every individual is created perfectly suited to that function for which God intended him. God knows us all exactly, and He has taken everything into account. For this reason it is important for each of us to seek the Head as to the exact place that God has designed for him. It is not a matter of looking over a list of vocational options and choosing the most lucrative or naturally appealing. It is a matter of discovering God's call. Not everyone can, or will, be the hand. And it is good for the Body that not everyone is a hand. If everyone was a hand, who would do the walking, the hearing and the seeing? But God has given to everyone a function as it has pleased Him, and for that function, and no other, are we held accountable. The hand is not accountable for what the foot does, nor is the foot accountable for what the hand is to do.

When every member of the body is functioning in its place there will be a rest in the body. The individual person will find true expression and fulfillment. He will feel a sense of belonging and accomplishment, and the body as a whole will be edified and built up properly. When everyone is in his place everything will be accomplished.

> *"For even as the body is one and yet has many members, and all the members of the body, though there are many, are one body, so also is Christ. For by one Spirit we were all baptized into one body, whether Jews or Greeks, whether slaves or free, and we were all made to drink of one Spirit. For the body is not one member, but many. If the foot should say, 'Because I am not a hand, I am not a part of the body,' it is not for this reason any the less a part of the body. And if the ear should say, 'Because I am not an eye, I am not a part of the body,' it is not for this reason any the less a part of the body. If the whole body were an eye, where would the hearing be? If the whole were hearing, where would the sense of smell be? But now God has placed the members, each one of them, in the body, just as He desired. And if they were all one member, where would the body be? But not there are many members, but one body. And the eye cannot say to the hand, 'I have no need of you'; or again the head to the feet, 'I have no need of you.' On the contrary, it is much truer that the members of the body which seem to be weaker are necessary; and those members of the body, which we deem less honorable, on these we bestow more abundant honor, and our unseemly members come to have more abundant seemliness, whereas our seemly members have no need of it. But God has so composed the body, giving more abundant honor to that member which lacked, that there should be no division in the body, but that the members should have the same care for one another. And if one member suffers, all the members suffer with it; if one member is honored, all the members rejoice with it. Now you are Christ's body, and individually members of it."*

I Corinthians 12:12-27

B. THE FUNCTION OF THE MEMBERS

God desires the Church, the Body of Christ, to be a growing, healthy and functioning body, where every member has his responsibility to the edification of the whole. In order to accomplish this, God has given to every individual in the body natural talents and abilities that are to be used for His glory. It is not accidental that individuals in the body have certain aptitudes and interests. These are all part of God's plan for that person's life purpose. Unfortunately so many people fail to look for ways in which they can channel these aptitudes and abilities into investment in the kingdom of God. God desires that all of these abilities be used for the glory of God *(Matthew 25:14-30)*.

In addition to natural talents and abilities, God also has given spiritual gifts that are to be operating in the House of the Lord. When we enter into the kingdom of God by the new birth, we are taken out of the natural realm and transplanted into the realm of the Spirit. While natural talents and abilities are helpful for the extension of the kingdom of God, natural talents and abilities will never be enough to get the job done *(Zecheriah 4:6).* For this reason, God distributes spiritual gifts to the members of His body that operate above the natural realm into the supernatural. They operate above natural ability by tapping into God's supernatural ability *(I Corinthians 12:7,11).*

On the basis of these things that God has given to the members of His body, God has further given to each member of the Body a ministry, or function, that is to add to the edification of the whole. The word "ministry" simply means "service" or "function". In every body there are many members and all the members do not have the same function *(Romans 12:4-5).*

> *"As each one has received a special gift, employ it in service one another, as good stewards of the manifold grace of God. Whoever speaks, let him speak, as it were, the utterances of God; whoever serves, let him do so as by the strength which God supplies; so that in all things God may be glorified through Jesus Christ, to whom belongs the glory and dominion forever and ever. Amen."*
>
> *I Peter 4:10-11*

In order for us to understand fully the way in which these ministries operate and their importance, we need to realize several things.

1. These ministries all find their origin in the Lord Jesus Christ. When Christ
came, He came as the fulness of the Godhead bodily *(Colossians 1:19, 2:9).* As the fulness of the Godhead, He manifested in life expression every gift, grace and ministry that would eventually function in the Church, His body. When Christ came as the fulness of the Godhead bodily, He had all the ministries functioning in their mature expression because He did not receive from the Father a *measure* of grace, or a *measure* of the Spirit, He alone received the fulness *(John 1:14; 3:33-35).*

As such Christ was the pattern for all ministry. If we want to know how a certain ministry is to operate in the Body of Christ, we simply need to look to Christ to find out how He operated in that ministry. Christ was THE:

Apostle *(Hebrews 3:1),*
Prophet *(John 4:19),*
Evangelist *(Luke 4:18),*
Pastor *(John 10:11),*
Teacher *(John 3:2),*
Elder *(Romans 8:29),*
Deacon *(Luke 22:27),*
Exhorter *(Luke 2:25),*
Giver *(Galatians 2:20),*
Ruler *(Luke 1:33),*
Shower of Mercy *(Hebrews 2:17),*
Worker of Miracles *(John 11:47),*
Healer *(Luke 6:17-19),*
Governor *(Isaiah 9:6-7),*
Intercessor *(Hebrews 7:25),*
Etc., Etc., Etc. . .

(NOTE: In part two of this book we are going to look at some of these ministries more closely and see how Christ is the pattern for each).

2. These ministries are merely an expression of Christ in you *(Colossians
1:27).* Christ is the *fulness* of the Godhead bodily and therefore as the Head, the fulness of all ministries is in Him. When we become attached to the Head by new birth, we become partakers of the fulness that is in Him. We ourselves do not contain the fulness, we only partake of a *measure* of the fulness that is in Christ.

> *"And the Word became flesh, and dwelt among us, and we beheld His glory, glory as of the only begotten from the Father, full of grace and truth . . . for of His fulness we have all received, and grace upon grace."*
>
> *John 1:14, 16*

66

As the fulness of the Godhead bodily, Christ was full of *grace* that enabled Him to accomplish and fulfill all of these ministries. When we are attached to the Head, we become a *partaker* of that *grace* that is necessary to fulfill the particular ministry that we have been given by the Lord.

"But to each one of us grace was given according to the measure of Christ's gift."

Ephesians 4:7

HEAD
FULNESS

BODY
MEASURE OF
FULNESS

Since this is the case, it is very important that we as believers recognize the ministry that we have been given, because we will receive grace for that ministry. Without the grace for the ministry, the ministry will inevitably fail because none of these ministries can operate effectively on a natural level. All of them have to be supported and underwritten by the grace of God. The grace of God in relation to service is simply the supernatural enablement of God. Paul recognized the grace that was upon his life, therefore he could move with confidence in the ministry which he had received from the Lord *(Romans 12:3)*.

"Through whom we have received grace and apostleship to bring about the obedience of faith among all the Gentiles for His name's sake."

Romans 1:5

"But I have written very boldly to you on some points, so as to remind you again, because of the grace that was given me from God, to be a minister of Christ Jesus to the Gentiles, ministering as a priest the gospel of God, that my offering of the Gentiles might become acceptable, sanctified by the Holy Spirit."

Romans 15:15-16

"According to the grace of God which was given to me, as a wise master builder I laid a foundation, and another is building upon it. But let each man be careful how he builds upon it."

I Corinthians 3:10

"For I am the least of the apostles, who am not fit to be called an apostle, because I persecuted the church of God. But by the grace of God I am what I am, and His grace toward me did not prove vain; but I labored even more than all of them, yet not I, but the grace of God with me."

I Corinthians 15:9-10

"and recognizing the grace that had been given to me, James and Cephas and John, who were reputed to be pillars gave to me and Barnabas the right hand of fellowship, that we might go to the Gentiles, and they to the circumcised."

Galatians 2:9

If we are to be successful as stewards of the manifold grace of God, we must be sure that we recognize the grace of God that is upon our lives. The grace of God goes with the calling of God. Paul tells us that when it comes to evaluating the grace that is on our lives we should be sober. We should be careful in our evaluation and estimation of ourselves and careful not to think of ourselves more highly than we ought to think. How many ministries have failed because they attempted greater things in God than that for which they had received grace. We must be careful to perceive God's grace in our lives, and then it will not be difficult to perceive the ministry that He has for us. We must remember that God never holds us accountable for that to which someone else has been called. He only holds us accountable for what He has instructed us to do. If I am struggling to be a pastor in the body of Christ but God has given me the grace to be an intercessor, then I will not receive the commendation of a good and faithful servant. God only measures us against what He has called us to be. He never rates us on the basis of what we do, only on the basis of how faithful we are to do His will for our lives. There may be those who attempted to be apostles in their own strength who will receive the judgment of an unfaithful servant in the kingdom of God, while there will be those who were singers in the choir who will receive the accommodation of the faithful steward and become the ruler of cities in the kingdom to come. Our placement in the future kingdom will not be dependent upon our natural talents and abilities, it will not be dependent upon the number of spiritual gifts we exercised, it will not be determined on the basis of the ministry calling that we had in this lifetime, *it will be determined on the basis of faithfulness,* that is, how faithful we were to what God told us to do. If we are judged faithful, we will be assigned areas of rulership in the kingdom of God *(Matthew 25:14-30).*

"I urge you therefore, brethren, by the mercies of God to present your bodies a living and holy sacrifice, acceptable to God, which is your spiritual service of worship. And do not be conformed to this world, but be transformed by the renewing of your mind, that you may prove what the will of God is, that which is good and acceptable and perfect. For through the grace given to me I say to every man among you not to think more highly of himself than he ought to think; but to think so as to have sound judgment, as God has allotted to each a measure of faith. For just as we have many members in one body and all the members do not have the same function, so we, who are many, are one body in Christ, and individually members one of another. And since we have gifts that differ according to the grace given to us, let each exercise them accordingly: if prophecy, according to the proportion of his faith; if service, in his serving; or he who teaches, in his teaching; or he who exhorts, in his exhortation; he who gives, with liberality; he who leads, with diligence; he who shows mercy, with cheerfulness."

Romans 12:1-8

3. These ministries functioning together will make up or comprise the fulness of Christ.

When Christ ascended on high and led captivity captive, He left the earth bodily, but He did not leave the earth without a witness. On the day of Pentecost the Holy Spirit was outpoured upon the expectant disciples and there took place the miraculous birth of the Body of Christ. At this time Christ distributed His ministry and fulness of grace to His body.

"Therefore it says, 'When He ascended on high, He led captive ahost of captives, and He gave gifts to men.' And He gave some as apostles, and some as prophets, and some as evangelists, and some as pastors and teachers, for the equipping of the saints for the work of service, to the building up of the body of Christ."

Ephesians 4:8,11-12

This distribution is seen in several beautiful New Testament pictures, the first being the Day of Pentecost itself. In *Acts 2,* when the Holy Spirit fell upon the waiting believers, there were some supernatural manifestations that took place simultaneously. There was the sound of a mighty, rushing wind and there were tongues like as fire. In the original language of this text the implication in the fire is that the fire appeared and then distributed itself among them in the tongues, one fire dividing itself and distributing itself among many. The fulness of Christ being broken and distributed to each member of the Body.

Another picture is in the New Testament Table of the Lord. When Jesus instituted the Last Supper, and identified the bread as being His body, He was teaching us something about the New Testament Church, the body of Christ. The first thing Jesus did was to break the bread which spoke of the fact that Christ's natural body was to be broken in death. After the breaking He distributed that bread to the disciples. This is exactly what Jesus did when He ascended on high. He took of His fulness and distributed it to His body *(Ephesians 4:8-12).* No disciple received the fulness of the loaf but they all received a measure of the fulness. Each became a partaker of the divine fulness. No one ministry has it all, but all have a fragment that they are to share with the rest of the body.

If we are to experience the fulness of Christ's ministry we must receive and acknowledge that which is in each member. God's desire is that the bread that was broken become one lump or one loaf again *(I Corinthians 10:17).* When the individual members of the body of Christ are in unity and harmony then the loaf is restored as whole and we can experience Christ's fulness.

"He gave some as apostles, and some as prophets, and some as evangelists, and some as pastors and teachers, for the equipping of the saints for the work of service to the building up of the body of Christ; until we all attain to the unity of the faith, and of the knowledge of the Son of God, to a mature man, to the measure of the stature which belongs to the fulness of Christ. As a result, we are no longer to be children tossed here and there by waves, and carried about by every wind of doctrine, by the trickery of men, by craftiness in deceitful scheming; but speaking the truth in love, we are to grow up in all aspects into Him, who is the Head, even Christ, from whom the whole body, being fitted and held together by that which every joint supplies, according to the proper working of each individual part, causes the growth of the body for the building up of itself in love."

Ephesians 4:11-16

In order for this to happen, we must begin to recognize and receive the ministry of others. We must recognize that we are members one of another *(Ephesians 5:30),* and we need each other to be what God has called us to be to the world. Christ only has one body. If the members of this Body are self-centered, full of striving, and critical of each other, the body is divided, the seamless garment of the Lord is rent, and the ministry of the body is rendered ineffective.

4. These ministries functioning together as the many-membered Body of Christ are to fulfill and complete the ministry of the Lord Jesus Christ.

When Christ was here on earth He ministered out of a heart of compassion seeking to save that which was lost. He came as the apostle sent from heaven. He came as the mouthpiece of God to a dying world. He came to proclaim the good news, to gather sheep, to instruct in the ways of God, to serve man where he was at, to exhort to righteousness, to give Himself as a ransom to many, to reach out to man in his need. Yet when Jesus was here on earth He was limited by the fleshly body of which He partook. He was confined to one geographical location, to one set of circumstances, to the needs of one small group of people at any given moment. God's love is for the whole world. Christ as the man on earth, could not reach out to everyone. More Christs or "anointed ones" would be needed to satisfy the heart of God. When Christ rose from the dead he provided the answer. Christ rose from the dead as the firstborn of many brethren. Now He desires to carry on and complete His ministry through His body, the fulness of Him that filleth all in all.

"And He put all things in subjection under His feet, and gave Him as head over all things to the church, which is His body the fulness of Him who fills all in all."

Ephesians 1:22-23

Christ as the Head is continuing to preach and heal and prophesy and teach and exhort and seek out the lost, but now He is doing it through His Body. The Book of Acts begins in a beautiful way. Luke writes of his former treatise, the Gospel of Luke, which is perhaps the most complete account of Jesus' earthly life and ministry extending from the birth of John the Baptist to the ascension of Christ. He refers to this treatise as being only a record of that which Jesus **"began** *both to do and teach" (Acts 1:1).* That three-and-one-half years of ministry was only a beginning. The book of Acts as well as Church History records all that Jesus continued to do and teach by the Holy Spirit through the Church of Jesus Christ, which is His Body.

Chapter 9
THE OFFICE OF THE DEACON

The dictionary defines the word "office" as:

"A particular duty, charge, or trust; an employment undertaken by commission or authority; a post or position held by an official or functionary; specifically, a position of trust or authority under a government." (Funk & Wagnalls)

When we apply this definition to the Church and the structure of the Church we find that there are only two recognized offices in the biblical, New Testament Church. There are many ministries, but only two offices, those of the bishops and the deacons *(Phil. 1:1)* or overseers and servants. We would like to look at these offices in depth to get a clear New Testament understanding of the place and function of them in the Church. We are going to begin with the foundational ministry upon which all ministry is built, the ministry of the deacon.

A. THE MEANING OF THE WORD

There are four main Greek words that shed light on this ministry in the scripture: diakoneo, diakonia, diakonos, and diako. The best way to begin to study any concept in the Bible is to examine the root words that are used in connection with this concept. One thing that is immediately apparent when we look at the root words in this case, is that our English word "deacon" is not a **translation** of the Greek word but it is a **transliteration** of the Greek word. That is, the translators have simply used English letters for the Greek word without giving the actual meaning of the Greek word. This should immediately raise a caution flag for us. Whenever we find a word that is not translated in the New Testament, but is transliterated, we can be sure that when the translating work was done on that passage there was a theological problem connected with that particular word.

Some good examples of this are words like baptism, bishop, apostle, evangelist, and deacon. The word baptism literally means "immerse, dip, or plunge," but in the 1600's when the Bible was brought into the English language, baptism was not always practiced in Christian circles by dipping, plunging or immersing. To avoid, therefore, raising theological issues over the validity of other modes of baptism, a neutral term was used that could be given any meaning desired by the interpretation. This became a very widely used word and kept the controversies alive.

This is exactly what we find with the word "deacon". The Greek word for deacon occurs many times in the New Testament and in most cases it is translated, but occasionally when this same word is used in connection with an official position in the Church, the word is not translated but it is transliterated. Evidently this area relating to the ministry, office and function of the deacon is also an area of wide interpretation and some disagreement. The only way to overcome some of these misunderstandings is to look at the biblical words that are used in conjunction with this ministry and see how they are used throughout the New Testament. The following is a summary of the definition and usage of these words in the New Testament.

1. Diakoneo — This word literally means "to be an attendant, to wait

upon." In the New Testament it is used of waiting on someone at a table as a waiter *(Luke 22:24-27)*; it is used in a general way of serving someone in any way *(Matt. 4:11; 27:55; Acts 19:22; II Cor. 8:19)*; it is used in the sense of caring for or taking care of *(II Cor. 3:3; Acts 6:2)*; it is used of helping or supporting someone *(Matt. 25:23; Luke 8:3; Rom. 15:25)*; it is used of the ministry of a church official.

"And let these also first be proved; then let them use the office of a deacon, being found blameless."

I Tim. 3:10

This word is translated several ways in the King James Version of the Bible. It is translated: minister, serve, administer, and used as the office of a deacon.

2. Diakonia — This word literally means "service or attendance as a servant."
In the New Testament it is used generally of all manner of service (Heb. 1:14; Eph. 4:12; Acts 6:4); it is used specifically of the service necessary for the preparation of a meal (Luke 10:40); it is used of the service or function of all New Testament ministries (I Tim. 1:12; Acts 20:24; I Cor. 12:5; Col. 4:17); it is used in the sense of aid, support or distribution especially of alms and giving to the poor (Acts 11:29; Rom. 15:31; II Cor. 8:4); and it is used of a specific ministry in the body of Christ (Rom. 12:7). This word is translated several ways. It is translated serving, ministry, ministration, relief, office, service, administrations, ministering.

3. Diakonos — This word literally means "a waiter, attendant, servant or minister."
In the New Testament it refers to the servant of someone (Matt. 20:26; 23:11; John 12:26); it refers to a helper or an encourager (I Thess. 3:2; I Tim. 4:6); and it refers to an official of the church (Phil. 1:1; I Tim. 3:8). This word is translated minister, servant, deacon. It is interesting that the apostles and other prominent Christians are seen in this capacity (Col. 1:23; Eph. 3:7; II Cor. 3:6).

4. Diako — This word is never found in the New Testament but it is significant in this study because it
is generally regarded as the root word on which the other three words are built. This word literally means "to run or to hasten on errands." This obviously serves as the foundation for all ministry or service.

When we put all of these words together with their references in the New Testament, it is clear that these words are closely related and that they are used in primarily two ways, an unofficial way and an official way. In the general or unofficial sense, they refer to any kind of servant ministries. At times they refer to the ministry in the home, the ministry of civil rulers, the ministry of angels, the ministry of various servants and the ministry of all believers regardless of their calling in the body of Christ. It is in this sense that every born-again believer is to have the heart attitude and characteristics of a servant. Every believer in order to be great in the kingdom, must learn to be skillful in service.

These words are also used in an official way, however. It is very clear from certain passages that when these words are employed they are referring to a special class of people who have proven themselves and were thus designated "deacons" or "literally "servants." These would be people who had obviously distinguished themselves in this capacity by their excellence and were utilized by the churches in certain designated areas of responsibility. This, then, became a specific office for which specific qualifications were given.

> "Paul and Timotheus, the servants of Jesus Christ, to all the saints in Christ Jesus which are at Philippi, with the bishops and deacons.
>
> Philippians 1:1

B. THE ORIGIN OF THE OFFICE

> "And in those days, when the number of the disciples was multiplied, there arose a murmuring of the Grecians against the Hebrews, because their widows were neglected in the daily ministration. Then the twelve called the multitude of the disciples unto them, and said, It is not reason that we should leave the Word of God and serve tables. Wherefore, brethren, look ye out among you seven men of honest report, full of the Holy Ghost and wisdom, whom we may appoint over this business. But we will give ourselves continually to prayer, and to the ministry of the Word. And the saying pleased the whole multitude: and they chose Stephen, a man full of faith and of the Holy Ghost, and Philip, and Prochorus, and Nicanor, and Timon, and Parmenas, and Nicolas a proselyte of Antioch: Whom they set before the apostles: and when they had prayed, they laid their hands on them."
>
> Acts 6:1-6

In this passage we have recorded for us the origin of the ministry of the deacons. Although this is not clearly stated in the passage, the use of the Greek words, the prominent position of this passage, the spiritual qualities for these seven, and tradition all seem to suggest that this is the case. If this is not the beginning of this new office, then we have no place where the beginning is recorded.

From this foundational passage we can glean many insights and guidelines for the establishment of deacons in the Church. First of all, the origin of deacons was a matter of practical consideration. They did not choose deacons just for the sake of having deacons. They did not choose *seven* deacons because they like the number seven. *They chose deacons to meet a particular need that their growth and expansion prohibited them from fulfilling.* In other words, the early Church developed in response to need. As long as the Church was small there was no such need. But as the Church grew and the responsibilities grew the oversight realized that they could no longer meet certain of the needs of the people and still be faithful to the unique charge that God had placed on them to feed the flock of God. The apostles of the early Church were not being proud or haughty when they looked for someone else with whom to share their responsibility, they were merely recognizing the area of service God had given to them in handling the Word. They were finding that they did not have time to do both. They would have to delegate some of their responsibilities to others. In delegating this responsibility they did not neglect their responsibility or cease in any way to be responsible, they merely used men of obvious character quality to assist them in meeting the needs of the people. This then did not elevate these seven men to equal status with the apostles or in any way establish a new realm of authority, but the deacons were given to the leadership to assist them even as the Levites were given to assist Aaron in the priestly office.

Secondly, the origin of the deacons was initiated by the leadership with the consensus of the people, and they were set in by an action of the leadership. The idea for deacons did not come from the people but God directed the leadership in the solving of a very real problem. Those in leadership saw a need and the way to meet that need best. They communicated their desires to the people; they asked the people to participate in the selection of suitable helpers; they prayed over those selected and they set them into their place of service. It is clear, that while the people were given a voice in the matter, the leadership had the final and directing voice in the matter. The apostles approved those who had been selected by the people because they met with the qualifications that were laid down by the apostles.

Thirdly, many later Churches seem to have realized the divine order in the selection of deacons for they also set them in to their Churches. We know that the Church at Philippi had deacons *(Phil. 1:1)*. The Church at Ephesus also seems to have followed this pattern because of the letter written to Timothy while he was in Ephesus *(I Tim. 3:8-13)*. In addition to these Scriptural inferences, early Church history tells us that this became a universal principle among the Churches.

C. THE QUALIFICATIONS OF DEACONS

It is interesting that God does not want just anyone to care for and render service to His people. He does not want just anyone to wait on tables. He does not take just any volunteer who wants the job. God is very particular about every person who has any responsibility in His house. When the apostles were looking for helpers they asked for men of honest report, full of the Holy Ghost and wisdom *(Acts 6:3)*. As the function of these men developed in the New Testament, Paul gave a little more concrete definition to their required qualifications. It is important that we see that these qualifications are not put forth as ideals to be aspired to by deacons nor is this office to be given to someone so that these qualities can be cultivated, BUT everyone who is set in as a deacon should already possess these qualities.

"Likewise must the deacons be grave, not double-tongued, not given to much wine, not greedy of filthy lucre; holding the mystery of the faith in a pure conscience. And let these also first be proved; then let them use the office of a deacon, being found blameless. Even so must their wives be grave, not slanderers, sober, faithful in all things. Let the deacons be the husbands of one wife, ruling their children and their own houses well. For they that have used the office of a deacon well purchase to themselves a good degree, and great boldness in the faith which is in Christ Jesus."

I Timothy 3:8-13

All of these qualifications can be summarized in terms of moral, domestic and spiritual qualifications.

1. Moral Qualifications

a. Not double-tongued *(I Tim. 3:8)*. This would imply that he is not a gossip. One who has a double tongue is one who says one thing to one person and gives a different view of it to another. Not being a person of gossip is vital to one who would know of the problems of different members because of his position.

b. Not given to wine *(I Tim. 3:8)*. This individual must be above reproach in terms of his personal habits. Whatever he does he will be a great influence upon others.

c. Not greedy of money *(I Tim. 3:8)*. This, as well as the above, is put in stronger terms than even in the qualifications for elders. Perhaps, it is because when the deacons are in a place of assisting and helping others, they may be tempted to accept monetary gifts from those to whom they minister.

d. Blameless *(I. Tim. 3:10)*. In every area of this man's life he must be above reproach. This would involve all business dealings and such. He must be an example to others of a godly life style.

e. Proven *(I Tim. 3:10)*. The word proved here means "to test, examine, scrutinize to see whether a thing be genuine or not." The office of the deacon is not given to promote maturity. Those given this position should already be living the life of a servant before they are entrusted with the title of the office of the deacon.

2. Domestic Qualifications

a. Husband of one wife *(I Tim. 3:12)*. The laws of God are a priority for this individual who has undivided affection.

b. Ruling his own house well *(I Tim. 3:12)*. This qualification is probably not to determine rulership ability as it is with the elder, but to determine the nature of the deacon's Christian walk. The deacon must first be a good parent, doing a good job at home.

3. Spiritual Qualifications

a. Full of the Holy Ghost *(Acts 6:3)*. Natural ability is important but it plays a second role to the life that is motivated and empowered by the Holy Spirit. It would be better to use someone who was sensitive to God and lacking some natural ability than to use someone who was relying on natural ability alone *(Zech. 4:6)*.

b. Full of wisdom *(Acts 6:3)*. Often times individuals working in the name of the leadership will need much wisdom because they will find themselves in situations where emotions are involved and where they know facts that they could use in a wrong way. They must know how to behave themselves wisely.

c. Grave *(I Tim. 3:8)*. This term denotes a seriousness of mind and character which should characterize his whole service. These people are to be such that they inspire the reverence, awe and respect of others.

d. Holding the mystery of the faith in a pure conscience *(I Tim. 3:9)*. This person must be spiritually right with God, so that along with material relief, he might also bring spiritual encouragement.

These qualifications indicate to us the importance that God places on all manner of service in the house of the Lord. In the Old Testament only those who had set themselves apart were to bear the vessels of the Lord *(Is. 52:11; I Chron. 15:12)*. In the New Testament the Lord is just as concerned over His house.

These qualifications in many ways closely resemble the qualifications that God has for elders in His house. In light of this similarity it should be noted that there is no mention of having an ability to teach, or ruling in the house of God *(I Tim. 3:2,5,12)*. It is clear that deacons are not those in authority in God's house nor are they the teachers who handle the Word, but they are, as their name indicates, the servant order in the House of the Lord.

D. THE WORK OF THE DEACON

When we have studied all of the references to "deacons" in the New Testament it becomes clear that *the general function of the deacons is the performance of various services of a practical nature in the Church, relieving the elders of burdens which might interfere with their ministry of spiritual oversight.* In the passage in *Acts 6* we find that the duties are mainly to aid in the distribution of relief to the poor. It was a practical service designed to free the apostles for the ministry of the Word and prayer. This passage seems to imply that these seven men did not necessarily do all the work themselves but they may have been given the oversight in these areas to make sure that the job was carried out in a systematic and impartial manner. *Acts 6:3* mentions that the apostles were looking for those that they could "appoint *over* this business."

In *Philippians 1:1,* when Paul writes to the Church to thank them for their special gift to him, he mentions this class of people in his greeting. This is a little unusual because it is the only letter where Paul includes the deacons in his address to a Church. Perhaps this is the case, however, because of the unique purpose of this letter. Paul was in receipt of a love offering that the Church at Philippi had raised and sent to him while he was in military custody in Rome. Now Paul responded with a letter of encouragement and thanksgiving. In addressing this letter to both the bishops and the deacons he seems to be acknowledging an important role that each had in the gift that he had received. If *Acts 6* serves as a pattern for us, it is likely that the idea to send an offering to Paul came from the eldership or the bishops while the deacons in the Church were the ones who organized it, collected it, and saw to it that the offering was delivered properly.

In the only other portion of scripture where the office of the deacon is mentioned, *I Timothy 3:8-13,* we have the qualifications for the office. No specific mention is made of the work of the deacon in this passage but we do notice that all of the qualifications listed are very much suited to this practical kind of ministry. Probably the most striking thing to note here is that teaching ability and ruling ability are not necessarily required of a deacon.

There are many practical ministries around the House of the Lord that could be done by others to relieve the oversight of a tremendous burden. Often times when a church is small, the pastor or pastors do it all. When a Church begins to grow, however, it becomes impossible for the pastor to handle every matter personally. There comes a time when help in natural areas becomes necessary so that those in spiritual oversight can truly give themselves to the Word of God and prayer and therefore have a real word for the people. There comes a time when someone else will do the bulletin, keep the books, type letters, answer the phone, arrange the weddings, keep the place clean, organize the ushers, give baby showers, operate the nursery and distribute to the needy. God has provided in the ministry of deacons a means through which all of these things can be done and, what is more important, they can be done *well.*

E. THE APPOINTMENT AND TERM OF OFFICE

One of the things that distinguishes the ministry of the deacons in the New Testament is the means whereby they are set into their place of service in the body. The only case of the setting in of deacons in the New Testament is in *Acts 6* where they were set apart by the laying on of hands of the oversight on the approval and in the presence of the assembly. Since this is the only case in the New Testament this must serve as a pattern for us.

Concerning the term of office for a deacon the Bible is silent. This silence in itself communicates a message to us. The silence seems to indicate that there was no specific term. This would imply that a deacon would remain a deacon as long as he did the work of a deacon and as long as he qualified under the original requirements for that office. It is clear that all those who began as deacons did not always serve in that capacity all their life. Philip went on to be an evangelist *(Acts 21:8).* It does seem likely that many who would have started out as deacons may have ended up as elders later on.

74

F. THE HONOR AND THE REWARD OF DEACONS

"For they that have used the office of a deacon well, purchase to themselves a good degree, and great boldness in the faith which is in Jesus Christ."

I Timothy 3:13

Paul tells us that for those who serve well there is honor and reward. There is a lot of meaning wrapped up in the phrase "those who serve well." For someone to fall into this category it would require diligence, faithfulness, responsiveness, sensitivity, thoroughness, and sacrifice. Stephen and Philip were such people. They were individuals who went above and beyond the call of duty. They were individuals who used every natural opportunity to minister spiritual realities. Because of this they become the best illustrations of the honor and reward of a deacon.

Paul says that those who serve well purchase for themselves "a good degree." This is not a bachelor's or a doctor's degree although these things are good degrees. This is a degree that God gives. It may mean that they gain a good reputation for themselves and are held in high esteem by others, but it may also mean that in serving well this becomes a good step into greater levels of ministry. They may be used to help other Churches establish similar ministries, thus finding a greater sphere of influence. The Greek word here means "step" and it could imply that the office, or at least the role of deacon, is preparatory for eldership. Many ministries in the New Testament seem to have begun in the role of a servant. Timothy served Paul *(Acts 19:22)* and John Mark served Paul and Barnabas *(Acts 13:5)*. The best example, however, is that of Philip who began as a deacon waiting on tables and ended up as a great evangelist *(Acts 8:5-6; 21:8)*. The Old Testament seems to suggest a similar pattern in the Moses/Joshua *(Ex. 24:13; Josh. 1:1)* and Elijah/Elisha relationships *(I Kings 19:19-21)*.

A second thing that Paul says is that those who serve well inherit great boldness in the faith. Stephen is a beautiful example of this. As a deacon he had opportunity to see many needs. As he was ministering natural things he was faithful also to minister to the spiritual needs of individuals. He had many opportunities to share his faith and his testimony with those in need. He had many chances to pray with people. As he was faithful God began to move in these situations and prayers were answered. Soon Stephen appeared as bold as a lion, doing great signs and wonders among the people *(Acts 6:8)*. This was not part of his job description, but it sprang from a life of service and devotion to the will of God. Stephen had so much boldness of faith that he was able to preach the boldest message in the book of Acts. He went from faith to faith as he was a faithful servant in the natural areas of responsibility.

G. THE OFFICE OF THE DEACONESS

"Women must likewise be dignified, not malicious gossips, but temperate, faithful in all things."

(NAS) I Timothy 3:11

There seems to be good evidence to support the fact that many women were set in as deacons in the New Testament Church. Here in I Timothy we see Paul making some special admonitions to women who would function in this capacity. The King James Version of the Bible would have us to believe that these admonitions are for the wives of those in the office of a deacon. Careful analysis of this passage, however seems to indicate that these additional qualifications are not to be applied to the wives of deacons but they, in fact, form a whole new classification of workers. This is evident for the following reasons:

1. The Greek term translated "wives" in the King James may be also rendered "women". The Greek word that is used here is a word that can be translated in two ways and is translated these two ways consistently throughout the New Testament. It can be either translated "wife" or "woman". Which word is used in any particular passage is the translator's choice and can only be determined by the context. The general rule applying to this word is that it should always be translated "woman" unless the context clearly implies that it is refering to a wife or wives. The King James translators as well as others have felt it should be rendered "wives" in this case. However, other versions, such as the New American Standard, translate it simply "women". This is probably the more accurate translation in this case. Since there is no possessive pronoun in the Greek and no article, there is really no grammatical justification to link them to the deacons that are mentioned in the above verses (I Tim. 3:8-10).

2. The term "likewise" that is used here is the same word that is used in verse 8 to introduce the deacons as opposed to the elders. In the context this term seems to be used to denote a transition from one class to another (See also: I Tim. 2:9; Tit. 2:3,6). If so, the new class here would be that of a deaconess.

3. It would seem strange that Paul would state the qualifications for the deacon's wife when he states no such qualifications for the wife of an elder. It is obvious from the New Testament that the role of an elder in the Church was much more important in terms of authority and responsibility yet Paul lists no qualifications for the wives of the elder. This apparent inequity would also suggest that, in verse 11, these women form a category all of their own.

In addition to the evidence from this passage in I Timothy, there is additional evidence that women did function in this capacity in the New Testament Church. First, it is clear from documents from the early second century that there was an order of deaconesses in the early church. One such indication is found in an early letter that is dated about 112 AD. This letter is a report from the governor of Bithynia, a man by the name of Pliny, to the Emperor Trajan in which he indicated that he had tortured two Christian hand-maidens who were called "deaconesses."[1]

Second, there seem to be several women who function in the work of serving in the New Testament. In all of these cases the Greek word "diakoneo" is used in some form. Note the following:

1. Phoebe (Romans 16:1-2). Phoebe is the clearest case in the New Testament because she is clearly a woman (i.e. "our sister") and she is called "a servant of the church". The word "servant" here is the same word that is translated "deacon" wherever the word "deacon" occurs. She is sent here as a helper in matters of business which corresponds to the deacon's role.

2. The ministering women (Luke 8:1-3). Several women who had been healed and delivered by Jesus evidently travelled with Jesus and His disciples at times and served them in the areas of material substance.

3. Dorcas (Acts 9:36-40). This woman was vitally involved in the tremendous ministry of ministering to the necessity of the saints. The New Testament does not call her a deacon but the ministry that she had related clearly to what a deacon would do.

From all these considerations it is easy to conclude that the New Testament Church did have many women who functioned as "servants of the church". To these women Paul adds a few additional qualifications besides those listed for the men. The additional qualifications, that are given here are, in many cases, included in those listed for the men, but they are obviously repeated here for emphasis. Not only would a woman functioning in this capacity in that day be subject to greater scrutiny by those in the Church, but these additional qualifications may speak of the fact that women have certain areas in which they may be more easily tempted. At any rate these qualifications have to do with the matters of gossip, emotional judgments and trustworthiness.

1. They are not to be slanderers. This terms describes one "given to fault finding with the demeanor and conduct of others, and spreading innuendoes and criticism."

2. They are to be sober. This means she is known for her sound mind and good judgment. She is not to be one who makes emotional judgments.

---

[1]Shepherd, M.H., "Deaconess", *Interpreter's Dictionary of the Bible,* Vol. 1, page 786.

3. They are to be faithful in all things. Many women because of their many, varied responsibilities, can get easily side-tracked. One who is set in as a deaconess should be known for the fact that when she is given a responsibility or an assignment she is always faithful to carry it out.

4. They are to be grave or reverent. She must handle herself in such a way that she commands respect.

There are many responsibilities in the Church that could be best handled by a godly woman for which there would be a great need for deaconesses. The Early Church evidently found this to be the case as well. In an early manuscript from the late third century, called the *Syria Didascalia,* we are given a few clues as to the function of some of these deaconesses in that day. In this manuscript it says that the deaconesses were used to assist in the baptism of women. It also says that they were especially used in the art of anointing and "to go into the houses of the heathen where there are believing women, and to visit those who are sick, and to minister to them in that of which they have need, and to bathe those who have begun to recover from sickness."[2]

In our days there are many other areas where women could be of tremendous assistance to the work of God through the Church. Any time we fail to use all of the ministries that God has set in the body, we hinder that body from reaching its full potential. Any time we fail to recognize true ministries in an individual, we hinder that individual from reaching his/her full potential. God wants to release a whole army of servants into the body of Christ. Every believer begins by having a servant's heart. From those who have demonstrated a servant's heart and attitude, the leadership, appoints choice servants to function in the office of the deacon.

---

[2]Shepherd, M.D., "Deaconess", *Interpreter's Dictionary of the Bible,* Vol. 1, page 786.

Chapter 10
THE OFFICE OF THE BISHOP

In the New Testament Church there are two offices designated and recognized by God, the bishops and the deacons. In the previous chapter we looked at the office of the deacon and we saw that the heart of a deacon is the foundation of all ministry in the House of the Lord. We saw that the word deacon basically meant a "servant", and the word emphatically describes the function of the deacon. Now we come to the second office in the New Testament Church, the office of the bishop. Here we are also going to find that when we define the word we automatically discover a great deal about the function of a New Testament bishop.

A. THE MEANING OF THE WORD

There are six main Greek word forms that shed light on this ministry in the Scripture. These words are familiar to us in their transliterated forms but in order for us to get a correct, biblical view, we must look at their meanings in detail and see how they are used in the New Testament.

1. Presbuterion — This word literally means *"assembly of aged men, or the order of elders."* This term is used to refer to the council or senate among the Jews known as the Sanhedrin *(Luke 22:66; Acts 22:5)*, and it is used of the elders or bishops of a local Church *(I Timothy 4:14)*. At times the King James Version renders it "presbytery" *(I Timothy 4:14)*.

2. Presbuteros — This word simply means *"elder, older person or a senior."* At times this word simply refers to a person who is advanced in years. He may be someone who is merely older than his peers or others around him *(Luke 15:25; John 8:9)*. He may be a person who is advanced in life such as a senior citizen *(Acts 2:17)*. In like manner the feminine form may refer to older women *(I Timothy 5:2)*.

At other times this word is used in the New Testament to refer to the forefathers in Israel who lived in earlier days *(Matt. 15:2; Mk. 7:3-5; Heb. 11:2)*. All those listed in the "faith chapter" are referred to as elders.

The use we are most concerned about in this context, however, is when this term is used to designate people of rank who are appointed officials of the people. Among the Jews this word had a general meaning but it also had a specific meaning when it referred to members of local councils in individual cities *(Josh. 20:4; Ruth 4:2)* or members of a group of people in the Sanhedrin *(Matt. 16:21; 26:3; 27:41)*. Among the early Christian churches this term was also used of official "leaders raised up and qualified by the Holy Spirit and appointed to have spiritual care of, and to exercise oversight over, the churches" (W.E. Vine).

3. Episkopos — This word means *"an overseer, superintendent, guardian or bishop."* It is a compound word in the Greek and comes from two words, the first being a preposition meaning "over" and the second a verb meaning "to look or watch". Together they mean "to oversee" or "to watch over." This word is used five times in the New Testament *(Acts 20:28; Phil. 1:1; I Tim. 3:2; Titus 1:7; I Pet. 2:25)*.

4. Episkopeo — This is the verb form of the previous word and it means *"exercising the oversight, to oversee, to care for, to look at, to take care of."* It is used of the kind of care we are to exercise over our own heart in "looking diligently" after our own inward condition *(Heb. 12:15)*, but it is used primarily in regard to the ministry of elders *(I Pet. 5:2)*.

5. Episkopee — This word literally means *"charge or care."* It is used of the position or office of an overseer *(Acts 1:2; I Tim. 3:1; see also Num. 4:16)*.

6. Sumpresbuteros — This word is also a compound word. It is used only once in the New Testament by Peter who refers to those whom he is addressing as *"fellow-elders"* or *"co-elders"* (I Pet. 5:1).

A careful study of these words indicates that there is a close connection between the word elder and bishop; in fact, in the New Testament local church they refer to one and the same office. The word bishop is a word that is descriptive of an office or a position, while the term elder refers to the stature and maturity of spiritual experience that the man who fills that office must possess. This close relationship of these terms is easily seen in general passages where both of these Greek words are used. Notice the following verses where the Greek word used is in brackets behind the English rendering.

> *"And from Miletus he sent to Ephesus, and called the elders [presbuteros] of the church . . . Take heed therefore unto yourselves, and to all the flock, over which the Holy Ghost hath made you overseers [episkopos]."*
>
> *Acts 20:17,28*

> *"And ordain elders [presbuteros] in every city . . . for a bishop [episkopos] must be blameless."*
>
> *Titus 1:5,7*

> *"The elders [presbuteros] which are among you I exhort . . . feed the flock of God which is among you, taking the oversight [episkopeo] thereof".*
>
> *I Pet. 5:2*

Shaff's Bible Dictionary puts it this way:

> "In the New Testament the term (bishop) is synonymous with presbyter or elder — that "bishop" is borrowed from the Greek and signifies the function, presbyter is derived from an office in the synagogue and signified the dignity of the same office. These presbyters or bishops of the apostolic period were the regular teachers, pastors, preachers, and leaders of the congregations."

B. THE ORIGIN OF THE OFFICE

When we looked at the office of the deacon in the last chapter we were able to find a clear account of the establishment of this office in the Early Church. The situation is quite different in relation to the office of the elder or bishop. We can search the book of Acts and we will find no such account of the origin of the office of elders, in fact, they are first mentioned in *Acts 11:30* as if their function was clearly understood by all.

Perhaps the reason for this is that the office of the elder was not a new office at all. It was not new to the New Testament Church. It was, in fact, something that was very familiar to the people because it had been functioning for several hundred years. It was an office that was common to every synagogue.

Since this is the case we can not look to the New Testament to find the origin of the office, we must go to the Old Testament. The first definition of the office of the elder comes under the ministry of Moses when first Jethro and later God, counseled Moses as to how to handle his people problem. It is important to have a good understanding of what took place in Israel's history because it seems that what God gave Moses back there He also desired to be established in the local Church. The way God was to take care of the people problem was through plurality of oversight. Moses' problem was that he was given oversight over more people than he could effectively handle. Not only was he sending himself to an early grave but the people were becoming weary. As Churches grow, every leader has to face this problem. It is a good problem, but a problem nonetheless, because if this problem is not handled properly God's work will not prosper. Into this situation came the counsel of Jethro *(Ex. 18)* and later the counsel of the Lord *(Num. 11)* to set qualified men over the people to help him with the charge that God had placed on him.

Let us notice some things about the elders in the Old Testament that will help serve as a pattern to us.

1. Elders were instituted as a matter of practical consideration. In Moses' situation the weight of the people had become more than he could bear. This is the same thing we saw with the origin of deacons. There is no sense in having an office if there is no function to go with that office. A Church needs as many elders as it takes to oversee the people effectively. A Church of seventy-five does not need ten elders. The demand should in a measure dictate the number that will be necessary.

2. Elders were always plural in number. Except for cases in the New Testament where a Church had just started, all the Churches eventually had plurality of eldership. In fact there is no place in the New Testament where an established Church is seen to have only one elder *(Acts 11:30; 14:23; 15:2,4,6,22,23; 16:4; 20:17; 21:18; etc)*.

3. Elders always had a specific function and charge. When elders are referred to in an official sense they always had a specific job description that demanded a good deal of their time and energy. They were not titular authorities; they were active, functioning leaders of the people.

4. The function of elders in the Old Testament seems to parallel that which was to come later in the New Testament Church.

a. They were leaders in war.
b. They were judges in disputes.
c. They were men of good advice and counsel.
d. They represented and maintained the community.
e. They were the authorities of various cities.

As *Interpreter's Dictionary of the Bible* says, "As parents wield authority in a family, so the elders wield authority in the life of the clan, tribe or local community."

5. It was necessary for elders to be in their place so that the people could find their place *(Ex. 18:23)*. Not only did the plurality of leadership make it possible for Moses to have an occasional day off, but the people also found their place. If every member of the local Church is going to find proper placement in the body it will take the ministry of more than one man *(Eph. 4:11-13)*.

> "If thou shalt do this thing, and God command thee so, then thou shalt be able to endure, and all this people shall also go to their place in peace. So Moses hearkened to the voice of his father-in-law, and did all that he had said."
>
> *Exodus 18:23-24*

All through Israel's history they operated their political and religious affairs under the supervision of elders. Later when Israel did not have political autonomy they still maintained an eldership. During the Babylonian captivity the synagogue was established as a vehicle for keeping the people of God distinct in a strange land. Each synagogue had elders over it to guide, govern and instruct the people of God.

This pattern for eldership was operating in the synagogue in Jesus' day. This seems to be the pattern that Jesus had in mind for the Church. W.C. Hayden in his book *Church Polity* says:

> "Elders, among Jews, were the rulers of the people, prominent men who took the lead in directing and controling affairs. The elders of a city correspond to our councilmen, just as we now call them 'city fathers'. The elders of the people were their representatives and rulers in government and management of affairs pertaining to public welfare. As an official term therefore, this word expresses the idea of government by men of age, prominence, experience and wisdom. It indicates that this office is one that imposes important duties and grave responsibilities, and that it should be filled by men who are competent to perform the work devolving upon them efficiently and successfully. It indicates that an incompetent eldership is a great misfortune and disastrous in its consequences."

C. THE QUALIFICATIONS FOR ELDERS

God is very particular when it comes to choosing just *who* is to oversee His House, because it is *His* House, and He wants to be the One who selects those who will rule over His House. In the economy of God no one just decides to be an overseer. Every workman in God's House must be divinely called *(Romans 1:1)*, for if a man is divinely called, he will also be divinely equipped. It takes supernatural enablement to be a New Testament overseer. Without this God-given equipment, no amount of preparation or schooling will do any good toward making men overseers. In fact, it does a great deal of harm when organizations ordain to leadership, men who are not called and equipped by God. Apart from being called and equipped by God, however, there are lists of qualifications that are given us in the Word of God, to which an overseer must measure up. We find such lists in *I Timothy 3:1-7* and *Titus 1:5-9*. *We should notice that the New Testament does not put these qualifications forth as an ideal to strive for, but they are listed as the standards for all elders.* These are qualifications that all elders MUST have *(I Timothy 3:2)*. Let us examine these qualifications, which cover moral, domestic and spiritual areas.

1. Moral Qualifications — There are certain qualities of character that must be manifest in the life of every individual who would seek to lead the people of God. There are attributes of character that are necessary to be found and there are attributes that are not to be found, in the life of such a candidate.

a. The elder is to be blameless *(I Timothy 3:2; Titus 1:6)*. This does not mean that he will not be blamed for things, but that he will not be guilty. Jesus was blameless and yet false witnesses blamed Him of many things.

b. An elder must be temperate *(I Timothy 3:2; Titus 1:8)*. In other words he must have his self under control, exhibiting self-control. To have self-control is to have the spirit under God's control. He should not be given to excess in any area of life. An elder should be a person of balance.

c. An elder is to be sober *(I Timothy 3:2; Titus 1:8)*. The elder is to be a man of infinite discretion and a sound mind. He is one who has his mind trained or cultivated toward wisdom and sound judgment.

d. An elder must be of good behavior *(I Timothy 3:3)*. This Greek word implies the thought of being orderly and modest. It is closely akin to the word which means "adornment". The elder must be above reproach in all his activities of behavior, right down to the way he dresses. He is continually in the public eye, and there will always be those who will seek to bring reproach to the man of God.

e. An elder is not to be given to wine *(I Timothy 3:3; Titus 1:7)*. This seems like a rather obvious qualification, but there are many ministries who have fallen over this very thing.

f. An elder is not to be a striker *(I Timothy 3:3; Titus 1:7)*. An elder is a minister in spiritual battles and is not to be given to physical displays. A man who still needs to brawl is a man who has not yet given all of his rights over to the Lord.

g. An elder is not to be greedy of money *(I Timothy 3:3; Titus 1:7)*. A man who has given himself wholly unto the Lord will have no need of extravagances. Money will never be the motivation for his decisions in life.

h. An elder is not to be a brawler *(I Timothy 3:3; Titus 1:7)*. He is not to be contentious, quarrelsome or argumentative. Again, such a man has not yet yielded his members and rights totally unto God.

i. An elder is not coveteous *(I Timothy 3:3)*. He is a man who has learned to be content in whatsoever state God has placed him. His desires are toward spiritual things and not temporal things *(I Corinthians 12:31)*.

j. An elder is not to be self-willed or *"so pleased with himself that nothing else pleases him and he* *comes to please no body" (Titus 1:7).* A man who insists on his own way is not open to God's way. A man who is self-willed is one "so far overvaluing any determination at which he has himself once arrived that he will not be removed from it" (Trench). The Greek word carries the connotation of one who is self-pleasing, dominated by self-interest and inconsiderate of others. It is the opposite of gentleness.

k. An elder is to be a lover of good *(Titus 1:8).* The word "men" that is used in the King James Version is not found in the Greek. An elder never has a good thing to say about any practice of evil because he has a Christ-like hatred for evil.

2. Domestic qualifications.
The elder not only has to have himself under control, but he must have his own home under control. If he cannot rule effectively in his own house, how can he qualify to rule in God's House?

a. An elder must be the husband of one wife *(I Timothy 3:2; Titus 1:6).* He must be a loyal husband living in a pure marriage relationship without adulterous relationships or attitudes. God has never condoned polygamy. If he is a man who divides his natural affections, he will also be prone to divide his spiritual affections and commit spiritual adultery.

b. An elder is to be hospitable *(I Timothy 3:2; Titus 1:3).* If one would break this Greek word down it would be translated "a lover of strangers". The shepherd must be able to call his sheep by name. To do this he must not be afraid to get involved with them on a personal level and have them into his home.

c. An elder is to rule his own house well, having his own children in subjection *(I Timothy 3:4),* having faithful children not accused of riot or unruly *(Titus 1:6).* What a terrible blight it is that pastors' children have often been the most unruly. The exhortation goes on, *"for if man know not how to rule his own house, how shall he take care of the Church of God" (I Timothy 3:5).*

3. Spiritual qualifications
The elder needs to have certain spiritual qualities if he is going to fulfill the ministry to which he has been called. It takes more than a good man and a good father, it takes a man divinely enabled and equipped.

a. An elder must be able to teach *(I Timotht 3:2).* This does not mean that every elder must be gifted as a teacher as described under the five-fold ministry, but every elder must be able to expound, proclaim, and communicate what God has done in his life relative to the Word of God. He must be able to communicate it in such a way that others will learn.

b. An elder is not to be a novice or young convert *(I Timothy 3:6).* For an elder in the House of God spiritual age is more important than physical age. The man who is newly planted lacks essential experience to lead others in the good and perfect way.

c. An elder must be of good report among the unsaved *(I Timothy 3:7).* The Church has a vital ministry to the unsaved. It is essential that the Church has projected a good image to those outside the Church.

d. An elder is to be just *(Titus 1:8).* In the etymology of this Greek word we find that it originally was used of persons who observed the custom, rule and right, especially in the fulfillment of duties towards gods and men, and of things that were in accordance with right. In the New Testament it denotes right conduct judged whether by the Divine standard or according to human standards of what was right (Vine).

e. An elder is to be holy *(Titus 1:8).* The Greek word used here is not the same word that refers to the holiness of God but it has some of the following connotations: "that quality of holiness which is manifested in those who have regard equally to grace and truth," those that are "religiously right as opposed to what is unrighteous or polluted," "those that are . . . pure from evil conduct, and observant of God's will" (Vine — Compare *I Thessalonians 2:10*).

f. An elder must hold fast the faithful word as he has been taught *(Titus 1:9;* See also vs. *10-14).* This not only speaks of the ministry of an elder, but it tells us that he must be personally established in the truth, not blown about by winds of doctrine.

g. An elder must be able to exhort and convince in sound doctrine *(Titus 1:9).* He must be able to bring the truth to bear on the everyday encounters with the people he meets. He is not just a source of academic information.

h. An elder must be patient *(I Timothy 3:3).* God knows that in dealing with people a great amount of patience is required if they are going to be brought to maturity. An elder must be willing to work effectively with people at all levels of maturity.

It is interesting that there is no actual age requirement for New Testament eldership. Since no specific age is mentioned it must be assumed that when a person has come to the level of maturity where he has all of the character qualities necessary to qualify, he is old enough to govern in the house of God. The spiritual maturity of the individual is far more important than the physical attainment of age. It is possible to be old and yet not wise *(Ecclesiastes 4:13)* and it is also possible to have wisdom beyond your years because of a heart of obedience *(Psalm 119:99-100).*

D. THE NUMBER OF ELDERS

Nowhere in the New Testament are we given a set number of elders that is to be considered the ideal for which we are to strive. We have noted already that in every Church there seems to have been a plurality of eldership *(James 5:14; I Timothy 5:17; I Peter 5:1; Phillipians 1:1; Acts 21:18).*

> *"For this cause left I thee in Crete, that thou shouldest set in order the things that are wanting, and ordain elders in every city, as I had appointed thee."*
>
> *Titus 1:5*

This plurality of elders does not necessarily mean that all elders will have the same responsibilities, the same sphere of influence or the same honor by people *(I Timothy 5:17),* but it does avoid the concept of a single ruler of a congregation and it distributes authority as well as responsibility among several. Plurality does not, however, negate the fact that one elder will obviously carry the responsibility of a chief position. One elder will carry ultimate responsibility. The home is an example of this. God has placed plurality of leadership in every home and yet there is one, the husband, who carries ultimate authority and responsibility. In the Church in the Wilderness it was always Moses and the elders *(Exodus 18:17-26; Deut. 1:14-17; Numbers 11:16-17).* In the Jerusalem Church it was James and the elders *(Acts 12:17; 15:4-7,12,13, 22).* In addition to these we have an example of the church at Philippi. The letter to the Philippians is addressed to the elders and the deacons indicating plurality, yet later as Paul writes he addresses an individual who he calls his "true yokefellow", singular *(Phil. 4:1-3).* There is a very delicate balance here. This one man is not a monarchial bishop but he is a man who is himself submitted to the eldership but who, for practical purposes of administration of authority, becomes the mouthpiece for the eldership even as James functioned in Acts 15.

E. THE WORK OF THE ELDER

The elder's main responsibility is the general oversight and care of the Church. This responsibility involves three main areas:

1. Ruling — The elders are the rulers of the assembly *(Romans 12:8; I Thes. 5:12-14; I Tim. 5:17; Heb.*

13:17,24). The word rule means "to be over, to superintend, to preside over, to care for and to give attention to." They are to the Church what parents are to a home. As rulers, therefore, they stand accountable before God for the state of the assembly *(Heb. 13:17).* This ruling however, is to be done with a proper spirit and attitude. Elders must remember that they are servants of the people not lords *(I Pet. 5:2-3)* who are set up by God to provide an example for the saints to follow *(Heb. 13:7).* This ruling may at times call for the exercise of discipline *(I Thess. 5:12-13; I Tim. 3:5)* but every action taken by the elder is to be with the best interest of the souls of the people in mind.

> *"Obey them that have the rule over you, and submit yourselves: for they watch for your souls, as they that must give account, that they may do it with joy, and not with grief: for that is unprofitable for you."*
>
> *Hebrews 13:17*

2. Shepherding — One of the charges that is consistently given to elders is that of shepherding or tending the flock of God *(Acts 20:28; I Pet. 5:2).* This responsibility is specifically given in five areas. First, they are to feed the flock *(Acts 20:28).* Second, they are to watch out for wolves *(Acts 20:29-31).* Third, they are to help the weak *(Acts 20:35).* Fourth, they are to minister to the sick *(James 5:14-15).* Fifth, they are to go before the sheep with their good example *(I Pet. 5:3).*

> *"Take heed therefore unto yourselves, and to all the flock, over which the Holy Ghost hath made you overseers, to feed the church of God, which he hath purchased with his own blood. For I know this, that after my departing shall grievous wolves enter in among you, not sparing the flock. Also of your own selves shall men arise, speaking perverse things, to draw away disciples after them. Therefore watch, and remember, that by the space of three years I ceased not to warn every one night and day with tears. And now, brethren, I commend you to God, and to the word of his grace, which is able to build you up, and to give you an inheritance among all them which are sanctified. I have coveted no man's silver, or gold, or apparel. Yea, ye yourselves know, that these hands have ministered unto my necessities, and to them that were with me. I have shewed you all things, how that so labouring ye ought to support the weak, and to remember the words of the Lord Jesus, how he said, It is more blessed to give than to receive."*
>
> *Acts 20:28-35*

3. Instructing — Elders are responsible to teach or instruct the Church *(I Tim. 3:2; Tit. 1:9).* They are the ones that are going to give stability to the Church and help bring a unity among the body. As such it is essential that their teaching be firmly based on the Word of God *(Heb. 13:7; I Tim. 5:17; II Tim. 2:2).* In their teaching they should be able to convince the gainsayers *(Tit. 1:9).* A real priority should be placed on the eldership coming to a place of doctrinal unity on questionable areas so that they can speak as one man.

F. THE APPOINTMENT AND TERM OF OFFICE OF ELDERS

Elders or bishops in the New Testament were not elected by a vote of the people. Elders were called by the Holy Ghost *(Acts 20:28)* and recognized and appointed by leadership *(Acts 14:23).* In new Churches it seems to have been the ministry of the apostle who founded the work to ordain the elders in that work. After a work was established new local elders were undoubtedly set in by the decision of the elders of that local assembly. Two Greek words shed some light on the ordination process. The first is "cheirotoneo". This word literally means "to stretch forth the hand" *(Acts 14:23; II Cor. 8:19).* As with all of the ministries in the Old Testament and the setting in of deacons in the New Testament, the elders are set into office by the laying on of hands. The second word is "kathisteemi". This word means "to ordain or to appoint" *(Tit. 1:5; Acts 6:3).* It usually signifies to appoint a person to a position giving them a charge. All through the scripture when someone was appointed to any place of authority they were appointed or set in by those in authority not by the people. Thus, all rule came from God down and not from the people up. (See; *Matt. 24:45; Acts 7:35; I Tim. 4:14; 1:18; Acts 6:6; Acts 13:1-3).*

There is no word in the New Testament about the length of an elder's stay in office. We must believe therefore, that unless a person voluntarily withdraws from the position, or he in some way disqualifies himself by the same qualifications that were initially required for the office, he remains an elder. It would seem likely that elders who are particularly aged may only function in an advisory capacity due to a a lack of physical strength, but their wisdom should always be highly valued.

G. THE HONOR OF ELDERS

The elders have a serious charge before the Lord and God holds them accountable on a very strict scale. The elders who have been given a charge by God but fail to fulfill their responsibilities will be dealt with by God. But it must be remembered that the elder is not the only one who has responsibility. Not only does the elder have an obligation to the congregation, but the congregation also bears responsibilities toward its leaders.

1. The people are to "know" those who are over them *(I Thes. 5:12).* In this sense the people are to appreciate the true value of their leaders and seek them out.

2. The people are to esteem them very highly *(I Thes. 5:13).* This esteem is not to be based on one's inner feeling or sentiment. It is a respect that is calculated and deliberate. It is having a respect for the office that God has placed in the Church.

3. The people are to submit themselves to God's anointed and appointed leaders. *(Heb. 13:17).* The elders will not be able to be what God has called them to be without the submission of the people.

4. The people are to support the ministry financially *(I Tim. 5:17; Gal. 6:6; I Thes. 2:6,9; II Cor. 11:7f; Phil. 4:10f; I Cor. 9:11-14).* How much may vary from place to place, but whatever the arrangement it should be such as to remove from the leader's mind all cause for worry over financial support.

5. The people are not to charge an elder with wrong-doing too hastily. By the very nature of their office elders are often exposed to misrepresentation and unjust criticism. For this reason God protects them by warning His people not to rebuke an elder *(I Tim. 5:1)* and not to receive an accusation against an elder except in the mouth of two or three witnesses *(I Tim. 5:19).* It should be noted, however, if the elder does fall and he is guilty of something worthy of rebuke, he is to be rebuked openly that others may fear *(I Tim. 5:20).* The public nature of their office demands public discipline.

6. The people are to remember their leaders and pray for them *(Heb. 13:7; I Thes. 5:25).* Elders are men ordained by God to exercise the general oversight and care of the local Church. They need all the prayer support they can get. It is a great responsibility before the Lord.

H. THE RELATIONSHIP OF ELDERS TO DEACONS

Because of many traditional concepts of elders and deacons there have been many misunderstandings as to how these two groups relate to each other. In some circles the deacons rule over the elders, in others, neither group rules over the other, and in yet others, these groups may not even exist. For this reason it is important to see how these relate to each other.

In some respects we have a pattern for this relationship in the Old Testament with the priests and Levites. The priests were charged by God to function in a certain office and to sacrifice for the people. However, this work involved a lot of other things. There was constant clean-up and preparation that had to be made. There were repairs that had to be taken care of. There were many minor tasks that had to be done among the people. To solve this problem God gave the Levites to the priests to help them to get everything done that was related to their charge *(Num. 3:5-10)*.

God has given deacons to the elders in the same way. In this regard the deacons are to serve the elders by assisting them in the outworking of their ministry. God has placed authority in the House of the Lord in the hands of the eldership. The eldership then is able to delegate authority to the deacons to fulfill specific areas of function in the body *(Acts 6:3)*. The deacons in this way are under the authority of the eldership and answerable to them for the charge that has been given to them. The authority of the deacons comes by their appointment by the elders into their place of function.

The office of the deacon is not a God-called position in the same way that we find among the eldership. The deacon is an individual recognized and appointed by human leadership. If for any reason an individual who has been functioning as a deacon ceases to function in that capacity he also ceases from the office of a deacon although he should maintain the spirit of a deacon. The deacon office is a "man-called" office and thus functions only as long as the responsibility is being fulfilled. The deacons are truly the servants to the eldership as their name implies.

Chapter 11
THE MINISTRY OF THE APOSTLE

When Jesus ascended on high He did not abandon the infant Church. Jesus had told the disciples that it was to their advantage for Him to go away because then He would send them the Holy Spirit who would empower them to fulfill His charge to them *(John 16:7-16)*. As long as Jesus was here on earth the body of Christ was confined to the human limitation of space and time; Jesus could only be in one place at one time. When Jesus was on earth He was the fountain-head of all ministry. He was the apostle, prophet, evangelist, pastor, teacher, shower of mercy, intercessor, ruler, deacon, exhorter and giver all wrapped up into one. He had the fulness of all ministry. But it was Jesus' desire that this ministry of life and healing be taken to the uttermost parts of the earth.

When Jesus ascended on high He made it possible for his ministry to reach the four corners of the earth. When He ascended He received of the Father the gift of the Holy Spirit, and in Acts 2 the disciples of the Lord were endued with power from on high. With this enduement from on high, God gave a visible sign of what was taking place in the heavenlies in regard to the ministry of the body of Christ. A careful study of the Greek text in Acts 2 indicates that there was a visible manifestation of a fire that separated, distributed itself and came to rest on each of them. The thought implies a singular flame that was dissipated as a part of that flame rested on each one there.

This is in essence what Jesus did with His ministry. When He ascended on high He broke down His fulness of ministry into smaller measures and gave a measure to this one and a measure to that one until the whole was invested. So He gave some apostles, some prophets, some evangelists, some givers, some deacons, some gifts of healing. He did not give the whole to anyone but He gave each a measure of the gift of Christ.Christ in this way continues to carry on His prophetic ministry through theprophets He has set into the body. He continues to carry on His teaching ministry through the teachers that He has called and equipped in the body, and so on.

Some, however, have been given ministries that relate to authority in the body. Some, Christ has given to oversee the function of the body and how the members of the body relate to each other. Some, Christ has given as builders to make sure that every member is functioning in the unique place for which God has designed him. In Ephesians 4, it tells us that these ministries are for the adjusting or the equipping of the saints to do their service and they are for the building up of the body of Christ.

> *"But unto every one of us is given grace according to the measure of the gift of Christ. Wherefore he saith, When he ascended up on high, he led captivity captive, and gave gifts unto men. And he gave some apostles; and some, prophets; and some, evangelists; and some pastors and teachers; For the perfecting of the saints for the work of the ministry, for the edifying of the body of Christ: Till we all come in the unity of the faith, and of the knowledge of the Son of God, unto a perfect man, unto the measure of the stature of the fulness of Christ: That we henceforth be no more children, tossed to and fro, and carried about with every wind of doctrine, by the sleight of men, and cunning craftiness, whereby they lie in wait to deceive; But speaking the truth in love, may grow up into him in all things, which is the head, even Christ: From whom the whole body fitly joined together and compacted by that which every joint supplieth, according to the effectual working in the measure of every part, maketh increase of the body unto the edifying of itself in love."*
>
> *Ephesians 4:7-8, 11-16*

The five main ministries that God has given for this purpose (which we will be from hence forth referring to as the five-fold ministry) include the apostle, the prophet, the evangelist, the pastor and the teacher. These we also call governmental ministries, because of the responsibility, accountability and authority placed on them by God.

The first of the five-fold ministry that we are going to consider is the **apostle.**

A. THE DEFINITION OF TERMS

In order to get a clear understanding of this ministry in the New Testament we must carefully look at the origin and use of this word. Both the name and the ministry of the apostle have been frequently surrounded by a halo. For this reason people have been somewhat reluctant to apply these terms to people. Yet, if we could understand some distinctions that exist between apostles and the actual function of the apostle, it would perhaps once again release this ministry with power to the body of Christ.

The word "apostle" (Greek—apostolos) literally means "one who is sent forth". This definition in itself, however, does not really help us because it is too general. All ministry should in a sense be sent forth. Why is this term singled out by Jesus and applied to a certain kind of ministry in His day? Perhaps the key for this lies not in the definition of the word itself but in the use of the word in the classical Greek world, where it was used to refer to four things:

It was used to refer to an emissary or ambassador; to a fleet of ships or an expedition sent with a specific objective; to the admiral who commanded the fleet or to the colony which was founded by the admiral. If a fleet of ships left Rome with the purpose of establishing a new colony somewhere, all of these were called apostles — the fleet, the admiral, the new found colony.

The particular truth that is emphasized by this usage is the relationship of those who were sent to the sender. All of these, the admiral, the fleet and the colony that was formed, represented a true image of the one by whom they were sent. In other words, they were faithful to transmit or reflect the intentions of the sender (Hebrews 3:1). The primary attitude of a true apostle, then, must be faithfulness.

This association and connection between the sender and the one who is sent is clearly seen in the New Testament. There is an old Jewish maxim that teaches "the apostle is the equivalent to him who has sent him". This is not seen as simply a matter of substitution, but rather, the one who commissions is seen to be present in the person. This is seen most vividly in the life of Jesus, who was the great Apostle sent from the Father to found a Church and faithfully represent the intentions of the Father (Luke 10:18; Jhn 13:16).

"He that receiveth you receiveth me, and he that receiveth me receiveth him that sent me."

Matthew 10:40

In the light of all of this, how significant it was for Jesus, after spending the night in prayer, to take twelve of his disciples and name them "apostles" (Luke 6:13). These were going to be ambassadors or emissaries of Jesus. They were going to go out under orders to found and establish a new colony, the Church, that would truly reflect the intentions of the sender. It would be a true representation of the Heavenly City with foundations, whose builder and maker is God. It would be a little bit of heaven on earth and it would be known as the faithful city (Isaiah 1:26).

An apostle then, is one who is sent forth with authority, who faithfully represents the purposes and the intentions of the sender.

B. THE LEVELS OF APOSTLES IN THE NEW TESTAMENT

The New Testament makes a distinction between several distinct classes of apostles. Two of these classes are no longer operating directly in the church, however, their influence forms the basis for everything else that does happen. There are four main levels of the apostolic ministry:

1. Jesus Christ — Jesus Christ was and is the chief apostle (Heb. 3:1). The Gospel of John is the Gospel of Jesus' apostleship. He was sent by the Father from heaven to accomplish the divine intention (John 3:16; 20:21). Jesus was absolutely faithful to represent His Father to us (John 4:34; 5:19; 5:30; 6:38; 8:28-29,42; 12:44-45).

2. The Twelve Apostles of the Lamb — This is a distinct group who were specifically chosen and commissioned by Christ in His earthly ministry after a night of prayer (Luke 6:12). These are referred to as the apostles of the Lamb and have a unique place for all eternity, their names being recorded in the twelve foundations of the holy city (Rev. 21:14). These twelve marked the beginning of a new age in God's dealing with man. They close off the age of the prophets and inaugurate the Church age, the age of the apostles (Matt. 19:28). In the Old Testament it was the prophets who wrote scripture. In the New Testament we find scripture being written by apostles. It is interesting that Christ in His earthly ministry never chose a prophet, a pastor, an evangelist, or a teacher. He chose apostles.

3. The Post-ascension Apostles — Ephesians 4 tells us that upon Jesus' ascension He instituted yet another category of apostles. This is the group that is to be functioning throughout the Church age or until *"we all come in the unity of the faith, and of the knowledge of the Son of God unto a perfect man, unto the measure of the stature of the fulness of Christ" (Eph. 4:13)*. These apostles are part of the body of Christ and if they are not functioning there will be a certain paralysis in the body *(I Cor. 12:28)*. The New Testament mentions many apostles who fall into this category. Our list would include:

Andronicus *(Rom. 16:7)*,
Junia *(Rom. 16:7)*,
James, the Lord's brother *(Gal. 1:19)*,
Barnabas *(Acts 4:36; 14:14; 13:2)*,
Titus *(II Cor. 8:23)*,
Epaphroditus *(Phil. 2:25)*,
Timotheos *(I Thes. 1:1; 2:6)*,
Silvanus *(I Thes. 1:1; 2:6)* and
Apollos *(I Cor. 4:6,9)*.

4. Those Involved in Apostolic-type Ministry — In addition to the above categories there seem to be quite a number of people in the New Testament who did apostolic-type functions at times who were never specifically called apostles. Probably the best examples of these are the seventy that Christ sent out to do basically what the twelve had done in previous experiences. This seems to answer the question about many in our day who have been instrumental in some apostolic work but who do not appear to be specifically called to that life ministry. There are many in this category in the body of Christ.

C. THE PREPARATION OF APOSTLES

God requires men fully prepared for His work in building His Church. The task of building God's House is the most important in all the world and God desires to use instruments that are well prepared. Second-rate spiritual instruments can only bring second-rate spiritual results. Too often in an individual's haste to get going in his ministry he wields an unskillful sword and thus does more harm than good. God will take every ministry through a time of preparation. Often-times the preparation will be long, but even in the natural realm, for someone who is going to handle delicate life-and-death matters (i.e. a brain surgeon), there is a long road of preparation.

God has a desire to make sure that those whom He would use in the ministry of the apostle have a good understanding of their own weakness. Because of their influence over the lives of people, they are going to need deep humility. Moses is an example of this in the Old Testament. God was going to make him an influence over a large group of people, but first God had to work a deep humility in his spirit. Moses had great training and wisdom in terms of natural things, but God had to bring him to the place where he had no trust in any of it to accomplish the purposes of God.

Paul had a similar experience. Paul was brought up a strict Pharisee with great learning and knowledge. Paul, like Moses, tried to fulfill his call in his own strength *(Acts 9:23-31)*. But Paul was not ready yet. Just having a prophetic word over him was not enough. There was some preparation he had to go through. God had some true wisdom and understanding to build into him, and this would take time. He would need more than the gift of preaching. Paul received his call the day of his conversion, but he was not ready to be sent out for some time.

Barnabas was a man who was converted shortly after Pentecost. He was characterized as a selfless man from the time he began his walk with the Lord *(Acts 4:36-37)*. He demonstrated a yieldedness to the Lord and a submissiveness to God's delegated authority. As he continued in the Church at Jerusalem he became a man of proven character. It is likely that he became one of the elders of the Jerusalem Church. About seven years after his conversion he was sent to Antioch to strengthen the work there.

Timothy was also one who was prepared by God. He was raised in a godly home and was most likely converted to Christianity on Paul's first missionary journey through Lystra. He was familiar with the rejection that apostolic ministry can experience when he undoubtedly witnessed the stoning of Paul in that city. He proved his submission and obedience to the local leaders, and when Paul came through again a few years later, he was ready to go. He was ready to begin preparing under the apostle Paul.

When you put all of these things together you find some keys that apply to practically all who would be used in this ministry.

1. The apostle will have a definite call of God to this ministry.
2. The apostle will have to have a thorough knowledge of the scripture.
3. The apostle will experience a period of preparation covering several years during which he will prove himself and his ministry on the local level by which he will gain the necessary wisdom, knowledge and experience.
4. The apostle will usually train specifically for a time under the ministry of other apostles.
5. The apostle will not be sent by God until the preparation is complete.
6. The call, and timing of the going of the apostle will be confirmed by the brethren among whom he is ministering.
7. The sending Church will participate and identify with the work of the apostle by the laying on of hands (Acts 13:1-3).
8. The apostle goes forth in the power of the spirit, often times in company with others, to do the work God has called him to do.

There is something else that seems to be a common experience among many of the apostles in the New Testament. Many apostles, it seems, were used of God in one of the other areas of the five-fold ministry. Paul, for example, was used as a teacher (Acts 11:25-26) before he was released to apostolic ministry. Peter seems to have had a pastoral emphasis in his ministry (John 21:15-17; I Pet. 5:1-3). These other areas of function can be seen as preparatory in the life of the apostle, to help expose him to avenues of ministry at home prior to his being sent out.

D. THE QUALIFICATIONS FOR AN APOSTLE

All of the governmental ministries must obviously qualify under the same list that applies to all elders (I Pet. 5:1). Because of the special emphasis of each, however, there will also be qualities that should be strong in the lives of those called to each individual ministry. This is certainly true of the ministry of the apostle. In addition to the qualifications mentioned in relation to all elders there are five qualities that should be very strong in one who desires the ministry of the apostle.

1. An apostle must have the heart of a father (I Cor. 4:15; Phil. 2:22). As a father he will nurture, admonish, nurse, cherish, and be gentle with God's people (Eph. 6:4; I Thes. 2:6-8,11).

2. An apostle must have a deep love for and loyalty to the church of God. His love must be greater for the Church than for his own ministry. (I Cor. 13).

3. An apostle must have patience (II Cor. 12:12). Because of his revelation and maturity it will be very easy for him to become impatient with the seemingly slow progress of those to whom he is ministering.

4. An apostle must not be given to self-glory (I Thes. 2:6; I Cor. 4:9; II Cor. 10:8). He must not make people dependent on him, he must make them dependent on the Lord.

5. An apostle must have a servant's heart (Rom. 1:1; Phil. 1:1). The attitude of a servant is a supreme regard for the happiness and well-being of others. As a servant, an apostle should be characterized by humility, sacrifice and faithfulness (I Cor. 4:9; II Cor. 10:18; 11:22-23).

E. THE MINISTRY OF AN APOSTLE

When you study what was done by each of the apostles named in the Bible you find a great diversity of ministry. Not all of the apostles did exactly the same thing, yet there are some things that seem to apply to most of those who fall into this category. The following points should help to summarize the ministry and work of the apostle.

1. The apostle will be involved in founding and establishing Churches on a proper foundation *(I Cor. 3:9-14; Eph. 2:20; I Cor. 9:1-2; 11:34)*. This may involve the raising up of new works or the strengthening of works already in existence *(Rom. 1:11; Col. 2:5-7)*.
2. The apostle is one who will be particularly concerned about doctrinal exactness *(Acts 2:42; 15:1-31)*. Much of their work will depend on right doctrine.
3. The apostle will have the signs of an apostle accompanying his ministry *(Rom. 15:18-19; II Cor. 12:12)*.
4. The apostle may be involved in Church discipline at times, particularly in relationship to the Churches he has founded *(Acts 5:1-11; I Cor. 5)*.
5. The apostle is involved in the ordination of ministries such as elders and deacons *(Acts 6:1-6; 14:23; Tit. 1:5)*.
6. The apostle is involved in the feeding and training of other ministries *(II Tim. 2:2)*. This at times involves choosing workers and sending them to other Churches and giving them special assignments *(Acts 16:1-4; Phil. 2:19-25; Col. 4:7-12)*.
7. The apostle is to be involved with caring for the Churches which he has begun *(II Cor. 11:28)*.
8. The apostle is used in presbytery, in the laying on of hands and the impartation of spiritual gifts *(I Tim. 1:18; 4:14; II Tim. 1:6; Rom. 1:11)*.
9. The apostle is not a dictator *(I Cor. 16:12)*, nor a lord over the sheep *(I Pet. 5:2)*, but as a father he is to help the members of the body of Christ come to maturity *(I Cor. 4:15-16; II Cor. 1:29)*.

It can be easily seen from all of this that there is a sense in which the apostle has to have some capability to operate in all of the governmental ministries. As he goes into a new community he will have to be able to do the work of an evangelist. As new converts come into the new church he will have to be able to feed them and teach them in the ways of the Lord. As ministries mature he will also have to serve as an example of the prophetic ministry. The five-fold ministries can be illustrated by the human hand. There are four fingers and a thumb. The thumb is like the apostle who is easily able to touch all of the other four.

F. THE RECOGNITION OF AN APOSTLE

God is vitally involved with every ministry that He has ordained. God in His sovereignty is the head over all and He is responsible for several things in regard to a person's ministry.

He determines the kind of ministry, the length of time the ministry functions and the sphere of influence that the ministry is to have. This applies to the ministry of the apostle.

God calls the apostle, he determines how long he will minister and the kind of influence he will have. Not all apostles will be received as such by the body of Christ world-wide. Paul was not *(I Cor. 9:1-3)*, but Paul did know where he was received as an apostle, and it was directly related to the places where he had produced apostolic fruit. It is possible for a man to be considered an apostle to one group, but not received as an apostle by another group.

The question remains, then, who should recognize an apostle? An apostle should be recognized by at least four categories. First, he should know it himself. He should know God's call on his life. Second, he should be recognized by his local leaders, that is, those of his local Church. A man's gift should be apparent to all. Third, he should be recognized by the people in his home Church, having a good report throughout. Fourth, an apostle should be recognized by those he has grounded and established in the faith. Apart from this an apostle needs no recognition except from God, and that is Whom the apostle is ultimately serving.

Chapter 12
THE MINISTRY OF THE PROPHET

The second of the five-fold ministry to be mentioned in Ephesians 4 is that of the prophet. Many have confined the prophet's ministry to the Old Testament age, and yet we are told in Ephesians 4 that the ministry of the prophet is necessary if the Church is to come to maturity. The prophet's ministry has been rarely understood by present day expositors. The whole subject of modern day prophecy has been given many varying definitions and for this reason it is often times equated with inspired preaching. It is clear, however, in the New Testament that prophets were more than merely preachers. If we are going to receive a prophet's reward in these days of visitation it is going to be important for us to recognize this ministry and receive a prophet in the name of a prophet *(Matt. 10:41)*.

A. THE DEFINITION OF TERMS

The ministry of the prophet is not a new ministry to the New Testament age, it has its roots in the Old Testament. In order to understand what a prophet is we must first understand what prophecy is. It is also important to know what prophecy is not. Prophecy is more than inspired preaching. In the Old Testament there are several words that are translated "prophecy". There are, however, two main words that help us to understand the nature of prophecy. The first word is "raba". This word occurs over 400 times in the Old Testament and it means "to bubble up, to gush forth or to pour forth". This word seems to emphasize the ecstatic nature of the prophetic word.

The second main Old Testament word that is translated "prophecy" is "nataf". This word means "to drop, to fall as drops of rain." Many times this word is applied to rain but several times it is used of prophecy *(Mic. 2:6, 11)*. In this case the emphasis seems to be on the divine origin of prophecy. Even as the rain falls from heaven to water the earth, God gave words to His prophets that they might be His mouthpiece in the earth.

In the New Testament the word that is used for prophecy is the Greek word from which our English word is derived "propheteuo" which simply means "to say or speak forth or fore". On this basis prophecy seems to involve two main aspects. Prophecy involves *forthtelling* which is simply speaking forth a message from God *(Heb. 1:1)*. Prophecy also involves *foretelling* which has to do with declaring beforehand something that will surely take place *(Jer. 28:9; Ezek. 33:32-33)*. All prediction is prophecy but not all prophecy is prediction.

The prophet then is a spokesman for God. He is to God what Aaron was to Moses. Moses was to speak to Aaron and Aaron was to speak to the people *(Ex. 4:15-16)*. Even as Aaron was to be a mouthpiece for Moses so the prophets were to be the ones who would speak as the mouthpiece of God *(Jer. 15:19; II Pet. 1:20-21)*. For this reason the words of the prophets were considered to be the words of God *(II Kings 17:13; 21:10; 24:2)*.

The prophet was in a sense the counterpart to the priestly ministry. The priests approached unto God in behalf of the people. The prophets, on the other hand, heard from God and approached the people on behalf of God. For this reason it is absolutely essential that a prophet be in a place of hearing the voice of God *(Num. 12:6; Hos. 12:10)*. The prophet must be one who stands in the inner counsel of the Lord *(I Kings 17:1; Jer. 23:16-22)*.

B. THE LEVELS OF PROPHECY

There are at least four levels of prophecy referred to in the Scriptures. In order to better understand the distinction between the gifts of the spirit, and the ministry of the prophet that is part of the gift of Christ, we must look at these four levels individually.

1. The Spirit of Prophecy *(Rev. 19:10)*. — The spirit of prophecy is the Holy Spirit's mantle of prophetic anointing which is given at various times to a believer or a body of believers which enables him to prophesy the Word of the Lord (the testimony of Jesus) and without which occasion of special endowment he would not normally prophesy.[1] All believers can function in this capacity and yet not all are prophets (Num. 11:29; I Cor. 14:24,31; 12:29). King Saul is a good example of this. When he came into the company of the school of the prophets, the anointing which was on them affected him, and he began to prophecy (I Sam. 10:10; 19:20,21). Suffice it to say that Saul was not, indeed, numbered among the prophets.

2. The Gift of Prophecy (I Cor. 12:10) — This is one of the nine gifts of the spirit and it operates under the same guidelines as any of the gifts of the spirit. It is a gift in which any believer can function and yet certain limitations are placed on this gift. When believers exercise this gift (Acts 2:18) it should be limited to the realms of edification, exhortation and comfort (I Cor. 14:3). Anything beyond this realm falls into a deeper realm of prophecy and should be reserved for the prophets. Operating the gift of prophecy does not of itself make one a prophet.

3. The Ministry of the Prophet (Eph. 4:11; I Cor. 12:29; Rom. 12:6) — As has already been implied the ministry of the prophet has to do with one's life calling, and is not limited to the areas of edification, exhortation and comfort. The prophet may also operate in realms of confirming guidance, rebuke, judgment, correction, warning and revelation which we will discuss more fully later.

4. The Prophecy of Scripture (II Pet. 1:19-20) — This is the highest form of prophecy, and it involves new revelation that becomes authoritative as Scripture.[2] It is God-breathed (II Tim. 3:16). This type of prophecy is totally inerrant and infallible. **This type is no longer being given today** (Rev. 22:18-19). All other forms and ministries of prophecy must be judged on the basis of their agreement with the prophecy of Scripture which is the infallible Word of God. Many prophecies uttered in Bible days did not have Scriptural authority, and therefore they were not preserved for us by God (Num. 11:24-30; I Sam. 10:10-11; 19:18-24; Acts 15:32).

C. THE ORIGIN OF THE PROPHETIC MINISTRY

God has always had His prophetic voices in the earth. Since the world began God has witnessed through the leaders of His people (Acts 3:21; Luke 11:50-51; Jer. 28:8; 7:13,25). Before the flood men like Abel (Luke 11:50-51), Enoch (Jude 14) and Noah (Heb. 11:7; I Pet. 3:20) prophesied to their generations. After the flood God used the patriarchs to be a witness and a testimony in the earth. Abraham (Gen. 20:7), Isaac (Ps. 105:9-15), Jacob (Gen. 48-49) and Joseph (Gen. 50:24) all prophesied the Word of the Lord. Later God used others prophetically including Moses (Deut. 34:10), Miriam (Ex. 15:20), Aaron (Ex. 7:1) and Deborah (Judges 4:4). Moses was to be an important figure in the development of this ministry because God would give him the guidelines by which all future prophets would be judged (Num. 12:6; Deut. 18:15-22; Luke 16:29; Is. 8:16-20).

It was really under the judicial leadership of Samuel, however, that the ministry of the prophet came into its own. Samuel was the last of the judges and the first of the prophets (Acts 3:23-26; Heb. 11:32; Acts 13:20). It was Samuel who inaugurated the schools of the prophets (II Kings 2:3-15). In establishing tne schools he created a new prophetic order of men who were educated in the Word, responsive to the voice of the spirit of God and worshipers of the most high God. The many prophets that would follow from Samuel to Malachi would owe a great deal to the work that Samuel did at the first.

From Samuel on, then, God has always had His prophetic voice in the earth. Nearly every king in Israel was given a personal prophet to keep him on the right path. During the intertestamental period, however, there seemed to be a prophetic dearth in the land. For 400 years there is no mention of the prophetic voice, but suddenly, as God's fulness of time approaches, once again the prophetic voice is heard and the word of the Lord comes to John (Luke 7:26-28).

Once the New Testament Church is established there seems to be a flood of prophets on the scene again. God was moving in the earth and there was a need for spokesmen. So we see this ministry carried

[1]Blomgren, D.K., The Laying on of Hands, and Prophecy of the Presbytery, pg. 36.
[2]Blomgren, D.K., The Laying on of Hands, and Prophecy of the Presbytery, pg. 39

into the New Testament by Judas and Silas *(Acts 15:32)*, Agabus *(Acts 21:10-13)*, and Ananias *(Acts 22:12-15)*. Every place where there was a strong Church there seemed to be this ministry functioning. We have prophets at Antioch *(Acts 13:1)*, there are prophets at Tyre *(Acts 21:4)*, there are prophets at Jerusalem *(Acts 11:27)* and probably at Corinth *(I Cor. 14:29)*. God was restoring a ministry that had long been dormant.

D. CHRIST, THE PATTERN PROPHET

Since the New Testament ministry of the prophet is a measure of the gift of Christ it is important to see Jesus as the pattern prophet. Not only was Christ called a prophet by God *(Acts 3:22; John 1:21,25; 7:40)*, but he was recognized by many as a prophet *(John 4:19; 6:14; 7:40; 9:17)*. Christ was clearly the speaking place or mouthpiece for God while on the earth *(Heb. 12:1-2)*. As such He only spoke those things which He had heard the Father speak *(John 4:19; 12:49; 14:10,24; 17:8)*. Not only did Christ declare God's message, but He also moved in the ministry of prediction *(Luke 11:49; Matt. 24:3-51)*. Christ was indeed **the** great prophet. This ministry of Christ has been given to the Church in the form of New Testament prophets *(Eph. 4:11-13)*.

E. THE MINISTRY OF THE PROPHET

In looking at the actual function of the New Testament prophet we again have only the Word of God to guide us. As we look at the condition of the Church today we may see no complete modern day example of the prophet's ministry, but that should never frighten us away from the Word of God. If this ministry has value in the Church we should covet its full restoration to the Church and we should be instrumental in bringing it about. From a careful examination of the Scripture there seems to be seven main things that characterize the ministry of the prophet.

1. A prophet's ministry will vary from prophet to prophet. No two prophets' ministries are exactly alike. This is seen first of all in the names and titles of the prophets. Sometimes they were called seers *(I Sam. 9:9)*, other times they were called messengers *(Is. 42:19)*; men of God *(I Kings 12:22)*; or servants *(Zech. 1:6)*. It is also seen in the varying modes of revelation in which the prophets operated. Some were visionary: they saw things. Ezekiel, Daniel and Zechariah were prophets of vision. Others were verbal: the Word of the Lord came to these perhaps in an audible way or perhaps they only heard it in their spiritual ear. Micah, Isaiah and others were verbal prophets. Then there were still others who received revelation while in a trance: Daniel, Abraham *(Gen. 15:12)* and the apostle John had experiences like this. Variety among the prophets is also seen in the ways in which they communicated the message that God gave them. Some just delivered the message verbally whether in spoken or written form. Others involved themselves in prophetic actions that dramatized their messages *(Is. 20:1-6; Ezek. 4:1-3)*. In the New Testament Agabus dramatized the binding of Paul with such a prophetic action *(Acts 21:11)*. There were still others whose whole life stories were to demonstrate God's dealing with His people. This is seen in the lives of Hosea and Jonah.

The main message that is here for us in all of this, is that in this ministry particularly, there is going to be a great diversity of individual expression. Every prophet was a little bit different from all the rest.

2. A prophet's ministry will involve revelation. Even as Nathan was used of old to point out certain areas of David's life that he could only have known by revelation, so the New Testament prophets will need to hear from God in a special way. This will involve revelation and insight into the Word of God *(Eph. 3:5)*. It will involve the revelation of facts and information about people's lives, their sins and their problems *(Acts 21:10-11; I Cor. 14:25)*. It will also involve at times the revelation of future events *(Acts 11:27-28)*.

3. A prophet's ministry will involve exhortation. Just as Haggai and Zechariah exhorted the people to build the ruins and the waste places in the days of old, the New Testament prophets should be continually exciting the people of God to finish the work *(I Cor. 14:3; Ezra 5:1; 6:14)*.

4. A prophet's ministry will involve warning *(Acts 21:8-11; 11:27-30)*. Often times God will reveal a thing to His prophets so that they can warn the people of coming danger. In this way God's people can be prepared ahead of time for what will transpire. Agabus prophesied a famine so the people of God could order their steps accordingly.

5. A prophet's ministry will involve the impartation of vision to the people of God *(Prov. 29:18* with *Jer. 14:14; 23:6)*. As God prepares to move upon His people He will give direction through His prophets. The prophet is to help prepare the way of the Lord *(Luke 1:76)*.

6. A prophet's ministry will involve grounding and establishing churches. *(Eph. 2:20; 3:5)*. The prophet, with the apostle, works on the foundation of the House of God. In this regard He also works in the confirmation of Churches *(Acts 15:32,41)* and the sending out of ministries *(Acts 13:1-3)*.

7. A prophet often ministers with like ministries in a multiple form. Many times in the New Testament we find prophets working in teams *(Acts 11:27-30; Acts 13:1; I Cor. 14:29)*. This undoubtedly would give some important checks and balances to a somewhat subjective type of ministry.

F. WARNINGS CONNECTED WITH THE PROPHETIC MINISTRY

There are basically two kinds of warnings in regard to the prophetic ministry, warnings to the prophets themselves, and there are warnings to the people of God in regard to the prophetic ministry. The people of God are warned to receive the ministry of the prophet *(Matt. 10:41)*. It is important to receive this ministry, for when we fail to do so, we cut ourselves off from further perfecting *(Eph. 4:11-13)*. Often prophets are not well received in their own country *(Matt. 13:57; Mk. 6:4)*. Unfortunately the "own country" has often been the Church.

A second warning that God gives to people is to be on the guard for false prophets. Strong warnings are given in both the Old Testament *(Jer. 5:30-31; 14:13-18; 23:9-40; Ezek. 13)* and the New Testament *(Matt. 7:15; Matt. 24:11,24)*. Probably because of the nature of the prophet's ministry in revelation and the gifts of the Spirit God gives us a stern warning. Do not judge a ministry by its signs and wonders. There are lying signs and wonders that will cause many to be deceived *(Mk. 13:22)*.

God also gives warnings to the prophets themselves. First of all, He warns them always to exercise discernment and self-control *(I Cor. 14:32)*. God wants them to use great wisdom with what He shows them and tells them, so that the body will truly be strengthened.

A second warning that God gives to prophets, is that they should allow their ministry to be judged *(I Cor. 14:29)*. No one is infallible, and the Bible teaches us that all prophecy is to be judged. There are six questions that can be asked that will help judge a prophetic ministry *(I John 4:1)*.

1. Is it in harmony with the Word of God?
2. Is it given in a good spirit *(Rom. 8:34)*?
3. Do his words come to pass *(Deut. 18:22)*?
4. Does his lifestyle reflect godliness *(Jer. 23:15-16)*?
5. Does the Holy Spirit within bear witness to the truth *(I John 2:20-21)*?
6. Has this been confirmed in the mouth of two or three witnesses *(II Cor. 13:1)*?

If any prophet insists that you follow him without submitting to the test, judge him a false prophet.

Chapter 13
THE MINISTRY OF THE EVANGELIST

There are certain terms and ministries that we are more familiar with than others. When we discussed the apostle and the prophet it was necessary to examine the Scripture to discover a dormant ministry in the Body of Christ. When we come to the next three of the five-fold ministry, the situation is a little different. Most Evangelicals have had some exposure to the titles "Evangelists", "Pastors" and "Teachers". This fact in itself means that most people have a reasonably good idea of what they think these ministries are like and what they think they ought to do. Unfortunately, it is possible to have a viewpoint that is shaped by tradition, rather than by a clear Scriptural understanding. In these cases it is a little more difficult for people to approach the Word of God objectively. There are too many traditions that are at stake. We must always be on guard that we do not nullify the effectiveness of the Word of God in our lives by holding fast to our tradition.

When we look at the ministry of the evangelist we have a special problem. Everybody has a view of what they believe an evangelist to be. You will have definitions of an evangelist that run all the way from someone who passes out tracts in front of a movie theatre to someone who does the work of an apostle.

Another thing that complicates the problem, is that of all the five-fold ministries in the Bible, the evangelist has the least recorded about him and apart from Christ we only have one good Bible example of an evangelist. In spite of this, however, we have to believe that the Bible has sufficient to say about this ministry, and we have to believe that the example we are given is to be a characteristic example of what an evangelist is to be.

A. DEFINITION OF TERMS

There are three main word forms that are used in connection with this ministry. They all come from the same root word and they all come from the Greek word from which we get our English word "evangelist".

1. Euaggelizo — This word literally means "to announce good news or glad tidings." This word is descriptive of the *ministry* of an evangelist. This word is used often in the New Testament especially under the ministry of Jesus *(Matt. 11:5; Acts 13:32; Rom. 10:15; II Cor. 10:16; Gal. 1:18; Eph. 3:8; Heb. 4:2)*. In a sense we all have this ministry, but the evangelist is going to be a specialist in this realm.

2. Euaggelion — This word means "the gospel or a good message." This word is descriptive of the *message* that an evangelist brings. Although many things can be good news, this word is especially applied to the good news of God's saving grace made possible in the death, burial and resurrection of Jesus Christ *(Matt. 24:14; Acts 20:24; Rom. 1:16; I Cor. 4:15; Eph. 1:13)*.

3. Euaggelistes — This word means "a preacher or messenger of good news." This word is descriptive of the *man* and is usually translated "evangelist" in the New Testament. This word is only found three times in the New Testament. It is used of Philip *(Acts 21:8)*. It is used in the list of the five-fold ministry *(Eph. 4:11)*. Finally, Paul instructs Timothy, an apostle, to do the work of an evangelist *(II Tim. 4:5)*.

We might visualize the distinction between these words in the following chart:

GREEK WORD	MEANING	DESCRIPTIVE OF:
Euaggelizo	to announce good news	THE MINISTRY
Euaggelion	the gospel or a good message	THE MESSAGE
Euaggelistes	a preacher or messenger of good news	THE MAN

B. CHRIST AS THE EVANGELIST

Luke's Gospel seems to be that of Jesus as the evangelist. The word "euaggelizo" occurs ten times in the Gospel of Luke and it only occurs one other time in the rest of the Gospels and that is in the Gospel of Matthew. Luke seems to give a summary of this ministry of an evangelist in relation to Christ in *Luke 4:18-19.*

> *"The Spirit of the Lord is upon me, because he hath anointed me to preach the gospel to the poor; he hath sent me to heal the brokenhearted, to preach deliverance to the captives, and recovering of sight to the blind, to set at liberty them that are bruised, to preach the acceptable fear of the Lord."*
>
> *Luke 4:18-19*

Here Luke lists six things that were going to characterize Jesus' ministry.

1. Preaching the gospel.
2. Healing the brokenhearted.
3. Preaching deliverance to the captives.
4. Preaching recovery of sight to the blind.
5. Setting at liberty them that are bruised.
6. Preaching the acceptable year of the Lord (the acceptable year of the Lord had to do with the jubilee and the year of release in Israel).

Luke portrays this as being the primary purpose for Christ's being sent. *(Luke 4:43; See also: Luke 7:22; 8:1; 20:1).*

This ministry of Christ the evangelist was given to the Body of Christ *(Eph. 4:11).* The Body of Christ is in desperate need of this ministry to be released and functioning in the body.

C. THE MINISTRY OF THE EVANGELIST

In order to get a Biblical understanding of the work of an evangelist we must look at the only post-ascension example that we have of an evangelist and glean principles from his ministry. Philip is the only one specifically called an evangelist *(Acts 21:8),* so it is to him we must look for the pattern. Philip's ministry in the book of Acts is confined to Acts chapter 8, but in that chapter we have some valuable insights to this ministry. From that chapter we can see four things that relate to the evangelist.

1. The preparation of the evangelist *(Acts 6:1-6)* — Philip did not just turn up at the door of the Church one day, and announce that the evangelist had arrived. There was much preparation that went into the making of an evangelist. There are several things that this chapter tells us about Philip. First of all, Philip belonged to a local Church. Jerusalem was his home at first, but after persecution broke out there, Philippi became his home. Second, we notice that in that home church he was a man of proven character. He was a good man, full of the Holy Ghost and wisdom. Third, we see that Philip was a man with a servant's heart. He was willing to work and he had a heart that was touched by the feelings of those around him. This heart of compassion motivated him to respond to the needs that he saw. Fourth, we find that before Philip moved out beyond the sphere of his own Church he proved himself as a deacon. *Those best equipped to handle authority are those who have really learned to submit to authority.* Philip was not over anxious about getting out and preaching, but in God's time he was forced out *(Acts 8:1-2).*

2. The public ministry of the evangelist to the lost (Acts 8:5-25) — In this chapter
Philip is truly seen as a messenger of good news. As he comes down to Samaria he is coming to a field that is ripe unto harvest. An evangelist is a reaper, and Philip is going to reap a harvest he did not sow. This harvest was sown in tears by Jesus and the woman at the well (John 4), but in Acts 8 this harvest is going to be reaped in joy.

As Philip comes down to Samaria it is clear that he has one main message, for there is only one main message to the soul that is bound in sin. All of his preaching is centered around Jesus Christ (Acts 8:5,12, 25 also vs. 35,40). Whether ministering to crowds, or ministering one-on-one, the message is always the same.

Philip's preaching was confirmed by signs and wonders (Mk. 16:15-20; Acts 8:6-7). This seems to be the mark of the evangelist. There were miracles, healings and the loosing of those that were bound by demonic powers. The message of the healing of the sin-sick soul brought with it the message of life, healing and deliverance to the whole man, spirit, soul and body. It was no doubt through these signs and wonders that God arrested the attention of the crowds in the city.

Philip's preaching resulted in the fruit of salvation (Acts 8:8). Not only was there great joy in the city, but it was properly founded on true repentance and faith, and a turning to God.

If Philip would have left them here, he would not have been a faithful evangelist. Instead he took them one step further. He took them into the waters of baptism. It is interesting how Philip always seemed to work water baptism into every message (Acts 8:12,36). He evidently knew that it was the seal of their faith.

Now Philip has a problem. For these new Christians to be introduced into the things of God properly, there is still the matter of the baptism of the Holy Spirit. Perhaps if he had been living in our day, and would have known by reading Acts 2:30-39 that the baptism of the Holy Spirit was for all that God would call, he would have gone ahead and prayed for these new converts himself. Since, however, this was Samaria, and these people were not entirely Jewish, he probably was not sure if it was proper to pray for them. Evidently at this point he sent word back to his home Church to send some ministry down. Peter and John came down and gave the necessary assistance, and evidently organized the new converts into a Church, for later we read of the Church of Samaria (Acts 9:31).

Several things are worthy of note in Philip's life and ministry that should characterize the evangelist. The first thing is that Philip recognized the limitation of his own ministry. He did not have to do everything himself. In the areas he was strong, he acted with authority. A second thing we notice is that he demonstrated a willingness to work with other ministries. He realized he was not on his own. He had a home Church to support him when he had need of help. He did not view himself as the whole Body of Christ wrapped up into one. A third thing is that Philip did not leave this group of converts unattended. The goal of such mass evangelism was a Church. Obviously it is a little different with individuals, but when a large segment of people turn to the Lord, you know God wants to plant a Church there. Philip did not leave until he had clear direction from the Lord to do so (Acts 8:26).

3. The private ministry of the evangelist (Acts 8:26-40) — An evangelist who is powerful behind a pulpit, but cannot work with people one-on-one, is out of balance in his ministry. Philip had a beautiful balance in his ministry, and whether he was in a crowd or with one individual, he was just as eager to share the good news. He knew the news he had to share would be just as good to one or to a hundred. An evangelist, then, should be an expert soul-winner. He should always be ready to share the good news wherever he finds himself (Acts 8:40).

An evangelist should always be keenly aware of the leading and prompting of the Spirit of God to be able to minister to prepared people. When Philip went down to Samaria, it was to a prepared people. When Philip approached to the Ethiopian eunuch he had already been prepared by the Word and the Spirit. It was an easy thing for Philip to reap this man for the kingdom. When the harvest is ripe, the fruit practically falls into the basket by itself.

An evangelist should, (as with all the five-fold ministry), have a familiarity with his basic tool, the Word of God. Philip had the kind of familiarity that he could preach Christ from every text. This was extremely important. The evangelist is a chosen workman, but the tools that God has placed in his hands are the Word and the Spirit. Without either one the job will never be properly accomplished.

4. The role of the evangelist in the Body of Christ *(Eph. 4:11-13)* — To this point we have centered on the ministry of the evangelist to the lost. This certainly is the main area of concern to the evangelist, but Ephesians 4 tells us that this ministry has also been given to the Church, the Body of Christ. The public ministry of the evangelist, then, involves mainly two areas. He is first of all given as a travelling ministry to the unevangelized, working as a kind of ground-breaker to prepare the way for other following ministries. Beyond this, the evangelist is given to the local expression of the Body of Christ for the perfection of the saints *(Eph. 4:12)*. The word "perfecting" here, means "to fit, complete, equip, put in order, arrange or adjust." It also means "to make one what he ought to be." In this sense the evangelist has the function of bringing the saints to a place of effective evangelism, helping to equip them to evangelize, and helping to make them what they ought to be in God.

This means that the function of the evangelist in the body does not involve evangelizing the saints. Never in the New Testament do we find the main meeting of the believers being used as a tool for evangelism. An evangelistic message to people who are already believers is not needed. The main purposes of the corporate gathering of the saints are the equipping and building up of the saints to do the work of the ministry, and the celebrating of the saints before their God. If an unbeliever happens to come into such a meeting, God can speak to him easily through whatever takes place *(I Cor. 14:24-25)*.

God is raising up true evangelists in these days. He is preparing the world for a great harvest. The field is ripe and there is still much land to be possessed.

Chapter 14
THE MINISTRY OF THE PASTOR

When God set different ministries in the body of Christ, He did it with great care, and in doing so He provided for a great variety of expression. God realized the tremendous variety of needs that exist among His people and He was very much concerned that all of those needs were met. Probably the most descriptive image that God could have given of His people to describe their absolute dependency on divine resource is that of "the flock". God often refers to His people as "a flock" *(Is. 40:11; Jer. 13:17; I Pet. 5:2)*. This term in the Bible does not always refer to sheep, but God seems to have sheep in mind when speaking of His people *(John 21:15; Matt. 26:31; Ezek. 34)*.

This figurative use of the term "flock" or "sheep" in relation to God's people is not necessarily the most favorable title that God could have applied to His people. There are a lot of things about sheep that make them something less than the most co-operative, independent, and noble of all creatures. Yet this is the picture that God chooses, and it is important for us to realize why God has made this choice.

There are many things about sheep that make them an appropriate symbol for the people of God. The first thing that is clear in the Bible about sheep is that sheep need special care. In fact, of all the animals involved in creation, it seems that from the beginning sheep were dependent on one outside of themselves for care *(Gen. 4:2)*. Sheep have to be tended *(I Sam. 17:20,28)*. They must be fed *(I Sam. 17:15)*. Most animals have instinctive ability to seek out food and water but sheep have no such ability. In the winter time, when the snow is on the ground, a goat can forage for itself but a sheep must be led to pasture.

A second quality about sheep that makes them a fitting symbol of God's people is that sheep have a poor sense of direction. Some animals can wander and can easily find their way home. There are some animals, in fact, that you can try to lose, and yet, given enough time, they will return home. A sheep will never do this. Sheep get lost easily *(Jer. 50:6)*. Once they get off track they usually must be sought after diligently *(Ezek. 34:12)*. The thing that really compounds the problem, however, is the coupling of the fact that sheep have no sense of direction with the tendency among sheep to wander *(I Kings 22:17; II Chron. 18:16; Ps. 119:176; Is. 53:6)*. This means that it is a common thing for sheep to get lost, and, unless they get help, they are in real trouble.

A third quality that sheep have, that parallels the people of God, is that sheep are of all animals some of the most defenseless. They have no claws. They are not powerful runners. Their jaws and teeth are not suitable for defence. Sheep on their own are susceptible to almost any kind of attack. They are open prey to wild animals of all kinds *(Matt. 7:15; Matt. 10:16)*. They are only safe when they are huddled together. This is why sheep must have folds and they must have shepherds *(Num. 32:24,36)*. Left to themselves they will never survive. Even if no wild animal hurt them, sheep will eventually die if they are not shorn of their excess wool *(Gen. 31:19)*.

The sheep is in need of special care, it has no natural sense of direction and it is absolutely helpless and defenseless on its own. In spite of all of this, however, sheep have always been viewed as a valuable possession. Even with all of these negatives, man has always concluded that the efforts of caring for sheep were worth it for the value that sheep were to mankind. Sheep do have some positive qualities that make them some of the best of domestic animals. Sheep produce meat, milk, and wool, which provide food, drink and clothing. They have an ability to follow *(John 10:4)*, to respond to the voice of the shepherd *(John 10:3)* and to flow together like no other animals. God wants His people to manifest these same positive qualities, but He knows that on their own they will never be productive. Because of this God sets pastors or shepherds over His flock to see to it that they become all that they were meant to be.

A. THE DEFINITION OF TERMS

The word "pastor" is only used once in the King James Version of the Bible *(Eph. 4:11)*. In this case, however, we do not have a strict translation of the Greek word that is involved. The actual Greek noun that is used here (poimen) occurs eighteen times in the New Testament and is always translated "shepherd". This word literally means "one who feeds, tends a flock or keeps sheep." In its history and development, there seem to be two primary connotations to this word. The position of shepherd was, first of all, a position of authority. In this sense there was rulership and government involved (II Sam. 5:2; Mic. 7:14). In fact, in the Old Testament times, the shepherds of God's people seem to have had military and political powers (I Chron. 11:6; Jer. 2:8; 25:34-36; 50:6). At times foreign rulers are also referred to as shepherds (Is. 44:28; Nahum 3:18). Even in Assyrian and Babylonian cultures the term "shepherd" was used figuratively of leaders and rulers of the people. In this sense rulership involved gathering the dispersed, righteous government, and caring for the weak.

The position of shepherd was, second of all, a position of service. This is a position of accountability. In this sense the shepherd was seen as one who nourished the flock and furnished pasturage or food. In a spiritual sense a shepherd would be one who supplied the necessary things for the well-being of the souls of his people. This involves sacrifice and humble service, visiting the sick, supporting the weak, nursing those with problems and providing the food and drink necessary for the sheep to be healthy and strong.

The verb form of this word (poimaino) also supports this two-fold usage. At times it seems to be referring to the governmental aspect of the function of a shepherd (Matt. 2:6). In this connection those who shepherd are given power and authority to rule (Rev. 2:26-27; 12:5; 19:15). At other times it seems to emphasize the caring and feeding aspect of this ministry. In this connection the shepherd is feeding (Lk. 17:7; John 21:16; Acts 20:28), caring, and gently leading the flock of God (Rev. 7:17).

Both the noun and the verb forms of this word seem to be directly related to another Greek word which is very likely their common root. This root word (poia) means "protect". The shepherd, then, is one who has responsibility to care for and protect the sheep from harm. In addition, Thayer says that the shepherd in a spiritual sense is "He to whose care and control others have commited themselves, and whose precepts they follow."

B. THE PATTERN FOR A PASTOR

The Church is a theocracy where God rules. God often refers to Himself as a shepherd and as such He fulfills that ministry to His people (Gen. 49:24; Ps. 68:7). He goes before His flock (Ps. 68:7), guiding it (Ps. 23:3), leading it to pasture (Jer. 50:19), leading it to rest beside waters (Ps. 23:2; Is. 40:11), protecting it with his staff (Ps. 23:4), whistling to those going astray (Zech. 10:8), gathering the dispersed (Is. 56:8) carrying the lambs in His bosom (Is. 40:11) and gently leading those that are with young (Is. 40:11).

When Jesus came, He put a face on God, and demonstrated the true shepherd's heart that was part of God's nature. Jesus came as a pattern by which those who would later be raised up as shepherds over God's people would have to measure themselves. Jesus came to demonstrate the Father's love for the flock of God. Jesus never once criticized the flock of God, but He only manifested a genuine love and compassion for them (Matt. 9:36; Mk. 6:34). Because of this He was willing to give His life (John 10:11) and lay down His life for the sheep (John 10:15). Jesus showed us the value that God places on even one sheep (Luke 15:4). He did not just see sheep as crowds of people but He had and took time for individuals.

Because of God's love for His sheep He is very much concerned that they are being cared for properly (John 21:15-17). He is concerned for individuals on all levels, and He has therefore appointed "undershepherds" to tend His flock (Eph. 4:11-13; I Pet. 5:2). These undershepherds must continually look to Jesus for the pattern of what it is to be a true shepherd of God's people.

C. THE QUALIFICATIONS FOR A PASTOR

It goes without saying that anyone who will be in a place of authority among God's people must qualify as an elder in the New Testament sense (I Tim. 3), but anyone who hopes to be used of God to shepherd or tend God's people must also have developed some specific skills and qualities that equip him in this area of service.

1. A pastor must be able to lead the sheep (John 10:4). When one leads another the implication is that he has himself gone that way before. If someone is going to lead God's people he must be one who has walked before the people in the ways of God. As such, anyone who leads, must be saved and filled with the Holy Spirit (John 10:1,3,9). These are basic requirements for the sheep (Acts 2:38-39). If the pastor has not experienced basic fundamental truths, he will not be able to lead others into them.

The principle is that the husbandman must be first partaker of the fruit *(II Tim. 2:6)*. If a pastor wants his people to pray he must first be a man of prayer. If he wants people to tithe, he must first be one who tithes. Leaders in God's house lead by example and lifestyle. Pastors must exhibit a lifestyle that the sheep can follow *(Heb. 13:7; I Pet. 5:2-3; I Cor. 11:1)*.

2. A pastor must be able to feed the flock and provide pasture *(Jer. 23:4; I Pet. 5:2-3; Ezek 34:1-3; Jer. 3:15; Acts 20:28)*. A shepherd must be able to provide the necessary food and water that will nourish, strengthen and build up the people of God *(Gen. 29:7; Ps. 23:2)*. This means that he must be one who is constantly involved in personal preparation and feeding in the Word of God. He must give himself to the Word of God and prayer *(Acts 6:4; Jer. 10:21)*. The food must be fresh if it is going to bring spiritual growth and refreshing to the people of God. Providing food also at times will involve exposing them to other ministries that will be able to supplement their diet with needed food *(Eph. 4:13)*.

Personal preparation in itself, however, is not the only thing that makes one a feeder. In addition, there must be an ability to communicate and to break down the food to various levels in the body *(Is. 40:11,29; John 16:12)*. A pastor is one ministry that has to be able to feed all levels from the very young to the very old. Every normal flock will have sheep at every stage of development.

3. A pastor must have a personal relationship with the sheep *(John 10:27)*. So often it is said that in order to be effective as a pastor there must exist a certain "ministerial aloofness". If this is so important, it is a wonder that Jesus had any success at all. It is true that a pastor will not be able to have an intimate relationship with everyone, and that there are many things he will never be able to share totally with others, yet, the Bible is clear that a true shepherd knows his sheep. A pastor should know the names of his people *(John 10:3)*. This can be a difficult task but a pastor who does not make this a priority is speaking volumes to his people by this neglect. Not only should the pastor know his people but he should allow himself to be known of them *(John 10:3)*. This means that he must identify with the people, sit where they sit and let them know that he is one of God's sheep himself *(Ezek. 3:15; Phil. 1:28-30)*. Without this relationship it will be difficult for the pastor to have a true heart of compassion for the sheep *(Luke 15:4)*.

4. A pastor must be willing to lay down his life for the sheep *(John 10:15; I John 3:16; Rev. 12:11)*. This means that there must be a deep commitment and loyalty that the shepherd has to the sheep. The sheep need to know that this is not just a job, but that it is a calling. They need to know that their shepherd is so committed to them that he would live and die for them. Commitment is a two-way street. *People will only commit themselves fully to one who is fully committed to them.* This commitment involves a pouring out of ones life and strength *(John 10:11)*. It involves caring for the sheep in times of need *(John 10:13; Ezek. 34:4)*. It involves staying with the sheep in times of trouble *(John 10:12)*. It involves visiting in the homes of the sheep *(Jer. 23:2)*. It involves a continual watchfulness for the safety of the sheep *(Heb. 13:17)*. In other words, the true shepherd is one who places the well-being of the sheep above his own life and ministry.

D. THE MINISTRY OF A PASTOR

Much of the actual work and ministry of a pastor has already been defined just by the very nature of the word and the qualifications of the position. There are four main words that summarize the work of a pastor: seeking, watching, caring and correcting.

1. The pastor is always reaching out, seeking that which was lost *(Lk. 15:4)*. There are many sheep who wander and go astray. The shepherd is one who never gives up on the lost one. This is why he is calling, visiting and exhorting those who have slacked off from their commitment and have gone astray.

2. The pastor is always watching for things that could cause damage to the flock *(Lk. 2:18)*. This watching involves a looking to the sheep for any problems that might arise,

checking for those that are hurting or limping. This watching involves looking out for wolves who may come to tear the flock, either from without, or within *(John 10:12; Acts 20:29)*. This watching involves vision, looking on the horizon, and reading the signs of the time. All of these areas have to do with the guarding aspect of the shepherd's ministry.

3. The pastor is always caring for those who are in need *(John 10:13)*. This may involve visiting the sick, making sure physical needs are being taken care of, assisting in financial planning, teaching principles by which to live, or giving comfort and consolation in times of bereavement. It involves a life commitment to reach out and touch the sick, the dying, the crippled, the poor, the widow, the fatherless, and all who are hurting.

4. The pastor is commited to correcting those who walk in a way contrary to the gospel *(Ps. 23:4)*. The shepherd has two tools, a rod and a staff. The staff is used for reaching and rescuing, but the rod is used for correcting and protecting. Discipline is the most difficult assignment for a pastor, or a father, or anyone involved in areas of responsibility, but discipline must be exercised if the immature are going to become mature *(Matt. 18:15-20)*. Discipline must be exercised in love, but the pastor who will not correct, admonish and exhort, is not a good spiritual parent, and in effect, is not loving the sheep at all.

All of these areas must be seen in balance in the work and ministry of a pastor. When they are so, the sheep will respond by giving themselves to the shepherd in loyalty and commitment. They will respond by providing wool and milk for the husbandman *(I Cor. 9:7)*. They will respond by reproducing themselves, thus producing more sheep. As a pastor is faithful with the sheep that he has, God will bless him with more *(Matt. 25:21,23)*.

E. CAUTIONS TO PASTORS

There are several cautions that God gives to those who would be pastors of God's flocks. God knows He is dealing with human beings who have weaknesses when He chooses shepherds for His people. Because these human beings have certain temptations that are common to them, He extends some warnings to pastors so as to protect His people.

1. Pastors must not neglect their own spiritual growth *(Jer. 2:8)*. So often people in leadership position are ruled by a busy schedule. Because of this it is very easy for them to neglect their own relationship to the Lord *(Acts 6:2-4)*. Pastors must never forget that they themselves are sheep and have need of a shepherd. The Lord will personally be their shepherd but they must carefully guard their relationship to the Bishop and Shepherd of their souls. Pastors will be the special object of satanic attack and therefore they, of all people, need to be guarded themselves *(Zech. 13:7; Matt. 26:31)*. Satan knows that if he can smite the shepherd, the sheep will be scattered.

2. Pastors must not be working for temporal gain *(I Pet. 5:2; I Tim. 3:3)*. When Jesus warned of false shepherds in *John 10*, it is interesting that all three of the illustrations He used had to do with money. He warned of thieves, robbers, and hirelings. A thief is one who steals by subtilty; a robber is one who steals by violence *(John 10:1,9&10; II Peter 2:3)*; an hireling is one who is just paid to do a job, but who has no heart for the sheep *(John 10:13)*. If money is the motive, the ministry will end in disaster.

3. Pastors must not be seeking worldly power *(Ezek. 34:4; I Pet. 5:3; Lk. 22:24-27)*. Many people look at the pastorate as an opportunity to be in command. They have a great desire to tell others what to do. Being a pastor is a position of authority, but it is also a position of humble service. One who is looking for a position of authority will expect people to wait on him and serve him, and he will ultimately be disappointed. The one who looks for a place to serve others, however, will be entrusted by God with a place of authority.

4. Pastors must not overdrive the sheep *(Gen. 33:13)*. Because pastors are God-ordained leadership, God takes the responsibility of keeping them ahead of the sheep in revelation, insight and life-style. To do this He has given them a heart that receives and comprehends truth easily and is able to apply it quickly. Often-times when a pastor receives a new insight he wants others to walk in it immediately, and he cannot understand it when the sheep do not immediately respond the way he did. A shepherd must be patient with the sheep. He must know the pace at which they can absorb truth, and he must not take them faster than their maturity will allow. This means that new insight must be introduced slowly if all are going to stay together as a flock.

F. JUDGMENTS ON UNFAITHFUL PASTORS

Pastors are ministries who have been appointed by God to care for His precious sheep. All pastors must continually realize that the sheep that are in their hands are not their own sheep. All of the sheep belong to the Chief Shepherd *(Jer. 23:1-2)*. They must realize that as far as God is concerned, there is only but one fold *(John 10:16)*. Because of this all pastors will be held accountable to the Great Shepherd for what they have done with the sheep *(Heb. 13:17; Ezek. 34:10; Jer. 23:1-2)*. If they are faithful they will receive a commendation. But if they are unfaithful they will receive judgment.

There are several judgments against those who are unfaithful as pastors over God's sheep. First of all, God will take the sheep from them *(Jer. 23:1-3; 10:21)*. Second, God will give those sheep to someone who will tend them *(Jer. 23:4)*. Third, God will bring his hand of judgment on the shepherds for mistreating His sheep *(Jer. 12:10-13; 22:22; 23:1-5; 25:34-38; 50:6-7, 43-44; Ezek. 34; Zech. 10:3; 11:3-9,17)*.

The ministry of the pastor is foundational to the building and establishing of the New Testament Local Church. Throughout the dark ages of Church history it has been this great ministry that has blessed God's people and brought them to the place that they are. God has a definite charge that He would like to make afresh to those who feel drawn to this service in the Body of Christ. He would make it through the words of Paul:

> *"Take heed therefore unto yourselves, and to all the flock, over the which the Holy Ghost hath made you overseers, to feed the church of God, which he hath purchased with his own blood. For I know this, that after my departing shall grevious wolves enter in among you, not sparing the flock. Also of your own selves shall men arise, speaking perverse things, to draw away disciples after them. Therefore watch, and remember, that by the space of three years I ceased not to warn every one night and day with tears. And now, brethren, I commend you to God and to the word of his grace, which is able to build you up, and to give you an inheritance among all them which are sanctified. I have coveted no man's silver, or gold, or apparel. Yea, ye yourselves know, that these hands have ministered unto my necessities, and to them that were with me. I have shewed you all things, how that so labouring ye ought to support the weak, and to remember the words of the Lord Jesus, how he said, It is more blessed to give than to receive."*
>
> *Acts 20:28-35.*

Chapter 15
THE MINISTRY OF THE TEACHER

Everything God does, he does on the basis of principles that He has laid down in His word. The life of the Christian, if it is going to be successful, must be ordered on the basis of these principles. Every Church must also be the pillar and ground of truth if it is going to be what it is supposed to be in the world. It is an interesting thing that in nearly every revival or reformation movement, the movement did not take hold until the truth around which it was built was carefully expounded from the Scripture. When Jesus gave the great commission to the Church, it did not involve just preaching the gospel in all the world for a witness, but it involved making disciples, or disciplined ones, of all nations and *"teaching them to observe all things whatsoever I have commanded you" (Matt. 28:20)*.

In this commission we find a strong emphasis on the work of teaching, and to meet this challenge God has given teachers in the Body of Christ. The teaching ministry is not a complicated ministry, but it is a very necessary ministry if God's people are going to *"come in the unity of the faith, and of the knowledge of the Son of God, unto a perfect man, unto the measure of the stature of the fulness of Christ" (Eph. 4:13)*. The teaching ministry is a very important ministry if babes in Christ are going to grow up into Him in all things *(Eph. 4:15)*.

A. THE DEFINITION OF TERMS

The main Greek word that is used in regard to the teaching ministry is the word "didasko". Often times this word is also translated as "doctor" or "master". The root word simply means "to instruct'. It relates to the process of holding discourse with others for the purpose of instruction. It refers to the process of explaining or expounding something. It involves the instilling of doctrine into others.

B. THE ORIGIN OF THE MINISTRY

There have always been teachers among the people of God in one form or another. Every time a father gave a word of instruction to his family, or a leader gave instruction to a people, the work of teaching was going on. Moses was a teacher of God's people, continually instructing them in the ways of God. In fact, God had given him this charge as part of the solution to his people problem *(Ex. 18:20)*. Moses' problem was the great amount of counseling that he had to do day after day. God told him that he could save himself a lot of counseling, if he would teach the people the very principles that he used in judgment so that they could settle their own affairs. So often people's problems are not totally their own fault. In many cases they have not had good teaching that will help equip them to deal with their problems.

From Moses on, the main responsibility of teaching seemed to be with the priests, at least until the time of the Babylonian captivity *(II Chron. 15:2-5)*. From the time of the captivity, however, the teaching ministry came into its own through the scribes. The scribes were to become the official interpreters of the Law, and were the experts at expounding the Scripture. In the days of the captivity when there was no temple, the local synagogue became the center of learning and instruction. The synagogue was not a place of sacrifice, it was a rallying place for the people where the Law could be expounded. It was here that the ministry of the scribe really began to flourish. During Christ's day this ministry was held in very high esteem.

C. JESUS AS THE MASTER TEACHER

Since the ministry of teaching is included as one of the gifts of Christ, it is good to look at the pattern for this ministry in Christ's experience. In many places Jesus is called a teacher. Nicodemus, a man of rank among the Jews, indicated that He was recognized by many as a teacher come from God *(John 3:2; 13:13)*. This was not difficult to see because Jesus spent so much of His time teaching the multitudes of people *(Matt. 4:25; 5:2; 9:35; 11:1; 13:54; 21:23; 22:16; Mark 10:1; Luke 20:21)*. Jesus taught everywhere he went (*Luke 13:26*). He taught in the synagogues, He taught in the streets. Every day He was teaching (*Mk. 14:49; Luke 19:4; 21:37*).

Jesus certainly was not the only one teaching in His day, but there was something different about Jesus' teaching. There was a power, there was an anointing, there was an authority that was not with the rest of the teachers of His day (*Matt. 7:28*). It is this anointed, authoritative teaching that God has given to His Church. The key to it is the same thing that made Jesus' teaching so unique. His teaching was not a success because of the great loud volume with which He lifted up His voice, because we know that Jesus was not loud or showy (*Matt. 12:19*). It was not a success because of the way He dressed, or His manner of presentation, because we know that He had no external beauty (*Isaiah 53:2*). What made Jesus Christ successful as a teacher, was the fact that He taught that which He had received from the Father (*John 8:28; 7:16*).

D. THE LEVELS OF TEACHERS IN THE NEW TESTAMENT

When we come to the area of teaching, it is important for us to realize that in the House of God, and in the Christian home, teaching must be going on at every level. No one could survive without some form of teaching. In the New Testament we have already seen that Jesus was the master teacher. The Holy Spirit also has this ministry in relation to the people of God (*Luke 12:12; John 14:26*). Among the body of Christ there will be many involved in the area of teaching, but not all will be considered teachers of the five-fold ministry stature.

Every believer in the body of Christ is in some way responsible to teach others how to live godly in Christ Jesus (*Matt. 28:20; Col. 3:16*), but that does not mean that every believer is recognized as a teacher in the body. Every elder is to be able to teach (*I Tim. 3:2*) even as every father is to teach those under his authority, but that does not make every elder or father a teacher in the Body.

God has set gifted teachers in the Church who function in a leadership capacity, primarily in this area of teaching (*Eph. 4:11; I Cor. 12:28-29*). Paul was evidently a teacher before he became an apostle (*Acts 11:26; II Tim. 1:11; Acts 18:11*) and when he was not involved in apostolic ministry he returned to this function (*Acts 15:35*). We know also that there were other teachers at the Church of Antioch (*Acts 13:1*). This is a very responsible position in the Body of Christ, and for this reason it is also one of great accountability (*James 3:1*).

E. THE MINISTRY OF THE TEACHER

The actual work of the teacher is adequately summed up in the definition of the term. The teacher is one who gives himself to the exposition of the Word of God, to instill in the people of God a love and respect for the Word, and to bring them to a place of maturity in the faith. There are, however, many aspects to this ministry that the New Testament further delineates.

1. A teacher needs to be continually taught, and open to teaching (*Rom. 2:21*). The teacher's life is one of study and personal preparation. If he is not able to be taught personally, he will not make a good teacher. A true teacher is taught of the Spirit of God (*I Cor. 2:13*).

2. A teacher should desire to see others come up to his level, and even surpass him (*Matt. 10:24-25*). Paul was able to tell the Ephesian elders "*I kept back nothing that was profitable unto you*" (*Acts 20:20*) and "*I have not shunned to declare unto you all the counsel of God*" (*Acts 20:27*).

3. A teacher must know the Word of God (*Mk. 12:24*). This is his basic tool. His job is to lead others in understanding. He can not do this if he has no understanding himself. He must be able to answer people's difficult questions (*Matt. 22:16-46*). He must be able to take the Word of God and apply it to life situations (*Mk. 9:14-29*). He must be able to establish and ground believers in the Word (*Heb. 5:12*).

4. A teacher must be able to teach by example (*John 13:13-14*). If a teacher does

not live what he teaches, he will have no more effect than did the Pharisees *(Matt. 23:1-3)*. This is the thing that separated Jesus from every other teacher. Jesus always did what He taught others to do *(Acts 1:1)*. Our greatest messages come out of what we **are,** not what we **say.**

5. A teacher needs to be very aware of his words. A teacher will have to use words carefully because they are the avenue by which he is going to communicate divine truth. It is a fact of life that because of his position, people will try to entangle him in his words, just as they did Jesus *(Matt. 22:15)*. *Matt. 22:15)*.

6. A teacher is excited when his teaching is in harmony with the will of God, finds its source in God's authority and reproduces an attitude of obedience in the hearers *(Deut. 4:5,14; 31:12-13)*. This is his greatest reward. When people's lives begin to change it makes all the effort worthwhile.

7. A teacher should be financially supported by those to whom he ministers *(Gal. 6:6)*. If a teacher is to minister effectively and with authority, he must have time to study and prepare. He will not have time if teaching is a secondary endeavor. Teaching will be his livelihood.

F. WARNING AGAINST FALSE TEACHERS

A good teacher can have a lot of power over people. He is one who handles the Word of God convincingly and therefore will be very influential in setting a path for the people of God. This is a place of great responsibility and therefore should be entered into with caution *(James 3:1)*. For this reason also God gives His people definite warning against false teachers. There are three kinds of false teachers that we must be concerned about.

1. Those who teach wrong doctrine *(II Pet. 2:1; II Tim. 4:3)*. Many people even enjoy strange and unusual doctrines, but the Bible is intolerant of those who perpetuate as truth things that are founded on anything other than the Word of God. It must be remembered that a true Biblical doctrine is everything that the Bible has to say on any given subject. There are many today who would take one obscure phrase from the Bible and build a whole doctrine on it. Against this we are warned.

2. Those who teach traditions of men as doctrines *(Mk. 7:7)*. Often times our heritage and upbringing can effect our doctrines. We have been told something so long that we are sure the Bible must teach it. Our doctrine can come out of our experience rather than totally from the Word *(Acts 5:1)*. The Bible warns us of this and admonishes us to be as the noble Bereans who received the Word with readiness of mind, but then they searched the Scriptures to see if what was taught was really the case *(Acts 17:11)*.

3. Those who teach with improper motivation *(I Cor. 4:15)*. There always have been, and always will be, those who teach for material gain *(Tit. 1:10-11; II Pet. 2:3)*. The Bible seems to imply that though at times these teachers may teach truth, yet it is also true that if these teachers felt it would be more prosperous to teach a lie, they might consider doing that. Often-times these teachers can deceive whole homes and gain a following for themselves. The Bible warns us of these. We must be careful of any ministry that is operating outside the checks and balances of the local Church.

At times we can look at negatives and be frightened, and yet we know that teachers are absolutely necessary to the Body of Christ. Teachers help us to stay on the right track and not get out of balance in our approach *(Is. 30:20-21)*. Teachers help keep peace in the House of God.

When Jesus ascended on high He gave gifts to men. The gifts that He gave His Church were valuable gifts. They were the oversight ministries in the House of the Lord. Each ministry has its own special value and the Church would be something less than what it was intended to be if any part were lacking. All the members are needed because each adds a dimension and supplies an emphasis that is not present in each of the others.

The APOSTLE is needed to GOVERN.
The PROPHET is needed to GUIDE.
The EVANGELIST is needed to GATHER.
The PASTOR is needed to GUARD.
The TEACHER is needed to GROUND.

No one member is more important than another. Let us believe God to raise up powerful, anointed ministries in all these realms that He might truly have a glorious Church!

G. THE RELATIONSHIP OF THE ELDERSHIP TO THE FIVE-FOLD MINISTRY

The New Testament does not deal directly with the subject of the relationship of the eldership to the five-fold ministry. Because of this it is difficult to make a definitive statement. There are several facts, however, that should help us in arriving at a Biblical conclusion.

1. The New Testament never uses the term "five-fold" ministry. The term "five-fold" ministry is one that has been applied to the ministries mentioned in *Ephesians 4:11*. This is the only place in the New Testament where these five ministries are listed together. In *I Corinthians 12* some of them are listed along with other body ministries. It is clear that these ministries are functions that different members of the body have been given by God, but eldership is an office into which one is actually installed.

2. There are only two offices in the New Testament Church. The two offices in the New Testament Church are those of elders and deacons *(Philippians 1:1)*. These offices are the only two that are described in detail with actual lists of qualifications. These are the only two offices necessary for order and structure to be brought to the House *(I Timothy 3:1-15)*.

3. The office of an elder is the only one to which we have an actual command to ordain as a governmental position *(Acts 14:23; Titus 1:5)*. No one ever ordained someone as a teacher, a prophet, a pastor, an evangelist or an apostle. God called many to these ministries but they were not ordained to that office.

4. Elders bear the ultimate authority and responsibility over the House of the Lord *(I Timothy 5:17)*. In the New Testament there is no man or group of men that are of greater authority in the local Church than its eldership. When Paul wanted to instruct the Church at Ephesus he called for their "elders". He did not call for the "five-fold" ministry. He did not call for "the pastor", he called for the ruling body of the church, the elders. When Paul reported to the brethren at Jerusalem it was an important footnote that *"all the elders were present" (Acts 21:18)*. When finances were sent to the Church it was placed, not at the twelve apostles feet, which had been done in the infant Church, but at the feet of the elders *(Acts 11:30)*. This was the case because the elders represented God's anointed and appointed leaders who were responsible and accountable for the affairs of the Church.

5. The only ministry to maintain a distinction from the eldership was that held by the twelve apostles of the Lamb *(Acts 15:2,4,6,22,23; 16:4)*. It must be noted, however, that no one is in the same category as these original twelve (see chapter 11) and therefore this is not to be a pattern, and was only the case in the Jerusalem Church.

Chapter 16
OTHER BODY MINISTRIES

The Church, as the Body of Christ, is filled with many unique and varied ministries. God has something for every member of His body to contribute to the success of the whole. There are ministries that range from helps to governments, with everything in between. It would be difficult to list all of the special ministries that exist in the Church. Nowhere in the Bible do we have such a list, but here and there we have partial lists and other allusions. There are intercessors, preachers, healers, and workers of miracles. There are counselors and administrators, helpers and showers of hospitality. There are singers and musicians, mothers and fathers in Israel. The list could go on and on.

In *Romans 12*, Paul deals with the area of body ministry, and he lists several ministries there that are important to consider in detail.

"For as we have many members in one body, and all members have not the same office: So we, being many, are one body in Christ, and every one members one of another. Having then gifts differing according to the grace that is given to us, whether prophecy, let us prophesy according to the proportion of faith; Or ministry, let us wait on our ministering; or he that teacheth on teaching; Or he that exhorteth, on exhortation: he that giveth, let him do it with simplicity; he that ruleth, with diligence; he that sheweth mercy, with cheerfulness."

Romans 12:4-8

In this passage Paul mentions at least seven different ministries in the Body. Upon careful examination we find that four of these have already been dealt with in some detail. Prophecy relates to those who have been given a prophetic ministry. We looked at the ministry of the prophet in Chapter 12. Ministry is the same Greek word that is translated service and relates to the ministry of the deacon. To wait on that ministry literally means "to serve". Teaching obviously relates to the ministry of teaching as was discussed in Chapter 15. Ruling involves the ministry of the elders in the Body of Christ who have been given this specific charge many places in the New Testament. We looked at the ministry of elders in Chapter 10 of this book.

At least three of these ministries, however, have not been discussed at all to this point. In this chapter we would like to take a brief look at these three important areas of function in the House of the Lord. Rather than give full exposition of these three areas, we are going to confine ourselves to a simple outline form. For further insight into these areas it would be very helpful to look up all the Scripture passages cited.

A. EXHORTERS IN THE BODY OF CHRIST (Rom. 12:8)

1. What does the word "exhortation" mean in the New Testament?

a. In the New Testament exhortation means an appeal, an entreaty, encouragement, consolation and comfort.

b. In the New Testament, to exhort is to admonish, or to urge someone to pursue some course of action. It means:

1. To appeal to, urge, encourage and exhort.
2. To implore, request, entreat.
3. To comfort and cheer up.
4. To try to console or conciliate, and speak to someone in a friendly manner.

c. In the New Testament an exhorter is one who is called to someone's aid.

2. Where do we find the pattern for the New Testament ministry of exhortation? The pattern for the New Testament ministry of exhortation is found in the Godhead.

a. The Father is seen as Comforter *(Rom. 15:5; II Thess. 2:16-17).*

b. The Son is seen as Comforter *(I John 2:1; John 14:6).*

c. The Holy Spirit is seen as Comforter *(John 14:26; 15:26; 16:7; Acts 9:31).*

3. What are some of the characteristics of this ministry? While we are all called to a ministry of exhortation *(I Thess. 5:11; Heb. 3:13; 10:25),* there will be those who have this function in the body *(Rom. 12:8).* Those who have the ministry of exhortation should find themselves:

a. Coming to the side of and encouraging people in times of tribulation, affliction, sorrow and bereavement *(Matt. 2:18; 5:4; I Thess. 3:2-3).*

b. Interceding for those that are sick *(Matt. 8:5).*

c. Encouraging people in things to come in relation to God's purposes *(I Thess. 5:16-18; Luke 3:18).*

d. Admonishing people when they are not entering into the full privileges of their inheritance *(Luke 15:28).*

e. Warning of impending danger and encouraging watchfulness *(Rom. 16:17).*

f. Exhorting and encouraging others to follow the ways of God *(Acts 2:40; 11:23; Eph. 4:1; Jude 3).*

g. Warning others of dangers they sense in the course they have set for themselves *(Acts 21:12; I Thess. 5:14; II Thess. 3:11-12).*

h. Coming to the side of those who have fallen, but have demonstrated repentance *(II Cor. 2:7-8).*

4. What is to be the attitude of one who is called to this service in the body?

a. They should minister in an attitude of meekness and gentleness *(II Cor. 10:1).*

b. Their motives need to be purely the interest of others *(I Thess. 2:1-8).*

c. Their heart should be full of a father's love *(I Thess. 2:8).*

5. What is to be our attitude toward those with this ministry?

a. We need to give heed to exhortation *(I Tim. 4:13).*

b. We should allow this ministry to be released by receiving exhortation *(Heb. 13:22).*

6. What is necessary for this ministry to operate effectively?

a. Those who minister must recognize that God is their source *(II Cor. 1:3-7).*

b. Those who minister must be familiar with the Word of God *(Rom. 15:4).*

B. SHOWERS OF MERCY IN THE BODY OF CHRIST
(Rom. 12:8).

1. What is a good definition of "mercy"?

a. It means "to feel sympathy with the misery of another, and especially sympathy manifested in an act." (Vine).

b. It is "the outward manifestation of pity; it assumes need on the part of him who receives it, and resources adequate to meet the need on the part of him who shows it" (Vine).

2. What are some of the ways in which the Lord is a shower of mercy?

a. The Lord is the source of all mercy *(Rom. 9:15-18; Eph. 2:4; Phil. 2:27; II Cor. 1:4)*, and has demonstrated Himself as a shower of mercy in the following ways:

1. By setting his love on us when we did not deserve it *(Deut. 7:7)*.
2. By pulling us out of the places of danger in which we were living *(Gen. 19:16)*.
3. By continually guiding and directing us in the right ways of God *(Ex. 15:13)*.
4. By continually exercising forgiveness for things we have done *(Num. 14:18-20)*.
5. By standing along side us in times of danger, distress and trouble *(Deut. 4:31; Psalm 31:7)*.
6. By having compassion on the misery of his people *(Judg. 10:16)*.
7. By delivering us from slaveries and bondages *(Ezra 9:9)*.
8. By punishing us less than our sin deserves *(Ezra 9:13; Job 11:6)*.
9. By putting up with our many failings and continuing to respond to our cry *(Neh. 9:17; 27-31)*.
10. By providing all our physical needs *(Psalm 146:7; 37:25,26)*.

b. Jesus, in His earthly walk, was called upon often to exercise mercy upon those in need and misery *(Matt. 9:27; 15:22; 17:15; 20:30,31)*.

3. What two things does the Lord expect from those to whom He shows mercy? LOVE and ACCEPTANCE *(Deut. 5:29; 7:9; II Chron. 30:9)*.

4. What is to be the believer's responsibility in relation to showing mercy?

a. We are all commanded to be showers of mercy *(Luke 6:36; Matt. 6:1-4)*.

1) We are all the objects of mercy, and this should inspire us to mercy *(I Pet. 2:10)*.
2) If we fail to be merciful to others, we will be judged without mercy *(James 2:13 with Matt. 18:23-35)*.

b. We are going to have to give an account as to our willingness to show mercy *(James 1:27; Matt. 25:31-46)*.

c. We are to pursue the virtue *(Pro. 3:3,4; Micah 6:8; Col. 3:12,13)*.

5. How does God regard this virtue?

a. Mercy is one of the weightier matters of the law *(Matt. 23:23)*.

b. God desires mercy over sacrifice *(Matt. 9:13; 12:7)*.

6. What are the rewards of this virtue?

a. It brings happiness *(Pro. 14:21,22)*.

b. It brings life *(Pro. 21:21)*.

c. It brings more mercy *(Matt. 5:7; II Sam. 22:26; Psalm 18:25)*.

7. Who are some good examples of this ministry in the Bible?

a. Dorcas *(Acts 9:36-42)*.

b. The Samaritan *(Luke 10:33-37)*.

C. GIVERS IN THE BODY OF CHRIST *(Rom. 12:8)*.

1. How could we describe the ministry of giving in the New Testament?
There are individuals in the Body of Christ whom God has blessed in material ways, that they might in turn share generously with those in need in the Body of Christ.

2. Where do we find the pattern and the chief example of this ministry?

a. In God Himself *(James 1:5,17; John 3:16; Matt. 7:11)*.

b. In our Lord Jesus Christ *(II Cor. 8:9; 9:6-15)*.

3. What is the principle that operates in this ministry?

a. God pours His blessing upon an individual that he might in turn bless others *(Gen. 12:2-3; II Cor. 1:3-4; I Tim. 6:17-19)*.

b. God gives certain individuals an ability to make money easily *(Eph. 4:28)*.

c. As we are faithful in this ministry God will continue to pour out His blessing abundantly *(Pro. 11:24-25; 22:9; 28:27; Isa. 32:8; Matt. 5:42)*.

4. What is to be the attitude and motivation of those involved in this ministry?

a. They should minister freely in this way *(Matt. 10:8)*.

b. They should minister willingly *(I Chron. 29:5; II Cor. 8:3,12)*.

c. They should minister liberally *(Rom. 12:8; II Cor. 8:2; 9:13)*.

d. They should minister as unto the Lord *(Matt. 25:40)*.

e. They should minister in love *(I Cor. 13:3; II Cor. 8:24)*.

f. They should minister before the Lord not before men *(Matt. 6:1-4).*

5. What are some cautions for those whom the Lord has called to this ministry?

a. There will be a temptation to withhold and store up when the Lord has blessed *(I Jn. 3:17-18).*

1) This will end in disaster *(Pro. 13:7).*

2) This will end in divine judgment *(Luke 12:16-23).*

b. There will be a possibility of being deceived by what blessings he has *(James 5:1-6; I Tim. 6:6-11).*

Whatever talent an individual has been given can be used in an important place in the House of the Lord. Secretarial skills, carpentry skills, photography, sewing, and "you-name-it" could all be used to extend the kingdom of God. We can either use our talent for purely worldly ends and, as it were, bury it in the earth, or we could invest it in the people of God and reap eternal dividends. God prefers the latter. When we build this way we are building with gold, silver and precious stones.

D. A WORD OF CAUTION

One of the dangers in becoming very precise and definite in our evaluation of various ministries in the Body of Christ, is that there can develop a tendency to become very selective and specialistic in our approach to problems. When confronted with a need we can excuse ourselves by saying that that is not our ministry. God wants us to realize that even though there are specialists in the body in certain areas, every Christian has a measure of responsibility in all of these areas. The fact that you are not an elder, does not let you off from meeting the requirements of an elder and ruling over your own circumstances. The fact that you are not a deacon does not free you from your responsibility as a Christian to serve. Every Christian is to be a servant. Every Christian is to be sent of God, with a word from God, to reach those separated from God. Every Christian should be ready to care for the hurting, and to instruct the babes. Every Christian is to exhort and encourage, to show mercy and to give liberally to the work of God. Over and above all that, God will also give a unique and special skill in one or two areas, where each of us can excel and abound in the work of the Lord.

E. FINDING YOUR PLACE

Once we realize that we all have an important place of responsibility before the Lord in all areas of ministry, we can concentrate a little more on the specific area in which God wants us to be particularly involved. Many people have a real struggle finding their "ministry" as if looking for a mystical "something" on the horizon. They imagine themselves in all kinds of strange situations that are absolutely foreign to their nature and makeup, thinking that God is going to have them do the thing they do the worst, and enjoy the least. They are like apple trees imagining themselves producing strawberries. It is ridiculous even to imagine. God wants His people to rest in the fact that He has not called them to be something that they are not. God wants us to be our unique selves all the while rendering honest service to Him. We do not have to struggle to be what we are. An apple tree does not have to struggle to produce apples, it comes naturally. A hand in the body does not have to strive to be a hand, it is a hand! As members of the body of Christ, God simply wants us to be released to be what we are.

There are, however, some things that we must recognize that will help us to be released in our areas of function in the body. There are ten things we all must recognize, that will help us to find and enjoy our place of function.

1. Recognize that you personally have an important place of function

and responsibility before the Lord *(I Cor. 12:7)*. There is something that God has for every member to do. He has given you this function as it has pleased Him *(I Cor. 12:11,18)*.

2. Recognize that God has made you perfectly suited to the ministry to which He has called you *(Eph. 2:10; I Cor. 12:27)*.
Your intelligence, your emotional make-up, your physical aptitudes and your very appearance are perfectly designed with your function in mind. A hand is made to grasp, a foot is made to walk, and each member of the body of Christ is uniquely made to fulfill their ministry.

3. Recognize that it is God who equips you with the gifts necessary to fulfill your ministry *(Rom. 12:3,6; I Pet. 4:10)*.
God gives the necessary spiritual gifts and the faith that we need to accomplish His charge. We need not fear that we will not be able to do what He has asked.

4. Recognize the headship of Jesus Christ and be subject to Him in all things *(Eph. 1:21-23; 4:15; 5:23)*.
No matter what ministry we have, all ministry depends on being in right relationship to the Head. If we are not able to walk in daily obedience to the Lord, we should not expect to be used in areas of responsibility in the body of Christ.

5. Recognize that all ministry equals and begins with service *(Luke 22:26-27)*.
The word ministry itself means "service". If we are looking for ways in which we can serve and strengthen others, we are going to find much to do in the body of Christ. Anyone seeking to exalt himself will find God working against him, but if he is attempting in his service to make others successful, God is going to exalt him *(James 4:6)*.

6. Recognize the area of service to which God is calling you *(Rom. 12:3-5)*.
As we become more familiar with the various ministries, and the type of people that must function in those ministries, we are better able to rightly assess and evaluate our own ministry. We are not to think of ourselves more highly than we ought to think, but we are to recognize the faith and grace that God has given to us.

7. Recognize that no one ministry is more important than another *(I Cor. 12:21,25)*.
We tend to rate ministries on the basis of their spheres of influence. We tend to make mental lists of that which is more important. God does not do that. God values them all equally. God's judgment of us is not based on **what** we are, but on **how faithful** we are with what He has given us to do. There will be one commendation for all, *"Well done, though good and faithful servant"* *(Matt. 25:21)*.

8. Recognize that all ministry develops over a period of time.
No-one begins with a fully developed ministry. Paul, Stephen, Philip, Timothy and Peter are all good examples of the development of ministry over a period of time. Begin by serving in obvious areas and God will give you further direction, promotion and recognition. Many make the mistake of desiring a title before they will function. Begin serving with whatever your hand finds to do, and your gift will make room for itself. Remember, promotion comes from the Lord *(Psalm 75:6)*.

9. Recognize that we will only be as successful as we are willing to sacrificially apply ourselves *(Rom. 12:10)*.
There is a cost involved for everything that we do in the Kingdom of God. It is the violent who are going to take the Kingdom *(Matt. 11:12)*. It is those who are willing to press in that are going to be successful *(Luke 16:16)*. Anyone who wants to be used of God must separate himself unto God *(Rom. 12:2)*.

10. Recognize that God is going to give you special grace or divine enablement to do His will *(Phil. 2:13)*.
No-one can truly be successful in his place of function without the grace of God. We are totally dependent on Him, but it is wonderful to know that His grace is sufficient *(II Cor. 12:9)*, abundant *(I Pet. 4:10-11)*, and free *(Matt. 10:8)*.

Chapter 17
CONCLUSION

God is doing some powerful things in His Church in these days. It is exciting to see God bringing understanding to His people. It is exciting to see proper order and structure come into His House. But we must constantly remember that the most important thing in the life of a Church is not order or structure. It is not a lot of people, good buildings, a big budget or a large Sunday School. **The most important thing in the Church is the presence of the Lord.** It is the presence of the Lord that God has promised to His House that will make the difference in our day between a Church that has life and a Church that merely has the name of one who lives *(Rev. 3:1)*. It is the presence of the Lord, not our structure, that will protect us in the day of storm *(Is. 4:5-6)*. It is important to have right structure, but structure in itself is like a body without breath *(II Cor. 3:5-6)*.

Moses realized the absolute necessity of being led and guided by the presence of the Lord. At one point God was angry with the idolatry of His people and He told Moses that He was no longer going to go with them personally, but He was going to send an angel to lead them on. Moses was very emphatic at this point. He let God know that He was not going to accept a substitute. He did not want angelic visitation, he wanted the presence of the Lord *(Ex. 32:34; 33:15)*. Moses was not interested in the dramatic. He was not interested in exhibitionism. He was not interested in programs for the sake of programs. Moses was interested in the presence of the Lord. He was interested in nothing else that would be a substitute for the presence of the Lord.

God has revealed to us that there is a promised land ahead of the Church. He has given leadership to His people even as he provided leadership in Moses. He has given us a pattern for the sanctuary. He has given us the sacrifices, the priesthood and the law, but, without the presence of the Lord in our midst, we are like all of the other nations, and we will never enter into what God has for us.

God's presence is not totally dependent on structure. Certainly our structure will make a difference in the degree to which God is freed to move in our midst, but God's presence is primarily dependant on the condition of our hearts.

God promises His presence to the humble *(Is. 57:15; Is. 66:2)*. God knows that if we remain humble before Him and His Word, that He can lead us and guide us into all truth. As soon, however, as we adopt a spirit of pride, thinking that we know it all and that we have no need of change, we will find God to be our enemy, and rather than leading us we will find Him resisting us *(James 4:6)*. God will not dwell with the proud *(Ps. 138:6)*. But to the humble He will show Himself strong.

God also promises His presence to the obedient *(Ex. 29:38-46; I Kings 6:12-14)*. If we are truly humble before the Lord we will want to obey His Word. If we are the kind of people that put a high priority on obedience to the commands of God, we can continually expect God to be in our midst exercising His Headship over the Church, which is His body. God desires to manifest His presence to us, but He will not dwell with the rebellious. If God has revealed His ways to us, and we are not seeking to conform our lives to His Word, we are in danger of losing His living presence in our midst.

In addition to humility and obedience, God responds to a thankful heart. For this reason **God promises His presence to a praising people** *(Acts 2:46-47)*. David tells us that God enthrones Himself in the praises of His people *(Ps. 22:3)*. When we praise God, He is exalted in our midst; the Head is exalted to His rightful place. It is interesting to note how, in the Bible, singing and praise broke the condition of barrenness *(Is. 54:1)* and those that refused to praise God became barren *(II Sam. 6:23)*. Singing and praise have the ability to break bondages and bring release to those who are bound *(Acts 16:25)*. This is all because God dwells in the praises of His people, and where God dwells, things begin to happen: people are set free in the presence of the Lord, and as a result more people are drawn in *(Zech. 2:10)*. When you have the presence of the Lord you do not need special gimmicks, dramatic acting, a great choir, or anything else to draw people. People will get saved just because of the presence of the Lord.

Another thing that will insure the presence of God in these days is **a willing heart to turn from evil ways of the past unto the right ways of the Lord** *(Ezek. 43:9)*. There is a sense in which anything that we do that is contrary to the Word of God is a sin in God's eyes *(James 4:17; Rom. 14:23)*. Once God has revealed truth to us, He no longer allows us the privilege of living on a secondary level. As He opens our eyes to areas of ignorance, He expects us to move on and walk in that truth (*Acts 17:30*). Sometimes that calls for some pretty major adjustments in our lives, but a spirit of obedience and humility, coupled with the grace of God, will enable us to turn from the old ways of tradition, to the right ways of God. As we do, God will confirm His word in our midst through a glorious manifestation of His presence.

One final ingredient that is vital to a release of God's power and presence in our midst is **unity.** Sometimes this is very difficult to maintain in times of change, because not everyone is able to change with the same speed. Some will always move slower than others, and it is these people that protect the others from being hasty and unwise. During a time of change, however, the slowness and deliberateness of individuals is rarely seen as a virtue. It is very easy for a leader who sees a truth, to want to force those who follow him to accept it and receive it as easily as he did. This will rarely happen. While sheep can be gullible, they also can be very stubborn. They are creatures of habit, they are products of their environment, and they will not change rapidly. Leaders must realize this, and see the importance of both moving slowly, and keeping a balance between the letter of the Law and the Spirit of the Law in their teaching. It is only by moving slowly that the unity of the Spirit in the bond of peace will be maintained (*Eph. 4:1-6*). This unity is absolutely vital if the people of God are going to experience God's richest blessings (*Ps. 133*). Every leader needs the wisdom of God plus the patience and longsuffering of God to see that everyone makes the transition, and to be unwilling that any should perish (*II Pet. 3:9*). As leaders maintain patience and hope firm to the end, with the Lord, they will reap a long-awaited fruit (*James 5:7*), and they will be able to look to the Lord and say "of those you have given me, I have lost none".